THE SEARCH FOR JOHN S

Mollie Gillen

The Search for
JOHN SMALL
First Fleeter

Mollie Gillen

Library of Australian History
Sydney
1988

LIBRARY OF AUSTRALIAN HISTORY
17 Mitchell Street, North Sydney, NSW. 2060

First published 1985
Reprinted with Corrigenda 1988

ISBN 0 908120 58 3
© Mollie Gillen

Text © Mollie Gillen

AUTHOR'S NOTE

I would like to reiterate my thanks to the
committee of the John & Mary Small Descendants
Association, whose gift to me after they were shown
the original manuscript helped to reimburse some
of the enormous personal expense of the years of
research that brought John's identity and
background to light. I have appreciated their
recognition of my work.

Printed in Australia by The Book Printer, Maryborough, Victoria

—Laws are everywhere made by the rich, and for the rich. The English Statute Book from one end to the other shows the indulgence of self-love and self-interest of the law-givers.

> —Minute, James Stephen 15 September 1841 enclosed in letter to Lord Russell (CO 137/256 no 234).

—It would be difficult to acquit the Government of a charge of gross delay and negligence in a duty that concerned a thousand of its subjects. To leave them on the high seas or at the other end of the world, without enquiry or assistance from May 1787 to January 1790—the earliest possible date at which supplies could have arrived by the *Guardian*—was nothing less than an act of criminal negligence and quite in keeping with the moral outlook of ministers who had proposed previously to send convicts to a probably worse fate on the west coast of Africa . . . The perfunctoriness with which the system was commenced . . . can neither be explained nor excused. . . .

> —Eris O'Brien, *The Foundation of Australia* (pp. 239-40).

—. . . a thriving infant empire, sprung for the most part from the mere superabundance of our distressed fellow-creatures, many of whom were driven to a breach of the laws of their native land from want of employment; but now, comfortable, industrious, and in hundreds of cases, wealthy settlers. . . .

> —*Friend of Australia:* Retired Officer of the East India Company's service, c. 1828 (p. 7).

PRM
Then, now, and always.

TABLE OF CONTENTS

ILLUSTRATIONS

ACKNOWLEDGEMENTS

It would take a separate volume to list everyone to whom my heartfelt gratitude is due for unstinting kindness and help in the course of research for this book. It is almost impossible to include by name all those without whose interest and enthusiastic assistance the work could never have been done. For fifteen years intermittently, the last ten in concentrated research, the clues have been followed in archives and libraries in Britain, Australia, Havana, the United States. Those who have helped me are too many and too widely dispersed to be named individually, but each of them will, I hope, accept my thanks in recognition of my debt to them: if all those who gave freely of time and of support will read between the lines, they will find their own names there, as they are and will remain in my mind and my memory.

First, perhaps, my most sincere thanks are offered to the staff at the Public Record Office at Kew and Chancery Lane, London, all of whom were endlessly patient and friendly. Far distant from them the director of the City Museum of Havana and the Canadian consulate there did all they could to help. The people at the British Library, (including the Newspaper Library at Colindale), the Guildhall, the Greater London Record Office (especially the Middlesex Record Office before incorporation), the Society of Genealogists, all contributed their time and interest to my work: librarians and archivists in many cities, either in person or by letter, in Birmingham, Exeter, Plymouth, Portsmouth, Hull, Kingston upon Thames, Edinburgh, Belfast, Dublin, gave me all the information they could find. The Duke of Bedford's archives were opened to me, as were the acquisitions of the Royal Marines at Southsea. In Australia, staff members at the Mitchell Library and the State Archives of New South Wales were never too busy to answer questions and produce documents. Private researchers confirmed details for me in places I was unable to visit. In this kind of research one makes many friends, some of them for a lifetime. Special thanks are due to Joanna Armour Richards of Sydney, without whose friendship and intimate knowledge of Australian archives the work would have taken twice as long to complete: and my gratitude to the generous interest of the John and Mary Small Descendants Association through the members of the committee.

To a measure of good luck some of the credit must go in that certain necessary documents survived until today. And I can only regret that so many beckoning side-paths, with promise of new insights into persons and events of the period but tangential to the main theme, had regretfully to remain unexplored further.

There are omissions in the story, not perhaps important but adding to the whole picture of the times, that would have been included had personal circumstances in the final year of work on the book not intervened to interrupt attention to minor details. I hope any such shortcomings will be forgiven and understood, and that all who had a part in bringing me to the completion of the work will feel their assistance has been justified.

There is more research to be done. In the small villages around Birmingham it might be possible to discover the marriage of John Small's parents, John and Rebecca Small. This and other discoveries I must leave to a later researcher.

I have thought it necessary to bring John Small "on deck", as it were, from time to time in scenes we know he took part in, though unmentioned by name. When writing a history of the inarticulate, a proper picture must be drawn to make the invisible man visible. Scenes that came alive in imagination when reading ships' logs and other contemporary documents would have been vividly alive to those who saw them with living eyes.

Permission to reproduce archival material has been instantly granted by the British Library, the Public Record Office, the New York Public Library, the Devon Record Office, the National Portrait Gallery, the Royal Marines Museum, to all of whom my thanks.

MOLLIE GILLEN
London (England) and Toronto (Canada)

1. PROLOGUE

On Thursday 17 January 1785 the Twelve Judges of England gathered in Westminster Hall in the chambers of the Lord Chief Justice, Earl Mansfield, to choose the circuits they would ride for the forthcoming Lent Assizes. This year the Western Circuit, covering with its 450-odd miles the second-longest circuit in distance from London, fell to the lot of Baron Hotham and Mr. Justice Buller, who would deliver the gaols of Southampton (Hampshire), Wiltshire, Dorset, Cornwall, Devon and Somerset of the "unhappy wretches" now awaiting trial on charges of varying gravity.[1]

Among the fifty-one men and women then being held for trial on capital charges in the High Gaol of Exeter were four men accused of the same crime—"feloniously assaultg James Burt in the Kings Highway feloniously putting him in Corporal fear and danger of his Life in the said Highway and feloniously and violently stealing and taking from his Person and agt his will in the said Highway one metal watch and Tortoise-shell case v. 30s one pruning Knife val. 6d and 5s his Goods". The men were named as Stephen Davenport, John Herbert, Robert Ellwood and John Small.[2]

The destinies of two of these men, who seemed to have first loomed up out of history with the appearance of their names on the pages of the big Devon Gaol Book, were to be tied intimately to those of some dozen other people, less intimately to hundreds more, men and women scattered across the realm living the day-to-day lives ordained for them by the society into which they had been born. None of them—many hardly more than children at this time—in the wildest of dreams could have imagined, or believed in, a future that would bring them together in later years from widely separated areas of England, Scotland and Ireland, and link their lives in a miserable endurance—though ultimately, in many cases, in an unexpected happiness and prosperity. They belonged to the mass of Britain's population denominated with unthinking arrogance by the privileged few as "the lower orders", almost as if they belonged to a different species. A few of them had received some education, and thus lived a little—but only a little—more comfortably than the rest. Most of

1

them, unable to read or write and with nothing to look forward to that would be any better than what they knew today, passed their time in a state of quiet, and sometimes not-so-quiet desperation.

The High Gaol at Exeter, in the grounds of the Castle, was a private gaol owned by Denys Rolle, father of the member of parliament for Devonshire, whose family had received it as a grant from the Duchy of Cornwall. The gaoler, James Webber, and after his death in 1784, his widow Mary, paid Mr Rolle £22 a year for the privilege of operating it, charging fees for food, clothing, coals, liquor, for release if acquitted, even for "easement of irons". It was a "crowded, offensive and destructive gaol", wrote the great prison reformer John Howard, after his visit there in 1783; parts of its three night-dungeons were seven or eight feet below ground, the stairs leading up to the men's room were "intolerably bad", and the surgeon was "by contract excused from attending in the dungeons any prisoners that should have the gaol-fever".[3]

The hapless prisoners awaiting trial at the 1785 Lent Assizes had at least escaped the ordeal of John Benwell, who had been committed at Exeter in October 1783 for horse-stealing; he would receive a free pardon in March 1785 at Oxford, whither he had been moved by writ of habeas corpus because "owing to a gaol fever by improper fetters he hath lost both his legs". Presumably he had not had the money to obtain easement of fetters. No wonder there were innumerable attempts to escape from every prison in the country, attempts severely condemned by the authorities as further indication of the low morals of the villains expected to stay decently and uncomplainingly where they had been put. There were many humane voices crying in a wilderness of indifference against the horrors of eighteenth century prisons: one can read the writings of Sir George Paul, foreman of the Gloucester grand jury, of the Reverend Henry Zouch, of Jonas Hanway, Dr John Jebb, the lawyer Basil Montagu, Dr William Smith, the Lancashire justice Thomas Butterworth Bayley, anonymous writers like *Student in Politics* and *Well-wisher*, all of them concerned about prison conditions and the effects of poverty. They had little practical effect except in isolated instances when even the government could not ignore outraged public opinion.[4]

Precisely where in the King's highway and exactly when Davenport, Herbert, Ellwood and Small embarked on their perilous escapade has long been a matter for conjecture. No transcript of their trial, such as those that can be scanned for Old Bailey sessions in London, has survived, nor has the indictment, which might have given ages and place of origin for each of the culprits, perhaps even a physical description. That the crime took place in Devon has always seemed likely from the Exeter location of the trial. Exeter gaol records are not notably accurate and have many omissions: the first appearance of the four men's names is in the Calendar of Prisoners in the High Gaol for 6 April 1785, when they had already been tried, but they were probably committed some time after the Summer Assizes of 1784 and, in fact, not long before they were to appear in the dock. This may have depended on how far distant from Exeter was the site of the crime, and the time it had taken to transmit the papers—and the prisoners—from that place to the seat of the Devon Assizes.[5]

Many of their fellow prisoners had suffered the miseries of the High Gaol for several months, some of them doomed, some of them to share a totally unexpected future. William Clarke had been in the prison since April 1784 and faced a charge of burglary. William Coombes, Robert Ruth, Thomas Acres and John Smith had been committed on various dates in August, all for highway robbery. Later arrivals were Mark Domingo, Samuel Lightfoot and John Dare, on separate charges of burglary. One Thomas Freeman had stolen £83 from his master in Plymouth. In November they were joined by an ingenious young fellow named John Bliss. He had captured the imagination of almost every newspaper in the kingdom when he was caught in Tavistock. He had evolved the brilliant plan of selling stolen Gloucestershire horses in Devon, and Devonshire horses in Gloucester. It was bad luck that a Gloucester shoemaker who had moved to Plymouth recognized a hired horse there as the property of a Gloucester baker, stolen some ten months earlier, and the whole scheme unravelled.[6]

The condition of these men while awaiting trial does not have to be imagined: there were enough horrified accounts, even then, of what they endured. "Convicts are generally stout robust young men", John Howard wrote in anger, "accustomed to free diet, tolerable lodgings and vigorous exercise. These men are ironed, thrown into close offensive dungeons and there chained down, some without straw or other bedding, spending sixteen or seventeen hours daily in utter inactivity and immersed in the noxious effluvia of their own bodies." In July that year a heartfelt plea from eleven men held in Leicester gaol under sentence of transportation would spur even a sluggish government to action, though only to remove them fairly promptly to one of the prison hulks.

"Confind [they wrote] this going on 3 Years in this Unhappy Prison on the Bare Allowance of two Pennyworth of Bread p^r Day, which is not Half sufficient to satisfy the Call of Nature the most Part of us being Young people, Neither does our misfortune End here for in Winter many of us has been forced to part with some part of our Little subsistance of Bread to Help to buy a Little Coal to make a fire to Warm our Benumbed Limbs that was Frocen by the Inclemency of the Season and Heavy Irons Together. . . . We must Certainly Perish in this our

4

Native Country Especially if we are to stay another Winter in this Cruel Unhappy Place For Had our sentences been Put in Execution as soon as we Was Cast our Punishment might by this Time been Over. . . . But instead of any Hopes we have Nothing but Dispair Before our Eyes Being almost starved to death with Hunger and some Bare footed and Bare Leg'd others Never a shirt to thier Backs and Almost Eaten up Alive with Vermin and . . . Nothing to Hide some of our Nakedness some being 100 Miles from Home and not a Friend in the world to Relieve them with a Farthing and them that Had a Few friends At first has Tired them Long ago. . . ."[7]

The Lent Assizes held in Exeter in 1785 opened on Monday, 14 March. On Thursday the 17th, the *Exeter Flying Post* announced the names of the eleven prisoners who had received the dread sentence of death: among them were the names of Stephen Davenport, John Herbert, Robert Ellwood and John Small, and against the names on the heavy pages of the Devon Gaol Book the ominous black asterisk of death was inscribed in the margin.

Before the judge left town, three of this four were among the lucky five granted a respite: but Robert Ellwood joined William Clarke, William Coombes, Thomas Freeman and John Dare on the gallows, with John Bliss, the horse thief, who only a week before his capture "had married a respectable farmer's daughter and taken a genteel house at Plymouth-dock".[8]

A clerkly hand prepared the report to the King's most Excellent Majesty, signed by Francis Buller on 26 March, in which he pleaded a reprieve, "circumstances appearing on their behalf at their Trials", for John Herbert and John Small, along with Mark Domingo, Edward Smith, Thomas Acres, John Smith and Robert Ruth, recommending that they be transported beyond the seas for seven years. And for Stephen Davenport, a Free Pardon.[9]

What brought these four men together for their fatal and unrewarding assault? Though no published report with details of the crime when it was committed has survived, one could suppose that in the pages of local papers that may have existed but are now lost there may have appeared an outraged paragraph about four villains who set upon an innocent wayfarer going about his lawful occasions. Could it have been in a moment of drunken bravado that they made the attack?—John Small would have a potentially dangerous tussle with the demon drink at a later stage in his life before he crossed the line back to law and order as Paterfamilias, Solid Citizen, Landowner and District Constable.[10] Or did the act arise from desperation and the direst poverty?

Who, then, *was* John Small, a man who seemingly sprang full-fledged into the records for an offence committed, with three companions, "in the King's highway", on some unknown road in the county of Devon?

Who were his companions in crime? Were they local lads, farm labourers, perhaps, on their way home from a night at the tavern? Were they apprentices, thinking to eke out their small wages by a spur-of-the-moment grab? Were they petty thieves, living precariously at other people's expense?

What were "the circumstances appearing on their behalf at their trials" that did not save Ellwood, but gained reprieve for Herbert and Small, and set Stephen Davenport free? And what of James Burt, the victim, going to or from his home with his small possessions in his pockets?

How, this far in time from a minor scene in the whole panorama of history, could these questions ever be answered?

By this act John Small was preserved as a person in countless recordings of his name, when less audacious citizens living their blameless lives have faded unknown and unremembered into the oblivion of the past. Apart from some details of his later life and certain family legends about his past (some fact, some patently legend), that, at this time, was all that seemed to be known of John Small. He was a name on that stark page of the Devon Gaol Book, a name printed in a few newspapers, a name in a surprising number of bleak official records, a statistic in the growing list of men and women from all over the country who were sometimes villains, sometimes only the deprived and desperate poor, all nevertheless equally victims of the savage criminal laws of England.

But who was he?

2. COLLEAGUES AND VICTIM

Where could one begin to look for, hope to find, a man with a name as little distinctive as John Small, a man of the 18th century born in the 1760s (his tombstone said he was 87 when he died in 1850),[11] who would be indubitably *this* John Small, traceable from childhood? Divers family legends said he was a soldier in the Black Watch convicted of disobeying an order about wearing (or not wearing) the kilt: a marine sergeant who came out with the First Fleet on HMS *Sirius* and brought his wife with him: a "ship's apothecary and paymaster to the troops" who came out on "HMS" *Charlotte:* sergeant in the New South Wales Corps in command of the personal bodyguard of Governor Arthur Phillip: from Scotland, connected with the Murrays of Atholl: "had a brother a lord" (this rumour half in jest but half-believed).

Family legends grow distorted, but they sometimes have a grain of truth at their roots, and subsequent research has enabled us to suggest, at least, possible origins for some of these distortions, some of them perpetuated in print. John Small did come with the First Fleet, though not on *Sirius,* and his wife was a First Fleeter too, though she was not his wife then, nor did she travel on the same ship. He did not come from Scotland, though his family may have: future research may fill the gap here. He came on *Charlotte,* but she was not one of His Majesty's Ships, but a convict transport vessel. And if he had been a soldier or marine, how to trace him now?[12] Great holes exist in public records. The careers of officers are often discoverable: of other ranks, seldom, if at all, and especially one who had lived and served in the 18th century. Finding him (even if possible at all) would be a matter of time, and persistence, but mostly of luck.

Knowledge of his companions in crime and their circumstances, and perhaps, too, of their victim, could throw a great deal of light on John Small himself, what manner of man he was, and why he turned to robbery. His companions—and his victim—had more distinctive names than John Small. Scanning contemporary London and local newspapers, one could make a note of Burts, Davenports, Herberts and Ellwoods and Smalls as they occurred, and hopefully search the parish

6

registers of Devon: a large task—he need not have been a Devon man, though the crime was committed there.

For a while a John Small baptized in April 1764 in the parish of Stoke Damerel, Plymouth, looked promising. This man's parents were John Small of HMS *Fame,* and Ann Angelly: John senior had worked during 1768 as a labourer at Plymouth Yard, and had been assigned to work on *Fame* "when on the rocks". But the promise caught on a snag. A John Small, no age given, had been buried in the parish five years later, in February 1769. Father or son? Or another John Small altogether? No clue slotted other information into place. Moreover, a chance scanning of a 1788 paper revealed a John Small of Plymouth who, with a companion was "in a sand barge at Mothercombe Back, [and], the tide being very rapid, the barge drove out to sea". The companion jumped onto a gravel bank, "but John Small, in the barge, sunk among the breakers, and was drowned, leaving several children, and his wife pregnant". Father or son?—or yet another John Small? And of course, now clearly not our John: in 1788 our John was toiling in the unfamiliar landscape of Sydney Cove.[13]

There were no pointers to possible Davenports, Herberts or Ellwoods. An Amos Burt, licensed victualler of Alphington, in the countryside on the outskirts of Exeter, was duly remarked—might he have had a brother or father named James? A James Burt, licensed victualler of St Budeaux Parish in Plymouth appeared on a slim and faded parchment recognizance form in a dusty box of Jurymen's Returns in the Devon Record Office at Exeter. This James Burt had stood surety on 19 July 1784 in the sum of £40 for the appearance of his wife Rebecca to answer a charge of assault laid against her by Sarah Labdon of the neighbouring parish of Egg Buckland. We had searched these records for the remote possibility that a juryman might have idly doodled something significant: our four highway robbers could have been committed in the latter months of 1784, too late to be recorded in the 1785 gaol records.[14]

Luck and persistence sometimes yield rich rewards. Why should one expect to find in the columns of a paper in *Dorset* more details of Exeter trials than Exeter's own paper? But one could never tell: no avenue should ever be left unexplored, no stone, as they say, unturned. It was almost as a last resort, at almost the last hour of a search in the West Country Studies Library in Exeter, that the *Sherborne Mercury* for March 1785 was checked, and this brought the first real break, effectively pinning the identification of our highwaymen's victim. Davenport, Herbert, Ellwood and Small, said the *Sherborne Mercury* unbelievably but in clear black and white on the 21st, had been convicted "for robbing James *and Rebecca Burt* of a watch, money, &c." (The jubilant italics are not the *Mercury's*.)[15]

So, if not precisely when, at least more precisely *where* the robbery took place could now be established. Listed in the Licensed Victuallers' Returns, proprietor of an alehouse in St Budeaux that looked across to Cornwall high above the River Tamar, Burt had been widowed in 1780 and left with a newborn child: he had married Rebecca Corham, aged 24, in January 1783. Members of Rebecca's family, gentry or near-gentry, appear frequently in the parish registers, sometimes designated "gentleman" or "esquire". Had our four offenders come on James and Rebecca after a night at their tavern? or were the Burts on an outing in another part of Plymouth when accosted?—Rebecca's earlier trouble had occurred in the parish of Egg Buckland. At any rate, that the robbery took place somewhere in Plymouth seemed to indicate that the men might have been seamen, and the naval port of Plymouth in 1784 and 1785 was full of unemployed sailors and marines after the enormous cutback in the forces at the end of the War of the American Revolution. The marine corps, for instance, dropped from 21,000-odd in 1783 to fewer than 5,000 next year, and by 1785 the Royal Navy was carrying only 22,800 men compared with 107,000 two years earlier. Had our four incompetent highwaymen been companions in the service?[16]

The only approach was a search through ship musters, thousands of them, name by name for likely years, hoping for more needles in this immense stack of hay. And it brought results. After hours of search through more than a thousand ship muster books, John Small and his companions began to emerge from the past. Robert Ellwood was the first to appear, his name leaping from the muster list of HMS *Europe* for April 1784. Ellwood was one of twenty-nine marines taken on board at Portsmouth for a passage to their own divisional base at Plymouth. Ellwood (149th company, new-raised in 1782) was included as one of a few other Plymouth marines from various ships recently come into port. He had been discharged from HMS *Nemesis* at Portsmouth on 25 April after a West Indies voyage, having embarked on her at Plymouth on 6 September 1782.[17]

He went on board *Europe* on 26 April, herself home after three years in the East Indies, and was discharged to his own headquarters at Plymouth on 4 May, doubtless eager for the fleshpots after hard months at sea. *Europe's* disapproving captain—by coincidence it was Arthur Phillip—noted in his log on 7 May an order for twelve lashes earned by a seaman "for attempting to stop a girl ordered out of the ship that had been brought on board to be debauched."[18]

Ellwood, less than a year from ignominious death, would have had time in his nine days on *Europe* to become acquainted with John Herbert, one of the captain's servants (as a matter of interest so also was Andrew Miller, later to be a First Fleeter, and Henry Brewer as clerk). No certainty exists that this John Herbert was the man with whom Ellwood would later be involved in the robbery: there are several other men of the same name on contemporary muster lists of Royal Navy ships. But the supposition remains possible.[19]

It seems inescapable fact, however, that Robert Ellwood would have had some acquaintance, however, slight, with Stephen Davenport, a marine corporal also attached to the Plymouth Division. Davenport, it would transpire, had had a long, adventurous and honourable career in the marine corps. His name, first coming to my attention on the muster roll of HMS *Caton*, was another needle poking sharply out of the haystack: it *was* possible, after all, to discover what manner of men John Small and his companions were, and it could yet be possible from these facts and others still to be discovered to deduce something of how and why they turned to robbery in the mid-1780s.[20]

Tracking Davenport's career through the muster lists was like fitting pieces of a jigsaw puzzle together. The picture that emerged saw him first as a private marine on HMS *Augusta* in 1777, engaged in the assault on Mud Island in the Delaware River, Pennsylvania, in support of General Sir William Howe's land attack on Philadelphia. Further diligent research might turn him up yet earlier, but for the purposes of this story it is enough to see him first in October 1777, perhaps as young as seventeen but possibly older, hot and dirty and tense as the guns roared all around and *Augusta* went aground trying to squeeze through a narrow channel made narrower by the enemy's defence works.[21]

The ship "lay quiet all night", said the captain at his eventual court martial, and the men were busy attaching cables and lightening her to catch next morning's flood tide, but the wind was unfavourable. At daylight the shore galleys began firing again. Mid-morning the captain noticed "an odd crackling kind of noise" and found his ship irretrievably in flames. No one had any idea of the cause. The master supposed the flaming wads from her own guns had set her afire. Her loss was termed accidental, and the captain and officers were acquitted. Christopher Marshall, retired druggist in Philadelphia, had noted the news of the day in his diary with quiet satisfaction. "It's said . . . that our fleet bravely repulsed the men of war and that our fire rafts had set three . . . on fire, and two were already blown up and destroyed. One of the said vessels, it's said, was the August, 64 gun ship. . . ."[22]

An American naval captain, Silas Talbot, another observer, said the explosion, heard 15 miles away, was mistaken for an earthquake. "[Augusta] had on board some live cattle and hay. The hay took fire from the wads of her own guns, and (the wind being high) the flames were so rapidly communicated to the ship, that the crew had scarce time to save themselves, before she blew up."[23]

Taking part in the battle on board *Eagle*, whose captain soberly reported "Augusta . . . was aground. . . . Saw Augusta take fire. . . . The

Augusta blew up", a young man named Michael Stanhope was serving as midshipman, soon to become master's mate. He was to play an important part in the life of John Small some five years later.[24]

Rescued from *Augusta*, the men were dispersed among other ships, and Davenport found himself on HMS *Somerset* doing service out of New York and Rhode Island. A year later, on 2 November 1778, guarding the entrance to Boston Harbour in an attempt to bottle up the French admiral le comte d'Estaing, *Somerset* was driven ashore in a hard gale "at the back side of Provincetown on Peaked Hill Bars". Many of the men were saved by the chance arrival of a boat engaged in bringing an exchange of prisoners to Admiral Gambier who was on board *Ardent*, but *Somerset's* captain, George Ourry, with most of his officers and about four hundred seamen, got on shore. On 6 November, they were "now going to march off to Boston". The delighted Americans managed to save all *Somerset's* guns, sails, cables, rigging and stores: and today some of her weathered timbers still lie on the beach and in the shallows of Race Point, where the great southward curve of Cape Cod Bay begins.[25]

Tantalisingly, gaps occur in the story: records in Royal Marines archives and other public repositories are abysmally few, and it is all the more frustrating to know, from the scraps that have survived, how thoroughly each man was documented in his day. In spite of diligent checking of ship musters from the North American fleet, Davenport has not so far been found among those men from *Somerset* distributed through the fleet after her loss: he may have been among those taken prisoner and marched to Boston, exchanged by cartel (Captain Ourry and his officers came to HMS *Renown* by cartel from Providence on 12 February 1779), or possibly wounded, sent to an American hospital. By some ship whose muster has not been traced he certainly returned to England during 1779, to appear—now promoted a corporal in the newly raised 129th company of the Plymouth division—on HMS *Dublin*, marked as having embarked on 9 November that year ("came on from Head Quarters 110 marines 1 captain 2 subalterns 4 sargins 2 Droomers").[26]

Here occurred the only blemish in Davenport's career. Against his name in the muster of *Dublin* on 27 December 1779 the dreaded R is written ("Run", the mark of a man who has deserted). But *Dublin* was Portugal-bound, and anchored in Plymouth Sound: "getting ready for sea" on the 25th, "employed unmooring" on the 27th, and "under way" on the 28th. Fourteen men were marked R between the 23rd and the 27th. Most of them, like so many seamen of the day, were probably caught ashore when the wind filled the sails, incurring an R that would be officially removed only after presentation of reasonable excuse. A plausible reason was usually accepted.[27]

A man with Davenport's good record would not have risked his career by deliberate desertion. At any rate, without his R, he was entered "late Dublin" on the muster of *Diligente* in Portsmouth at the end of March 1780, and in June was discharged to *Monarch*, where he served until the end of September. Other service followed, untraced except for a passage from Portsmouth to Plymouth on *Cormorant* in December 1780, and on 5 October he went into HMS *Nymph*.[28]

One ship blown up beneath him in 1777 and another wrecked in 1778, Davenport (a veritable Jonah) was now to encounter further disaster. *Nymph* caught fire at Tortola in the West Indies on 28 June 1783. "The fire rag'd so violently," the Admiralty was informed, "the Greatest exertions of the officers and company prov'd ineffectual." Only three men were lost, but a subscription had to be raised to clothe the survivors. Davenport eventually found himself on *Caton* and an uneventful voyage back to England. He was discharged to Plymouth headquarters on 4 November 1783 and paid in mid-February 1784: his later record remains untraced until that fateful day at Exeter in March 1785.[29]

On 10 February 1783 a letter had gone to the commanding officers of the marine corps at Chatham, Portsmouth and Plymouth. "You are directed and ordered, as any parties of Marines are landed from ships at the several ports, to discharge such as belong to your division on their arrival at Headquarters, as shall appear to you from their age, size, or any other consideration unfit to be continued in the Marine service. . . ." Preliminary articles of peace between Great Britain and France, Great Britain and Spain, and Great Britain and the United States of America had been signed at Versailles on 20 January, and the manning of a vast army and navy would no longer be necessary. An Order in Council specified still further reduction to take effect on 1 September. Only the healthiest and fittest men were to be considered for retention in the Corps, none to be discharged who were over five feet six inches in height or under forty years old. The new strength of the Corps would be limited to 4,480 men, including officers. For one reason or another, Stephen Davenport found himself discharged and unemployed at the end of 1783 after at least six years of unblemished and eventful service, and probably more.[30]

Some feeble recognition of the devastating effect of this flood of unemployed sailors crept into the minutes of the Navy Board on 6 February, when it was suggested that officers at the various naval yards might look into the possibility of allowing discharged boatswains, carpenters and servants a small gratuity for making themselves useful there, to avoid a situation "in many instances injurious to the public for want of proper employment". The authorities expected the worst from the increase in unemployment, though making no provision for its unfortunate victims. Magistrates in London were warned on 13

February to give orders for nightly searches of "reputed bad houses" and the arrest of any disorderly persons.[31]

The effect of the cutback was dramatically illustrated only a year later when a London magistrate wrote to Evan Nepean, under secretary of state for the Home Office, about seventeen men he had caused to be apprehended "for laying on the Brick Kilns at Bow Common and stealing potatoes for sustenance out of a field adjoining". They were sent overnight to the prison at Clerkenwell for security, but the justice, John Staples, "persuaded the farmer to forgive them", and gave them each sixpence to buy food, "my mind revolting at the idea of convicting and committing them for not paying the penalty". All the men had been at sea, and Staples judged "necessity only to have been the cause". Such charity was not often encountered. One thinks of Elizabeth Beckford, First Fleet convict, *aged 70,* "taken instantly" in London in *January 1787* with a 12-pound Gloucester cheese, sentenced to transportation for seven years and embarked on 26 January (she died on board the transport six months later).[32]

Davenport and Ellwood had both now been discovered as marines of the Plymouth division, and a possible John Herbert had served in the ship on which Ellwood was briefly a supernumerary passenger. All had been discharged when their ships returned to port after the cutback in manpower: at any rate, their names have not been found on any ship between then and the date of their conviction. How many potatoes had *they* been obliged to steal without discovery until their arrest for a greater crime? Not petty thieves, these men, but destitute and probably desperate. And what of John Small, who so far had not been found, either as seaman or marine?

3. TOO MANY JOHN SMALLS

The hunt for John Small through the columns of hundreds of the old ship musters led· to many wrong turnings and dead ends, with no promise of final success. Though Davenport and Ellwood had been marines of the Plymouth division and the family legend hinted that John might also have been a marine, he could have been serving in the Royal Navy in another capacity as John Herbert seemed to have been: or not at all. Every occurrence of the name, therefore, had to be followed as far as possible, tracing a dozen John Smalls from ship to ship.

With the recurring family legend of a possible Scottish ancestry, that John Small from Edinburgh who showed up as "schoolmaster" on HMS *Superb* in March 1783 could have been promising, except that there was no evidence that the man convicted in 1785 could read or write. This Scottish John Small, tracked back from ship to ship through earlier years, was in any case found to be too old when he first appeared, a volunteer at the age of 27 on *Invincible* in 1778. A 22-year-old John Small, also from Edinburgh, joined *Leocadia* in May 1784, but proved to have been still on board through the months of 1785 when our John was languishing in Exeter High Gaol. There was a John Small from Aberdeen on *Alcide*, but he was 35 in July 1779, was discharged in October 1780, rejoined the Navy on *Alcmene* in March 1782, collected his bounty and deserted at the Nore two months later. A John Small picked up by the pressgang at Cowes in November 1780 served on the *Sulphur* fireship, did harbour duty at Plymouth on *Warspite*, and was discharged "unserviceable" in March 1781: another John Small, also trapped into the service by the pressgang in January 1781 in Guernsey, was transferred from *Monsieur* to *Diligente*, from *Diligente* to *Courageux*, thence to *Belleisle* and back to *Monsieur*, was still on the latter ship when she was paid off in March 1783, and then disappears from the records, probably into the anonymity of the Royal Navy cutback. The John Small on *Sultan* in 1783 died in Bombay in March 1784 and the one on *London* died at Port Royal, Jamaica, in July 1782. John Small, volunteer from Leatherhead, Surrey, ordinary seaman aged 20 in

January 1782 on *Courageux*, looked promising: he was set aside for checking in parish registers if more evidence seemed to fit him to our John. There was a John Small briefly held on *Diligente* in 1782 who seems to have been an American prisoner of war and ended up in Forton prison at Portsmouth: not much chance of finding his antecedents if he happened to have been the convicted John.[33]

The John Small, no identification given, landing at New York from *Europe* in 1779, turned out in a later and more complete muster list to be Major John Small bringing over part of the 84th Royal Engineers to fight the rebel Americans. Major John Small was born in the district of Atholl, Perthshire, in 1726, and an offshoot legend (perhaps from eagerness to prove our John's respectability) that has had some currency had identified the convict John as a supposed son of the army officer. But when he died (now Major-General) in Guernsey in March 1796 after his 1793 appointment as lieutenant-governor of the island, his comprehensive will clearly showed that he left no descendants: his considerable property in Nova Scotia was bequeathed to named nephews, not a black-sheep convict son, legitimate or illegitimate, in Australia. This interesting fancy may, however, account for the suggestions from time to time that our John was connected with the Murray of Atholl clan. This John Small was also an officer of the Black Watch, accounting for another of the distorted legends that clustered in family lore.[34]

Disappointments. But there were bonuses—names that would later ring with fame or notoriety in world contexts not yet existing. Horatio Nelson, midshipman on *Seahorse*, 18 years old in 1775: Fletcher Christian, (later to be a *Bounty* mutineer) one of the complement of *Eurydice*, midshipman in 1783 but made master's mate in May 1784. There were the names that would become a part of Australian history. John White, surgeon on *Sulphur* in 1780, recommended for another naval appointment in 1783 by the captains of *Dragon* and *Termagant*, who were tartly told by the Admiralty that Mr White would be considered in his proper turn when a peace arrangement was concluded. Nicholas Anstis, to become known as the rascally officer on two convict ships, *Lady Penrhyn* in 1787 and *Surprise* in 1790, first appeared as coxswain on *Aetna* in January 1779, volunteer aged 26 in 1780 on *Porpoise*, stepping up to master's mate and then master, and was discharged to become master on *Worcester* at Bombay in January 1783: Denis Considen, surgeon's mate on *Champion* in 1780, served with Anstis on *Porpoise* and joined *Superb* as surgeon in 1783. Daniel Southwell appeared as midshipman on *Aurora* in 1783, William Bradley as lieutenant on *Ariadne* in 1784: William Faddy, marine second lieutenant on *Champion* from 1780 to 1784: Captain Lieutenant Watkin Tench of the marines on board *Mediator* in 1783 and *Diadem* in 1785.

And William Balmain, who went as surgeon's mate on *Nautilus* for the survey of the Das Voltas coast of Africa in 1785, in one of the government's last attempts to find a destination for England's convicts before the final decision that sent them to Botany Bay; he would go out to that place on board the transport *Alexander*.[35]

A possibility: John Small, private marine on board *Andromeda* in January 1778, discharged to Haslar naval hospital in August and not found on any later muster. But he was a Portsmouth marine of the 51st company, and the men were seldom moved from company to company, much less from division to division, except for possible promotion as Davenport was. As the names slid by beneath the glancing eye, imagination supplied a background of crowded deck, tarred rope, flapping sail, the splash and surge of sea noises, bursts of gunfire and the rough unshaven faces of once-living men who may have been comrades of John Small. Who were Ludovicus Petticam, Lion Mariner, Antrim Bulstrode? Who Hump Swindle and John Plumpy and Thomas Stumpy? Who Samuel Dreamer, Careless Copping, Tibbits Cricks, John Freshtops, Boæthius Cancer? Joseph Peevish, John Topless, Silas Kettle and Dark Vessell? Who Orange Wigginton and Timothy Milky, Zodiack Lenie and John Rhubarb? What were their families, their hopes and aspirations, their ultimate end? Did they ever know, had they ever served, briefly or for long months on any of his Majesty's ships of the Royal Navy with the John Small who was now eluding discovery?[36]

And then—moment of triumph—John Small, private marine of the Plymouth division, coming aboard HMS *Medway* on 1 February 1781 and serving until 19 October 1782 when he, like his Portsmouth namesake, was discharged sick to Haslar, the naval hospital at Portsmouth. But was he returned to service in ships on whose musters we might yet find him? Was he discharged unfit? Did he perhaps die in hospital, yet another of the John Smalls who had proved to be not ours?[37]

The frustration with which a researcher encounters the gaps in the records is galling. Those who complain of paperwork today may not realize how great a snowstorm of paper engulfed the 18th century, little of which has survived. Printed forms accompanied seaman and marine throughout their service life. There were forms to record each man's enlistment, forms to certify that a surgeon had examined him, forms in which the recruiting officer swore that enlistment procedures had been properly carried out. Forms announced that he had permission to travel from this place to that, other forms exempted him from the attentions of the pressgang. A printed form went with him ashore to infirmary or hospital or sick quarters, a printed form told his captain he was now cured and ready to resume his duties. When he left the service, he carried a printed form announcing his honourable discharge, and a ticket to claim what pay, if any, was due to him. Lists were kept of hospital patients, even if they were only in private quarters, lodged in houses belonging to suitable landladies in the town. Some First Fleet names jump out: John Poulden, first lieutenant of marines discharged to Haslar, spent a month early in 1781 at the house of Mrs Richards at Stonehouse: George Worgan, surgeon, by special request, "went into the country" instead of staying in hospital in mid-1782: James Campbell, captain of marines on sick leave in August, also went into the country and "never appeared at the Hospital".[38]

Most of the myriad forms and papers have swirled into the past, only a few pages remaining from which we can discover how thoroughly the authorities kept track of their men. In their day Robert Ellwood, Stephen Davenport and all the John Smalls were fully documented: but no document, at that point in our research, was found to exist for any of them except their listing in the ships' musters and pay books. One can go to Haslar today and see the solid old buildings and a few of the solid old wooden beds: but those Haslar records that managed to escape the hazards of loss and destruction for two hundred years were lost in 1940s bombings, the Entry Books and Dead Books that might have told whether John Small of *Medway* failed to survive his stay there, or was released, cured—even the "five vouchers and different scraps of paper" produced to the Board by one incompetent agent as his sole records for four months of 1782—all are gone, and there are no tombstones to search at Haslar, the bodies buried indiscriminately in unmarked graves until 1859.[39]

There are columns on the double-page spread of the musters for the clerk to record particulars of each man of the ship's complement: bounty paid, number on the books, entry date, appearance date, whence and whether prest or not, place and county where born, age at the time of entry, quality (rank or rating), date of discharge, death or desertion, and the various amounts advanced in cash or supplies to be charged against a sailor's pay. Some of the clerks were meticulous, writing in the details for each seaman under every head, but almost never for the marines, for whom it was sufficient to indicate their division, it being assumed, correctly, that individual records of marines would be kept at their headquarters. But those marine corps divisional books that could easily be consulted in 1783 by a Timothy Kelly needing to prove he had joined in 1775 have long since vanished. To "Comrade Kelly" in September 1783 wrote "Your most Affectionate Friend, Thomas Munro Serjeant" to say that "Captain William Henvill having retired upon half pay I thought the safest & most Expedicious method to procure you a Certificate as above signed by Lieut & Adjt Martin & hope will have the desired Effect. Remember me to all Enquiring Friends." And in a postcript, "Remember me respectfully to my old Friend and Messmate Benjamin Pewtriss as does likewise Serjt Pierson."[40]

Occasionally a more careful clerk would enter the company to which a marine belonged, and on *Medway* John Small was shown as belonging to the 33rd company. By some freak of fate, records of enlistments that included the 33rd company from 1763 to 1782 have survived at the Public Record Office.[41] But without knowing birthplace or place of enlistment for our John Small, how—even if a John Small appeared in these lists—could we be any more sure than before that we had found the right man? Besides, the document was unavailable, in use to another reader at the time of application. However, here on *Medway* we had, without doubt, a John Small who belonged to the Plymouth division of the marine corps as Ellwood and Davenport did. It would be interesting and might even be profitable, to look at the records of HMS *Medway*—log books, paybooks, captain's and admiral's journals—and find out something about this part of the life of one of the John Smalls. Perhaps he *would* turn out to be the right John Small—perhaps some tiny clue would appear, to tie in with one or other of the insubstantial family legends. We followed the movements of HMS *Medway* on this voyage with much hope, and with a strong sense of kinship with this private marine named John Small.

4. HMS MEDWAY

On 1 February 1781, HMS *Medway*, anchored in Plymouth Sound, received on board eighty-four men to make up her complement of 420. Thirteen of these were men from the Plymouth headquarters of the marine corps: among them was one John Small, private marine, the first appearance in surviving ship musters of a man of this name belonging to the Plymouth division. On the 4th, *Medway* sailed to join the Grand Fleet at Spithead under Admiral George Darby, who was preparing to escort a huge convoy of merchant ships to besieged Gibraltar, where provisions were fast running out.[42]

There was some delay caused partly by bad weather—in "heavy gales and violent wind" several navy ships were driven around to St Helen's: partly by the nervous apprehension of attack by Holland and France if the Grand Fleet left the Channel defenceless: partly by the unwieldy convoy gathering at Portsmouth and Cork.

Medway's captain, Harry Harmood, kept his seamen busy reefing sails and his marines exercising with small arms until the signal for sailing was made on 13 March, and the fleet, with "32 sail of the convoy", straggled down the Channel to collect the storeships coming from Ireland.

From the captain's log and other sources we followed John Small on the voyage. Captain Harmood snapped at the heels of his unruly charges the length of the Channel, firing signal shots to order them back into line, to follow in his wake, to stop going too far ahead. They moored in Cork harbour for a week while the main body of the Grand Fleet had been ordered to hover outside waiting for the 97 Irish victuallers, one of which managed to dismast herself crashing into *Medway*. Sailing on 27 March, Admiral Darby missed an encounter with the fleet of the French admiral the comte de Grasse ("25 sail of line, with 180 transports, besides several ships armed *en flute*") which had left Brest for the West Indies on the 22nd, an encounter that might have altered history and for which the Admiralty came in for scathing criticism in the Commons. "What was the consequence? . . . we had lost our islands: Sir Samuel Hood had been defeated, or nearly so, and our losses and disgraces were completed by the surrender of Lord Cornwallis's army at Yorkton."[43]

But the voyage across Biscay and down the coast of Spain was full of tension. This John Small would have heard the sound of guns coming through the fog from time to time, and "the fleet ringing bells and firing musquets", and would have wondered whether a battle was about to begin. The Spanish fleet at Cadiz had offered a possible threat: John Small might have shared his admiral's relief when "looking into the harbour, he saw the Spanish fleet lying peaceably at anchor". A missed opportunity, Charles James Fox would say bitterly afterwards. "[Darby] might have arrived time enough to fall upon the rear of the Spanish fleet, which after a cruize of two months, was returning in very foul condition to Cadiz."[44]

Just after midnight on 2 April the cutter *Kite*, sent ahead by Admiral Darby, brought news to the people of Gibraltar of the fleet's imminent arrival. (The lieutenant on *Kite* was Philip Gidley King, who would be a First Fleeter and eventually governor of New South Wales.) "The garrison are noisy with tumultuous joy," wrote Samuel Ancell, an army clerk stationed on Gibraltar, in his journal. The excited populace crowded to every vantage point, and as the heavy morning fog lifted on the 12th, "the fleet appeared as thick as a wood", gently riding out of reach of the enemy guns, "the men of war and merchant vessels, amounting together to near 100 sail, stretched all along the Barbary coast. . . . The British fleet are safe arrived, with England's banners triumphantly flying."[45]

Did *Medway's* John Small (*our* John Small?) spare a moment to marvel at the great range of African mountains behind the fleet, and the sharp wedge of the Rock before it, as everyone tensed for action? "The convoy . . . were in a compact body, led by several men of war, their sails just enough filled for steerage, whilst the majority of line-of-battle ships lay-to under the Barbary shore, having orders not to enter the Bay lest the enemy should molest them with fire-ships."[46]

The Spanish batteries, which had been menacing but silent until now, began "blazing like a volcano," and the stunned people of Gibraltar found themselves under a terrible bombardment that was to last for weeks to come. Navy ships, however, which immediately began escorting the victuallers into the bay to land their cargoes, suffered little damage. Enemy guns elevated to their highest pitch could not reach the main fleet, which was careful to stay beyond their range, but enemy galleys—"gun boats each of 20 oars and a long 26-pounder in the prow"—darted with mosquito tenacity among the shipping in the bay, too small to be hit except by a lucky shot from the ships' guns, and in fact unable to do much actual damage: though "these insect swarm of gunboats . . . render our days and nights infinitely miserable and alarming." These, and the 20-odd fireships stationed in different parts of the bay, kept the frigates and cutters cruising throughout the night, as well as boats from the ships.[47]

The cargoes, despite the difficulties, were unloaded in record time. The garrison had no vessels to assist the navy: "it will be necessary to have a Lieutenant and long boat from every ship in the Fleet," wrote Admiral John Ross to Darby on April 14th. Men of the garrison worked at the docks. "Our people are assidously unloading the shipping," wrote Ancell, "as the fleet is not intended to remain long here. We work day and night to get the provision landed; one party from sun-rise to sun-set and another from sun-set to sun-rise."[48]

There would have been plenty of work to keep John Small alert: standing guard between officers and men on board; keeping watch over the crew to guard against desertion or damage to the ship, exercising with firelock and bayonet. Beyond these routine duties on board, marines would be needed in the boatloads of sailors rowed ashore to help in landing the cargoes. So energetically did everyone work that by the 16th Admiral Ross was able to report to Darby that several vessels had been entirely cleared. "Such was the diligence of the British sailors," wrote one observer", ". . . that the cargoes of 50 vessels were landed in ten to twelve days." On the 20th, the wind sprang up, and "our fleet [was] set to sail with all the empty transports."[49]

Medway sailed for home from Gibraltar on 21 April, "43 ships of the convoy in company." By 23 May she was off Land's End, on 4 June at Spithead, on the 13th anchored at Plymouth in Cawsand Bay. For the next year she was one of the cruisers roving the home seas in defence of England, from the coast of Guernsey down the Bay of Biscay as far as Cape Finisterre at the northern tip of Spain. There were periods in harbour—a week in Plymouth in July, a fortnight in Torbay in September, all November at Spithead for repairs, two weeks in Plymouth again in December. Several times she took from tenders a few prisoners of war, French and American, to be landed at her next English port, and John Small, if he was one of the marines called on to guard them, guarded them well: there were no escapes. Once she chased and boarded a strange sail which proved to be a Jamaican packet. A sailor was lost overboard. Several seamen, including marines, were sent to hospital from time to time. Twelve lashes were ordered on various occasions to seaman or marine for drunkenness, disobedience, insolence or theft: one furious marine earned himself a second dozen by hitting the boatswain who had administered the first twelve. This John Small was an exemplary soldier: no misdemeanor is recorded against his name in the ship's books.[50]

In mid-January 1782 Captain Harmood was succeeded by Alexander Edgar. On 7 May *Medway* sailed again on a specific voyage, and reached

Madeira on the 26th, boarding any unidentified ship encountered on the way—more work and danger to cause a quickened heartbeat in John Small and his fellow marines. On 4 June the ship was anchored in Praya Bay on St Jago in the Cape Verde Islands for four days.

On June 24 *Medway* crossed the equator, and on 25 July she anchored at St Helena, where she remained for twelve days. Not a whisper of the name Napoleon had reached the world in 1782 when, a boy of thirteen, he was still attending the military academy at Brienne. For *Medway's* John Small and the ship's company, staring over the deck-rail as they would have been, St Helena was a fascinating small island of crags and gorges, a deep slash between the sharp peaks of mountains, its roadstead busy with shipping from a variety of exotic places, British since 1659 and a possession of the East India Company, "the true and absolute lords and proprietors of the island" under a charter of 1673.[51]

Medway left St Helena on 6 August. The voyage home took just over two months, with no ports of call on the way. On 26 September she was some eighteen miles off Flores in the Azores, too far for her crew to see land. Was there someone on board who could conjure up for this John Small and his companions the ghost of Sir Richard Grenville, who fell into the hands of God in the battle with the Spaniards nearly two hundred years earlier?[52]

On 14 October the ship passed the Scillies 40-odd miles distant. On the 19th, at Spithead, thirteen sick men were sent to the great naval hospital at Haslar: one of the two marines was John Small. And here, for the time being, we lost him.

The ship's company had been paid on board up to the end of May 1781. Full wages for John Small at that time had amounted to £3, swallowed up entirely by deductions: £1.13s.1d. for marine deductions plus 1s.5d. for "stoppages"; 19s. for "slop cloaths supplied by Navy"; and automatic deductions of 4s.3d. and 2s.2d. for the Chatham Chest and Greenwich Hospital. No deduction is shown for tobacco (perhaps he did not smoke?) or bedding, which he probably brought on board with him, the cash deduction having been made from his shore pay. After his discharge to Haslar in October 1782, his full wages for the rest of his time on *Medway* once again equalled his deductions: "Cloaths in Quarters", 2s.1d. (perhaps issued during one of the ship's periods at Plymouth after May 1781): clothes issued by the Navy, 2s.1d.; and the usual Chatham Chest and Hospital deductions, 6s.3d. and 3s.2d., a total of 16d.6d. The only reward for his twenty months of service was his sustenance on board ship. If he was discharged at this time, he would seem to have been cast upon the world, unemployed, without a penny in cash, in October 1782.[53]

But could he have been released from Haslar to service on board some ship not yet searched? And *was* he the John Small we sought? There had already been so many namesakes—though *Medway's* John Small was the first Plymouth marine of that name to show up. It could not be left at this point, taken for granted that we had found our man: the interminable checking of musters had to proceed. And—confusion more confounded—two more John Smalls, both Plymouth division marines, appeared, one on the books of HMS *Lively*, the other on HMS *Perseus*. The John Small on *Lively* entered 15 June 1781 and served on voyages that took him to North America and the West Indies until December 1782. The John Small on *Perseus* made his appearance on board at Plymouth on 9 August 1783: after a voyage that took him to ports on the north east coast of Ireland, he was discharged to sick quarters at Liverpool as "unserviceable" on 2 February 1784.[54]

Lively's John Small could not be the same man as *Medway's* John: *Medway's* John had already been four months at sea when *Lively's* John was boarding at Plymouth. Clearly there were two Plymouth marines of the same name. But the man on *Perseus* could have been either of them, returned from their different voyages and re-assigned to sea duty in the latter part of 1783. Or was there yet a *third* John Small, Plymouth division marine?

There had been moments of triumph and excitement when the victim James Burt was identified, and when Davenport and Ellwood were pinned down as Plymouth division marines, and when our John Small was almost certainly identified as also a Plymouth marine. To find the clue that would pin his identity to one specific John Small out of so many, the checking of the musters, it seemed, would have to continue.

But at this point the research was diverted to a different area, and brought the most tremendous discovery yet, equipping our John at a stroke, as it were, with a birthplace and birth date, with parents, brothers and sisters, and a boyhood environment. Chance re-reading of a 1951 family letter—"As far as I know the Smalls came from Birmingham"—gave emphasis to a published statement in a 1926 book whose other statements, demonstrably inaccurate, had lent disbelief to the possibility of a Birmingham origin. But *two* pointers to Birmingham could not be ignored. The trail that led to England's second city found our John Small at last.[55]

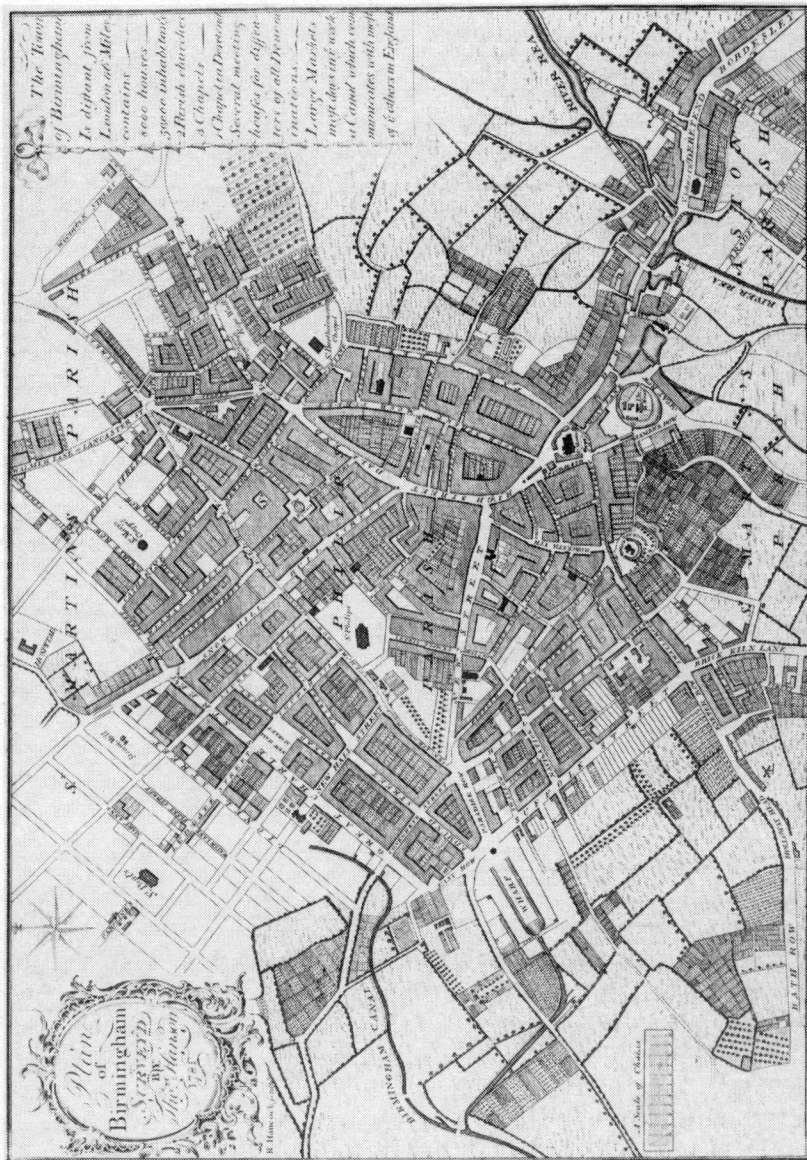

Birmingham in 1781, the year of John Small's enlistment. Holloway Head, where his parents lived, appears bottom left.
Courtesy British Library.

A South View of BIRMINGHAM from the turning house Chappel side Deritsky

1. St. Martin's Church
2. St. Philip's Church
3. St. John's Chapel
4. St. Bartholomew's Chapel
5. St. Mary's Chapel
6. St. Paul's Chapel

7. Free Grammar School
8. The Workhouse
9. Theatre in New Street
10. Hotel and Assembly room
11. Navigation Office
12. Mr. Turner's Rings work

View of Birmingham, England, showing the fields lying behind John Small's family home, as they appeared in 1785.
Courtesy British Library.

We went to Birmingham with hope, but not much expectation: there had been so many false trails. John Small's age on the tombstone in St Anne's churchyard in the Sydney suburb of Ryde—it has since been moved to the Field of Mars cemetery—was given as eighty-seven: making allowances for an old man's shaky memory, a search in the low 1760s might be expected to find him if he were there.

The moment of discovery stands in the memory in sharpened focus. Microfilmed names from the registers of St Martin's parish church, in endless eye-straining sequence, had slipped by with hopeless irrelevance, and then, suddenly, as if lit by a special spotlight, there was the entry in the baptismal register, undeniably right. *John son of John and Rebecca Small baptized 11 December 1761.* If we had not yet found the man, at least we had now found the boy.[56]

The family names that followed for brothers and sisters gave reason for even more certainty. For John Small, the convict of 1785, gave these names to his own Australian-born children in a direct sequence: Rebecca for his mother, John for his father (and himself), Mary for his first sister (and his wife), William for his first brother, and Thomas, Sarah and Samuel. (There was a little brother Joseph baptised 11 May 1771, but no child who could carry this name to the Antipodes was born (or is at any rate on record) to John Small in Australia after Samuel.)

A possible eldest sister, Ann, baptised in June 1749, may have been the first child of John and Rebecca Small: she and William were registered to the father only, before the law demanded the inclusion of the mother's name. It was not until 26 June 1751 that the church clerk would have to write in the register, "From hence, the Parents Christian Names are first mentioned", and Mary, John, Thomas, Sarah, Samuel and Joseph are all recorded as children of *John and Rebecca* Small. But there is no other John Small in the parish rate books or the registers of either St Martin's or the beautiful little cathedral church of St Philip, where the only child of John and Rebecca to die young was buried. While the registers tragically record the births and almost immediate deaths of so many other babies, John and Rebecca lost only one out of nine, a little two-year-old Sarah, and gained another Sarah ten years later. The family came of good healthy stock, or got good mothering, or was lucky, or all three.

The family that emerged from the pages of the old Birmingham registers of two centuries ago was therefore as follows: *Ann*, daughter of John Small, baptised 21 June 1749, St Philip's Cathedral (she was eleven years old before John was born and may have left home for marriage or domestic service before he had had time to know her): *William*, son of John Small, baptised 26 December 1750, St Martin's (a William Small and his wife Sarah were bringing for baptism babies born during these years: he may have been a brother of father John): *Sarah*, daughter of John and Rebecca Small baptised 26 December 1752, St Martin's (and Sarah, daughter of John and Rebecca Small buried 17 September 1754, St Philip's): *Mary*, daughter of John and Rebecca Small, baptised 1 April 1755, St Martin's. *Thomas*, son of John and Rebecca Small, baptised 1 October 1759, St Martin's: *John*, son of John and Rebecca Small, baptised 11 December 1761, St Martin's: *Sarah*, daughter of John and Rebecca Small, baptised 11 September 1764, St Martin's (this Sarah would be the one our John would remember): *Samuel*, son of John and Rebecca Small, baptised 4 August 1766, St Martin's: and *Joseph*, son of John and Rebecca Small, baptised 11 May 1771.

John and Rebecca and their growing family lived in the Edgbaston quarter of Birmingham in Holloway Head (it still exists), a continuation of Smallbrook Street on the road to Worcester. In the parish rate books for the years 1756 to 1763 John Small's name appears without a break, and again in 1764 and 1766. There are long gaps in the pages where no names at all are entered: but it seems likely that John Small senior lived consistently in this neighbourhood, his children baptised in the parish from 1749 to 1771.[57]

Holloway Head (named for the *holloway* or deep passage dug in the centre of the road by the passage of many travellers and often below house level until partially filled in) ran down the hill from the imposing parsonage of the Reverend Richard Dovey, rector of St Martin's. It held a huddle of small houses whose tenants—the names scarcely varying from one year to another—were unrated: probably invisibly marked "poor", as the visible entry in the rate books for Kingston upon Thames in the late 1770s marked James Squire, a man who was to be a First Fleet convict and neighbour of John Small junior in a yet-uncolonized New South Wales.[58]

Today's church of St Martin's-in-the-Bull-Ring is on the same site as the old church, and of similar design, only larger. For more than 700 years there had been a St Martin's at the centre of Birmingham, its steeple clearly visible in the early days, above the warren of small streets where the people lived and worked, perhaps clustered around an early village green. It is possible that the church existed as early as 1250, but certainly it was there in 1285 when two fugitives are said to have sought sanctuary within its walls. One could stand at the top of a small hill and look down past the church's slender steeple to the rectory, over the moat around the Manor House, and beyond them to fields and woodland. The area was the centre of a market place, a platform for public speakers, a gathering place for pedlars, public houses, pleasures and the common people.[59]

The church itself, to which John and Rebecca brought the baby John for his baptism on a cold December day in 1761, had by then been shorn of some of its early Norman charm, its original sandstone encased in three thicknesses of red brick, its windows only recently destroyed to allow for roof-raising and the installation of galleries. That stairways had to be crammed into ancient chapels, that wall paintings were blotted out with plaster, and that the floor was overcrowded with seats ("pews where no *pew* should be") was taken to indicate "the continual increase of people, and that a spirit of devotion was prevalent among them." St Martin's six bells, increased to ten in 1758, were a source of pride, but when the elegant small cathedral church of St Philip's was built in 1715 and later brought its six-peal bells to ten, St Martin's promptly added two more. As early as 1737 it had taken a Town meeting to order alternate ringing of the bells by the rival churches rather than together in a noisy louder-than-thou contest.[60]

John Small and Rebecca may have been newcomers to Birmingham—no marriage is recorded in parish registers, though of course it could have taken place in any of the small surrounding villages. They may have come to the community, then numbering about 25,000 souls, because of its employment opportunities in the 1740s-50s, when a man would soon be able to earn from 7s. to £3 a week, a woman 2s.6d. to 7s., and a child 1s.6d. to 4s.6d. Nail-making was probably the city's chief industry, at least up to the mid-18th century, though Birmingham was fast becoming a centre for various manufacturing industries. The great Soho works two miles distant were opened in 1762 by the engineer Matthew Boulton and a group of enthusiastic scientists full of ideas for making objects from metal and other material in new and better form. In partnership with this initiative, but remaining in his native Glasgow, was James Watt: and a recent arrival in Birmingham, Dr William Small, a minister's son from Carmylie in Angus and no relation to our John, came in 1765 to practise medicine, fresh from an appointment as professor of natural philosophy at Williamsburg University, Virginia, and to become technical adviser to Boulton.[61]

Arthur Young, agriculturalist and author, friend of George III, passing through in the late 1760s, "was no where more disappointed than at Birmingham; where I could not get any intelligence even of the most common nature, through the excessive jealousy of the manufacturers". The French traveller Faujas de St Fond was happier in 1784, marvelling at Birmingham as "one of the most curious towns in England. If any one should wish to see in one comprehensive view, the most numerous and most varied industries, all combined in contributing to the arts of utility, of pleasure, and of luxury, it is hither he must come."[62]

A Birmingham boyhood was no bad gift to John Small from his parents, poor though they may have been. Behind the houses in Holloway Head, fields perisiting almost to the end of the century saw the corn stand green through spring and summer. Here the young John would most certainly have played, and may well have helped at harvest time to rake the sheaves ready to be stooked and loaded onto the heavy horse-drawn wagons for storage in barns and silos. He was still a babe in arms in 1762, too young to enjoy the exhilaration of a "large concourse of people" gathered when war was declared on Spain: his mother, busy with her children, might not have been among them, but the gathering and the rejoicing would have been an event in the life of his father. The cheerful bells that rang all day long on 29 July 1768 may have brought to the little seven-year-old a glimmer of understanding of the importance of his Majesty's decision to build a canal in Birmingham. So rapidly did work proceed that just over a year later the young John, bright-eyed in the light from the bonfires, could have rejoiced with the writer of some fine and heartfelt doggerel:
"Eighteen months have scarce run
Since the work was begun
How pleasing the sight!
What a scene of delight!
As the barges come floating along;
Then cease from your toil,
Nor hammer nor file
Be handled today
All care shall away,
While bonfires are blazing,
(What can be more pleasing?)
All free-cost to gladden the throng."
Little boys can skip and dance, infected by the excitement of their elders and the heightened sense of festival.[63]

The 1760s saw some of Birmingham's worst winters: in January 1767 there was a tremendous fall of snow, and in November 1768 "the greatest flood in forty years" after 36 hours of unceasing rain swelled Deritend Brook and burst the Pool Dam at nearby Hockley.

In January 1764, heavy rain flooded the town with melting snow, and gales of wind tore up trees, ripped off tiles and blew chimneys down.

John's parents may have been concerned by the distress and damage from the storms, but for a child there is always excitement in the wild extravagances of the elements. A tree lying tumbled on the ground in a tangle of torn branches and perhaps bearing soggy nests and drowned baby birds stays in a toddler's memory.

Was John Small senior affected by the 1765 proclamation against the poaching of deer and rabbits, reward five guineas for information leading to conviction? Trade was bad in 1766 before the canal reduced freight costs and brought in goods at London prices, and there was an increase in crime and public disturbances in protest against the high price of bread. A subscription was raised to supply the poor with six pounds of bread for sixpence until the lower price of corn allowed bakers to offer similar prices. "A worthy gentleman" in June 1767 paid carriage for five tons of rice and one ton of pickled pork to be sold at London prices.

Throughout the decade there were feast days and celebrations, when the crowd shouted to honour royal birthdays, drank success to Frederick the Great, and marked victories with fireworks and illuminations. And there was always Guy Fawkes day, when the constables put up bills to warn against the inevitable throwing of "serpents, squibs and rockets," those joys of mischievous small boys. Sometimes the circus came to town, and there were balls, exhibitions of curiosities, conjurers with magic tricks: if the little John could not afford to see the performances, some of the electric excitement would reach through to the outskirts of a gathered crowd and tingle the nerves of the small hanger-on.[64]

Beyond his ken, probably, the city's progress was marked by the completion of a general hospital in 1768, by a musical festival, a circulating library, the Lighting and Cleaning Act. Orders were given to make streets safer, with prosecution for people who failed to cover cellar doors, or who left obstructions on the pavement, both traps for unwary travellers. Citizens were advised to throw ashes rather than water on the snow to avoid falls and broken limbs, as most of the town was "on a declivity": did this edict spoil the fun of sliding on the ice for Birmingham urchins? Street lighting was opposed at first as "unjust to the poor and partial to the rich", though one correspondent argued oddly, "Lamps frequently give a Villain an opportunity of perpetrating mischief, which is prevented by darkness."[65]

Those of us with known ancestry cling to our family record, a lifeline mooring us to the past and assuring our identity in the present. Even primitives take refuge in the enveloping security of a tribal spirit past, their continuity and identity assured through their communal legends. The blood coursing in the veins of John Small, of John Herbert, of Stephen Davenport, of Robert Ellwood, of all the men and women whose history is no more than a name on a scrap of paper, was the rich and living blood of a hundred shadowy ancestors who knew themselves to be alive and lusty in their own time, whose blistered hands had spaded the earth, wielded a hammer, whose blistered feet had tramped fields and pathways, who had climbed rigging and pulled on oars, who were warmed by fires, chilled by bitter winds, stung by salt spray, who had rioted with companions, singing and cursing, swearing, and drinking, loving and dying: each of them one of the myriad strands of British life that make the fabric of today. And one may wonder, perhaps, if a tree still stands somewhere in England or Scotland planted by a great-great-great-great-grandfather, a far removed uncle . . . or part of a wall whose stones were gathered and set by hands that carried the blood of an earlier John Small or Stephen Davenport or John Herbert, or of poor hanged Robert Ellwood; hedgerows now hoary and mossed with age beneath whose younger leaves an ancestor one day ate his meagre lunch, a building whose beams carry the chisel marks of some simple, vigorous Davenport, Herbert, Ellwood or Small. Ancestors, recorded or unrecorded, are alive in each one of us in the consciousness we know as "I".

An old man who could not read or write has left no memoirs, and those of his sons and daughters, grandsons and granddaughters, are long gone who might have remembered and recounted the old man's tales and reminiscences. What did he tell them of "when I was a boy?" His background beyond his Birmingham boyhood—and even that—cannot truly be painted in except by using the wider screen of his day and age, against which John Small's clear line to antiquity would show up only faintly, but it would be there nevertheless for a discerning and imaginative eye.

Current descendants of a star-studded lineage—or even of a merely worthy lineage, one bearing names that remain in history books, that had identifiable influence in their own day—trail their ancestry like proud pennants. The line that stretched back from John Small had its own individuality, its own family memories built up as sturdily as any who were to be embedded in history books, but without record except in the fading ink of parish registers and graven on now-illegible tombstones.

Yet in John Small's line there would have been figures noteworthy in their own circumscribed sphere and their own fleeting time—a grandfather known to his cronies as eccentric, or obstinate, crusty or witty or wise, or touched with wanderlust: a grandmother or great-grandmother whose contemporaries saw her as thrifty, or tight-lipped, a dreamer, a beauty, a comfortable person to those in trouble, or a person beset with illness: an ancestor somewhere renowned for his strength: of unusual stature: inventive: much-married: a sharp dealer: tragically struck down. One who had the courage of his convictions and suffered for them. Perhaps a John Small was envied for a green thumb, was admired as a teller of tales: who, though inarticulate, watched the sky and marvelled: or one with clear and musical voice that never reached beyond the village gathering places.

Portraits seldom exist of those without the means to commission them. Did some village genius ever make sketches of the boy John, of his mother Rebecca, of a little sister, fragments admired momentarily, treasured awhile, and lost? Young John was inheritor of unrecorded genes, as definitive and as inescapable, if less happily fortunate, as those of his more illustrious contemporaries. The difference lies in opportunity, education, energy, health, wealth, circumstance. The candle of the "lower orders" was a small flame, put under a bushel of obscurity by their self-styled betters, but in its day it often briefly glowed, lighting up a corner. This John was indubitably the *nth* John Small, scion of a long line. His descendants have a right and claim to this lineage, and a right to boast of it and cringe from it equally with those who have in their recorded lines ancestors of shame as well as of glory. Whether John Small's fall from grace was his own crime or that of the society in which he lived may always be a matter for debate.

His birthplace and family now known, we could picture his boyhood. His teen years—where and how spent? His early manhood—was he *Medway's* John or *Lively's* John? It was time now to search the recruitment lists for *Medway's* John, private marine of the Plymouth Division, 33rd company (the only one of the two actually given a company number on the ship musters). That record would—might—show this John Small, at last, as the John Small we sought. Or not.

We knew that *Medway's* John belonged to the 33rd company, Plymouth division. We knew that *our* John came from Birmingham. It was time now to look at what still survived of the records of the 33rd company: if a Birmingham John Small should show there, we had found our man without doubt. If not, where to turn next? Would we find that *Medway's* John had, after all, been our John, our blood still to be fired by his adventures at Gibraltar? Or was he *Lively's* John?—or the John Small on *Perseus*? Was there *any* way of being certain?

6. RECRUITMENT

By the almost miraculous survival of just this fragment of all the recruitment musters, there *was* a way to be certain: and because we now had discovered his birthplace, we would be able to distinguish between the two. And there they were . . . both of them—*two* John Smalls, *both* belonging to the 33rd company of the Plymouth division. John Small (1), whip maker aged 18, from Newry, County Down, five feet eight inches in height, with light brown hair, fair complexion and "hazle" eyes, had enlisted at Dublin on 23 August 1780. *And John Small (2), bitt maker aged 19 from Birmingham, Warwickshire, was entered as joining the service at Birmingham on 16 April 1781: dark brown hair, five feet six inches tall, fair complexioned, and with the same "hazle" eyes as his namesake.* Without the prior discovery of his birthplace, we could never have been certain that the Irish boy was not our John Small.[66]

Medway's John had been at sea for some ten weeks before Birmingham's John heeded the recruiting call. So the John Small we sought was the man on *Lively*. Which man entered *Perseus* at the end of August 1783 would yet have to be discovered.

An addition to the picture of the young John's probable appearance comes down to us from the future, out of a reporter's interview with one of his sons, described more than a hundred years later, when that son was aged 92. The reporter wrote: "There can be no doubt that much of the strength and individuality of the [Small] race has come from its patriarchal head." What he saw in the son was "a shrewd and intelligent face. Fine black eyes, with the somewhat hard, unfathomable expression often characteristic of the color, a large and slightly aquiline nose, arching eyebrows and a firmly-moulded mouth . . . features which have faithfully transmitted to at least half a dozen members of the Small family casually introduced to us." Did the black eyes come from a dark-complexioned mother?—and perhaps some of the other features too?[67]

A bitt maker. A skilled man, then: had he been unskilled, he would have been entered as "labourer", as so many others were. We could now picture his teen years, passed in apprenticeship to some Birmingham master in the craft of bitt-making. And what sort of bitt, or bit? *Bitt:* "one of the strong posts firmly fastened in pairs in the deck . . . of a ship, for fastening cables, belaying ropes . . . the chief pair . . . used for fastening the cable while the ship rides at anchor". *Bit:* "the movable boring piece of a drill (brace and bit)". *Bit:* "the part of a key . . . which grips the levers of the lock". *Bit:* "the mouthpiece of a horse's bridle".[68]

Birmingham was a canal town, and the barges were docking and undocking at the wharves: they would have a need of ship bitts. But Birmingham was the very heart of the metal manufacturing industry. Did John Small make drill bits, lock bits, bridle bits? Was he carpenter, then, or metal-worker? And why did he leave the trade he knew, for the marine service? Was he bored with monotonous, tiresome work at the forge? Was he lured by the call of high adventure in romantic, far-distant places?

A very brief history of the service he entered in April 1781 will fill in the background. The marine corps had been established, effectively, in the form that survived until recently, by an Order in Council dated 5 April 1755, when 5000 marines were raised under the Admiralty, in 50 companies to be quartered in three permanent divisions, at Chatham, Portsmouth and Plymouth. An Act in the same year called for "the better regulation of His Majesty's Marine Forces while on shore" ("Are not the Marines a corps which must be trained to the service on shore as well as to service at sea?" a House of Commons committee asked in 1833. "To act advantageously . . . must they not be trained to the same discipline as His Majesty's troops? . . . Is it not the order of the Admiralty, that the drill of the Marines, and the discipline of the Marines on shore, should be the same as of the troops of the line?")[69]

But the origin of the marines is usually dated a hundred-odd years earlier, at October 1664, when Charles II's Order in Council directed "that Twelve hundred Land Souldiers be forthwith raised, to be in readiness to be distributed into his Mai^ts fleets prepared for Sea Service . . . to be put into One Regiment under one Collonell, one Lieu^t Coll, and one Serj^t Maior & to be divided into Six Companies each Company to consist of Two hundred Souldiers, and to have one Capptaine, one Lieu^t, one Ensigne, one Drum, foure Serjts & foure corporalls, And all ye Souldiers aforesaid to be armed with Good fire locks, all which Arms Drums, & Colours are forthwith to be prepared & furnished out of his Mai^ts Stores; the Care of which is recommended to ye Duke of Albemarle his Grace Lord Generall of his Ma^ts Forces." The original marines carried army rank: marine privates were privates in the army. But these special "sea souldiers" were known as the Admiral's Regiment until 1685 when the Lord High Admiral succeeded as James II and the regiment became known as Prince George of Denmark's Regiment: Prince George had married Princess (later Queen) Anne in 1683. From then until 1755, regiments for sea service were from time to time raised, incorporated in regiments of the line, or disbanded, as wars waxed and waned.[70]

In 1747 (just prior to total disbandment in 1748) it was ordered that marine regiments, both those in existence and those to be raised in future, should come under the authority of the Admiralty. In 1755, on the outbreak of the Seven Years War, marines were once more needed: an act of Parliament for "the speedy and effectual Recruiting of His Majesty's Land Forces and Marines" set the scene for the marine corps as we have known it. From this date, the marine corps was fully under the control of the Admiralty.[71]

What induced the young John Small, bitt maker, to join the marine corps? Perhaps the canal along which the barges came to his city from unknown parts aroused curiosity, gave him a taste for seeing other places: or perhaps talks with the bargemen who told of sophisticated exciting London and Liverpool, and the roistering sailors who filled the taverns with wild tales and exotic artifacts. Perhaps the glamour of a recruiting party caught his youthful imagination, when the bills were posted all over town offering a bounty to likely lads, and a uniform, and adventure, and a stirring call to serve their country. Perhaps, even as a youngster, he had tagged happily along in the wake of the scarlet-coated men, dreaming about a scarlet coat of his own some day. But in his later teen years there was no call for recruits. In 1774 Parliament had reduced navy strength to 16,000, including only about 4500 marines. When the war with America demanded a large increase, he was probably still an apprentice and an apprentice could not be accepted in the service. By 1781, when he answered the call, the navy vote for 90,000 seamen included 20,000 marines.[72] The younger brothers and sisters at home were enough for his parents to care for, and a young John might have felt he could be less of a burden, even if the family were to lose the small wage he may have been bringing home (he could well have been barely out of his apprenticeship). And freedom, and adventure, for a still teenage lad, sing a loud and powerful siren song. Or, of course, he could have joined out of simple patriotism.

A marine recruiting party would differ from that for the navy in little else than that the navy could use pressgang methods to take men against their will for seamen: the marines almost always called for volunteers. At the time and place appointed—most likely a tavern or village square—the rendezvous would be opened by hoisting the colours, while fife and drum sounded to attract a crowd. Men had already been posting bills around the neighbourhood to attract likely recruits. The posters appealed to courage and patriotism, with a high sense of adventure, calling to "All young men of respectable Character, good countenance, robust Health. . . . All Dashing High-spirited Young Heroes who wish to obtain Glory in the Service of their Country . . . to enlist in the Navy or the Marine Corps. . . ." In another war with America yet in the future, "What a Brilliant Prospect does this Event hold out to every Lad of Spirit, who is inclined to try his Fortune in that highly renowned Corps, the Royal Marines", announced a poster for the War of 1812 (the marine corps had become "Royal" in April 1802). "Lose no Time then, my Fine Fellows, in embracing the glorious Opportunity that awaits you."[73]

Some who answered the call were lads eager for adventure in *any* of the services: a dozen years after John Small joined the marines, Parson Woodforde at Weston in Norfolk found his boy Tim Tooley vanished in the night, "All his Cloaths gone also. It is thought that he is gone to Norwich to enlist himself, as his Head has long run on a Soldiers Life." Six days later Tim returned from Norwich "with a Cockade in his Hat, and says he has entered himself in the thirty third Regiment of Foot. Poor Fellow, he appeared happy & looked well."[74]

So might John Small have looked, after entering himself in the thirty third company of marines.

Expenses for the marine recruiting party would not be very much different from those submitted by the navy officer who was recruiting in 1771 for HMS *Marlborough:* for a couple of men "paisting and distributing a Quantity of Invitation Bills" at 3s. a day: for the rendezvous room (a guinea a week): the cost of "an Ensign Staff, Jack Staff, Trucks & Hallyards to hoist the Colours on opening the Rendezvous", 13s. 6d. The ensign and jack cost £1.18s.8d., the drum and fife 5s., stationery for all the letters and forms needed, £6.18s.9d., with postage adding another 7s. Unforeseen expenses included "a New Oar for the Galley having lost the Old one", and "a New Oar having broke the old one going through Bridge", each at a cost of 8s. The marine recruiting officer however, would not, as the navy officer did, have had to pay out 3s.6d. to an informer for each suitable man rounded up from a hiding place to be impressed as a seaman, nor 6s.9d. for the hire of a horse to locate a likely seaman reported hiding in a neighbouring village: nor 3s.6d. for "Coach hire (being in danger of having them rescued) and a Boat to put them on Board". (In January 1758, however, a Derby man seized by a marine recruiting gang had been shot dead while attempting escape.)[75]

Recruiting procedures in 1781 probably varied little from those set out in Acts passed in earlier years "for the better supply of Marines and seamen" and "for the better payment of the Army and their Quarters", and "for the Regulation of His Majesty's Marine Forces while on Shore". No man would be accepted who was under five feet four inches tall, who was not able-bodied and fit, who was "a known Papist". Between 15 May and 15 October, no labourers might be enlisted if certified by a minister and churchwarden as employed in harvesting.

Rigid rules governed the records to be kept, the payment for clerks to make the mandatory copies, and their dispatch to the Secretary at War or the Admiralty. The new recruits were due their pay from the time of acceptance (those sections of the Articles of War against mutiny and desertion having been read to them) provided they appeared at headquarters within a certain time (30 days if more than 200 miles distant). Until they could be sent to the company and division to which they were assigned, they were to be quartered locally in inns, alehouses, livery stables, victualling houses, but strictly not in private houses. The owners of the accommodation were compensated at a shilling a day for privates, who were each to receive a daily shilling for their provisions, and were to be given candles, vinegar, salt, small beer or cider, and allowed the use of fire and utensils for the preparation of their food.[76]

When the time came to transport the recruits to their destinations, a waggon would be hired at a shilling per mile per waggon with five horses or six oxen, or with four oxen and two horses (so precisely spelt out were the regulations), and less in proportion for smaller vehicles: and a carriage was to be provided to carry the arms, clothes and accoutrements of the men, no carriage allowed to be burdened with more than a hundredweight. Birmingham recruits probably went by canal to Liverpool for a passage by sea to their respective headquarters as the cheapest mode of travel.[77]

The papers now lost by which we could have instantly, and without the long search, have pinned the identity of the two John Smalls, and their physical appearance, were carefully made out, the gaps between the printed words carefully filled in for each recruit by the relevant official, and the small snow-drift of papers that would have gathered around each John Small then began to accumulate. If the actual papers on which our John's name and description were inscribed have disappeared, the surviving papers of other men of his day and his circumstances clearly show a mirror-image of his own. "I [*John Small*] do make Oath, that I am a Protestant, and by Trade a [*Bitt maker*] and to the best of my knowledge and Belief, was born in the Parish of [*Birmingham*] in the [*County*] of [*Warwickshire*] and that I have no Rupture, nor ever was troubled with Fits, that I am no Ways disabled by Lameness or otherwise, but have the perfect Use of my Limbs; and that I voluntarily inlisted myself to serve his Majesty, king GEORGE the Third, as a private Soldier in the [*Third*] or [*Plymouth*] Division of Marines, on the [*16th*] of [*April*] 17 [*81*] and that I am not an Apprentice, nor belonging to any Militia, nor to any other Regiment, or to his Majesty's Navy; and that I have received the inlisting Money which I have agreed for." This seems to have been two guineas at that period.[78]

Along with this paper, signed with name or mark of the new recruit, went the statement of the justice of the peace. "These are to certify, that the above said [*John Small*] Aged [*19*] Years [*5*] Feet [*6*] Inches high [*fair*] complexion [*hazel*] Eyes [*dark brown*] Hair, came before me, one of his Majesty's Justices of the Peace for the County aforesaid, and acknowledged that he had voluntarily inlisted himself to serve his Majesty king GEORGE the Third, in the [*3rd*] or [*Plymouth*] Division of Marines, on the Day of the Month and Year abovementioned: He also acknowledged he hath heard the Second and Sixth Sections of the Articles of War read unto him, against Mutiny and Desertion, and took the Oath of Fidelity mentioned in the said Articles of War." With the surgeon's certificate ("I have examined the above Man and find him in every respect fit for his Majesty's service"), the new recruit was ready for dispatch to his headquarters.[79]

Thus shepherded to Plymouth, John Small would begin shore training in the use of arms, drill routines, guard and sentry duties and dress regulations: in the short period before he was embarked for sea duty (probably the six weeks from the beginning of May to mid-June) there was time for little else. The "Dashing High-spirited Young Heroes" may have amused themselves carving their names in sentry boxes and making holes with their bayonets: sympathised with those who had altered their uniforms and the cock of their hats to their own taste—a bit more rakish?—and were threatened with court martial if discovered: scrupulously attended Rollcallings after seeing a delinquent absentee forced to wear a Cap of Confinement until recalled to duty: surreptitiously observed the disorderly women smuggled into barracks against orders by drunken marines just back from a long East Indies voyage: observed the order to "NCOs drummers and privates of both Battalions to have their hair cutt immediately . . . to a patteran . . . shown to the Barbers who are to be answerable that no alteration to be made in futer on less [unless] by order any man who presum to cutt he hair short will be severly punishd".[80]

With the rest of the new recruits, John Small had been issued with a full kit of clothes on arrival, entitled to "one cloathing" for each year of his service. Owed several outfits after a long voyage away from Britain, a returning marine might be offered a sum of money (20s.) for each "cloathing" due. In 1757 it had been observed that under regulations issued in November 1729 and still extant, a foot-soldier was to receive in his first year a good full-bodied cloth coat, well lined, which might serve for the waistcoat in the second year: a waistcoat: one pair of good Kersey breeches: a pair each of good strong stockings and shoes: two good shirts and neck-cloths, and "a good strong hat, well laced", at a total cost of about £1.17s. As marines were "generally less-sized Men than the Foot-Soldiers," this cost could be estimated at 3s.4d. less per man. With fine economy, one shilling was allowed for the cost, in the second year, of making last year's coat into this year's waistcoat.[81]

In 1775, the kit ordered at Plymouth included four good white shirts, four pairs of good stockings (two white, two worsted), one check shirt, three pairs of good shoes, one pair of long gaiters, Hessian tops, and one pair of short gaiters: two pairs of good Prussian drab drawers, one brush, wire, picker, turnkey, etc.: one set of uniform knee and shoe buckles, one knapsack, two black Manchester velvet stocks. In 1783 a navy captain ordered for each of ten marines coming aboard his ship a marine jacket (7s.2d.), shirt (5s.6d.) and shoes (5s.6d.): navy slop clothes, waistcoat (5s.3d.), breeches (4s.9d.), shirts (3s.10d.), frocks (3s.5d.), trowsers (3s.5d.), stockings (2s.3d.), and shoes (5s.).[82]

John Small's shore pay was about 3s.6d. per week before stoppages for clothing, "and the 12d. in the Pound to be disposed of as His Majesty thinks fit, and One Day's Pay in the Year for *Chelsea Hospital*, and such other necessary Deductions as shall be directed . . .": also for tobacco and for a "cure" if he should contract venereal disease. If marine pay in those days is confusing for us today, it was evidently so for many of John Small's contemporaries. Shore pay was received from the pay master of the marine forces, sea pay from the treasurer of the navy. An impassioned commentator wrote anonymously in 1757 about the pay system for marines, after studying the latest statutes and regulations.[83]

"As to the Methods of Paying and keeping the Accounts of His Majesty's present MARINE FORCES, I am really so much in the dark about them that I hardly know what to say in such a Degree of Certainty as it is proper to be in a Case of National Concern. . . . I cannot find out what PAY any Noncommissioned Officer or a Private Marine is to RECEIVE, either *Daily, Weekly*, or *Monthly*. . . . The *Account* of each *Marine* is not only to be divided into TWO PARTS, but these Parts are to be kept by different persons in distant Places, as if they were distinct Accounts and not at all dependent on each other. . . . The *Scheme* is so INGENIOUSLY *contrived*, that neither the Treasurer of His Majesty's NAVY nor the Pay-Master of the MARINE FORCES can tell whether their ACCOUNTS of this Marine-Pay are RIGHT or WRONG. . . . During the time on shore, each marine is to receive Pay twice per week . . . at the end, to receive or be accounted with for his Arrears of Pay as mentioned in Statute III, and when he goes to sea, another Account of his pay is to be opened and charged with any over payment or debt on his land account, as well as with slop-cloathing &c. received by him from the Purser &c. on board ship; which account is to be closed when he returns to Quarters, but before this can be done, there must be about four computations made of Time, Pay and Stoppages for every man's account while at sea." . . .

"I have likewise read other printed *Regulations* and *Instructions* made and given by the . . . commissioners in October 1756, *relating to Marines serving on board His Majesty's ships;* but I cannot there find what PAY each Noncommissioned Officer and Private Marine is to RECEIVE, or what DEDUCTIONS are to be made from the Pay, when on Shore, or at Sea . . . what LAW a Marine is to plead for the Recovery of his PAY, if detained from him, or what DEDUCTIONS it is liable to, are matters equally unknown to me. . . .''[84]

In mid-June 1781 the order came to embark on HMS *Lively*. Equipped with a bed and sea-chest and the "usual" two-months' advance wages (an adjective deplored by the anonymous writer as uninformative), John Small now entered the next phase of his career, probably confused, but probably excited too, on the way to obtaining that "Glory in the Service of their country" the posters had promised to "every Lad of Spirit".[85]

Marine uniforms. Drawn by Charles C. Stadden.
Courtesy Royal Marines Historical Society.

7. HMS LIVELY

"Received on board 12 marines and a serjeant", reported the captain's log of HMS *Lively* at Plymouth on Friday 15 June 1781. She sailed next day, with 62 seamen and 12 marines of her complement of 80 on board, and at the end of her voyage in December 1782, five of her original group of marines—William Drake, Richard Barnett, David Butler, William Putty and John Small—and 16 of her original complement of seamen were still serving, some from as early as October 1779.[86]

Two days earlier, John Manley had succeeded William Carlyon as captain, as he had succeeded John Inglefield in his turn. *Lively*, a 12-gun sloop of some 206 tons, had been purchased (probably built) in 1779, and from her commissioning had spent her first 18 months or so "cruizing up the Irish Sea", in and out of Appledore and Milford Haven, across to Guernsey, over to Cork, up to Dublin and Carrickfergus and Liverpool. The entry of John Small and the other marines in June 1781 was the first time *Lively* had borne marines as part of her complement: but she had carried for 14 months the young Samuel Hood as master's mate, who in October 1780 would go to his cousin Lord Hood's *Barfleur*, eventually as second in command, to retire with the rank of vice-admiral.[87]

So John Small began his sea experience, butting down the Channel in thick fog, anchoring at Fowey in Cornwall in strong gales with showers of rain, out again towards Ushant, standing in for Brest on the way, where 15 French sail of the line were observed to lie with yards and top-masts struck (very different from the huge fleet under the French admiral the comte de Grasse which had readied at Brest in March and slipped away unmolested while the Grand Fleet had lain off Cork waiting for the Gibraltar victuallers). There were occasional exciting moments from chases when strange sail were encountered: and (one imagines, for any fleet until identified was potential danger) times when all eyes turned to "a fleet on the NW quarter thought to be Admiral Darby's fleet" returning from Gibraltar, but which turned out to have been the West India fleet coming home. And so, back to Plymouth, from mooring to mooring: eight days in port, six at sea, 19 in port, five at sea, nine more in

Early map of the West Indies, showing Key Sal (top left) and Havana (extreme left), with reefs on which HMS *Jupiter* grounded along the Cuban coastline south of Key Sal.

Courtesy British Library.

Die Ankunft des Königlichen Prinzen William Henry von | L'Arrivé du Prince Guillaume Henry fil du Roi
Engelland zu Newyork in Amerika 1781. | d'Angleterre a Nouvelle York en l'Amerique 1781.
den 10 October. | le 10 Octobre.

Arrival of Prince William Henry at New York, September 1781. The artist has depicted the prince's ship HMS *Prince George*, though he actually landed from HMS *Lively*, perhaps one of the smaller ships in the scene.

Courtesy New York Public Library.

port before leaving England behind on the first long voyage of John's career.[88]

He attended every muster since joining the ship, and the days and weeks in port would have been strenuous, noisy, busy weeks for John Small and his fellows, accompanying boatloads of dockyard workers and seamen to and from the ship amid the banging of caulkers jamming in oakum to block cracks in the seams, the smell of tar, the sound of carpenters' hammers, the shouts and bangs and thumps—and curses—as barrels and boxes were loaded on board, carpenter's and boatswain's stores, food, beer and water; standing guard as all the stores were stowed in their proper places on board. On one short cruise out of Plymouth, "saw a large fleet". . . "gave chase after an unknown vessel" . . . "saw the Grand Fleet anchored off the Sound": a period in which *Lively* moved from anchorage to anchorage for various naval purposes and took on men to build up her complement for a final sailing on 29 July, bound for North America, and who knew what adventures?[89]

There was not much to occupy the time of a marine on board while at sea, except to exercise small arms from time to time (and take care of them—a year earlier on another ship a marine had been docked 40s. for losing his firelock and bayonet overboard):[90] to stand duty at designated points on board between men and officers: perhaps to be stationed at strategic places with an axe to cut away rigging, sails, masts, toppled in a dangerous tangle in a storm. On board, marines were treated as seamen under the command of the captain, with the same pay and deductions, furnished with Navy slop clothes as needed (deducted, of course, from their sea pay), mustered with the ship's company. They were not required to do seamen's duty, but in fact a few learned even to furl sails and to go aloft, though this was purely voluntary. (Some captains actively encouraged this kind of participation, seeing in such volunteers a source of trained seamen when their complement needed increase.) Many of the marines, out of sheer boredom, did some deck duty. John Small took his share of stowing "hammacoes" each day in the deckside netting, learned to splice ropes, made "robins" (the small plaited rope-bands rove through the eyelet holes in sails). He may even have helped the ship's surgeon in some minor jobs (whatever tales did he tell his grandchildren that made them think he had once been "ship's apothecary"?).[91]

So, at the end of July 1781, *Lively* sailed down Channel again and into the fresh gales of the North Atlantic, noting the Lizard, Land's End, the St Anne's light at Scilly, last glance at England for everyone on board. They would all, without fail, have peered to see this last contact with home, quite apart from the regulations that required a log report of such sightings. It was an adventurous 44-day crossing, with guns fired at strange ships before they showed neutral colours, of chases by frigates that turned out to be Royal Navy ships, occasionally sailing in company for a few hours. Then at last, on 11 September, they saw the famed American coast with the strange names, Nantucket, "the High Land of Never Sunk and Sandy Hook", where the ship's clerk recorded in his own phonetics the presence of British vessels, "President, Huzza and Zeberah . . . Peral . . . Oystrige".[92]

On 21 September, Admiral Thomas Graves arrived at Sandy Hook after his failure to make effective battle with the French off Chesapeake Bay. And on the 25th, Admiral Robert Digby wrote from Sandy Hook on HMS *Prince George*, "I find the Lively Brig who sailed after us has been here some considerable time. I am now waiting . . . to get over New York bar but am afraid the wind will not serve us to Day." Next day. *Lively* was to have a signal honour: "At 10 a.m. . . . recd HRH Prince William Henry and Admiral Digby . . . and made sail for New York". The shallower draft of *Lively* got her over the bar safely, and she landed her distinguished passengers at the North River next day. One imagines the seamen, and particularly the marines in their smart scarlet, drawn up in ship-dressed order to honour Royalty. If only John Small could have kept a journal of that eventful day: but there seems no doubt that his nearest and dearest would have heard the tale many times in days to come: especially when in 1830 that prince became William IV, King of England.[93]

What did he see of New York, if he landed there briefly for a few hours of freedom and sight-seeing? Prince William, just turned sixteen, was not impressed. "The town is built in the Dutch way, with trees before the houses", he wrote to his father the king. "The streets are in general narrow and very ill-paved. There is but one Church, all the others being converted into magazines or Barracks." New York was a rowdy, tough, miserable city, entirely ruled by the roistering military under Sir Henry Clinton, commander-in-chief, where robberies and muggings abounded and rebels cruelly huddled in prison ships, to the lasting shame of the authorities, before the more humane regime of Sir Guy Carleton restored order and decency. *Lively* was 40 days in port, moving from Sandy Hook to Staten Island to New York: John Small on one shore visit may have ventured into "Canvas Town", a ragged collection of tents and huts on the site of the fire of September 1776, giving refuge to roughs and toughs, preying on citizens already subject to strict and merciless British military rule. William Putty and John "Nickles", both marines, received a dozen lashes for drunkenness on 15 October . . . after a visit ashore? But New York offered a new and strange way of life, new scenes, new accents, for the boy from Birmingham after months at sea, new memories to store away. And there were better areas into which he might have ventured, to gape at the mansions of the great families of the city, the Waltons, the Delanceys, the Hallecks.[94]

It was back to England for *Lively*, that swift sailer, with dispatches for the Admiralty, leaving behind the stately gathering of the fleets under Admirals Graves and Drake and Digby: seeing, on the day of her departure on 20 October "the whole fleet under Admiral Digby" sail for the Chesapeake with 25 sail of the line, three 50s, four 44s, and 6000 troops to attempt the relief of Cornwallis. *Lively* went straight into the fury of storms, squalls, strong gales, carrying only 55 of her complement. On 30 October her bowsprit was sprung by a heavy sea: she lost the sprit sailyard, the jib off the boom, and a man overboard, an unlukcy volunteer seaman, William Moore. Just over a week later, strong gales carried away the main topmast, main top gallant masts, the foresail yard, and split the fore top gallant sail. "Employed getting wreck down and fore topsail yard and main top mast up," says the log laconically. One does not imagine John Small and his marine companions were sitting idle during the crisis.[95]

On 14 November, with Dartmouth five or six leagues distant, a gun was fired for a pilot, and Captain Manley went ashore with his dispatches. He also carried letters from Prince William. The prince had told Captain Manley, said the *Morning Chronicle* of 16 November, "Here's a letter for my father, another for my mother, and letters for as many of my brothers and sisters, as I had time to write to; and pray give my compliments to Sandwich, and tell him, we are just going to fight the French *in earnest*". John Small could not write. Did he persuade a more competent fellow seaman to send word, in his name, to the family in Holloway Head, Birmingham?

Lively was to spend the next 173 days in port at Plymouth—plenty of repair work to be done after that rough North Atlantic crossing. For part of the time *Medway* was also in port. Did the two John Smalls ever meet? (How would they have greeted each other? "Irish, eh?" ... "A Brummagem boy, then!")*Lively* went briefly to sea on 4 April 1782, with a new master (David Swan), to accompany a convoy to the Downs. In May she spent seven days at St Peter Port, Guernsey, to bring back 32 French prisoners destined for Mill Prison at Plymouth, six of whom were discharged into HMS *Swan*. (Did they elect to join the Royal Navy?) While at anchor in Plymouth Sound, a French sail of truce ran on board of *Lively*, and carried away the fore topsail yard, main top gallant mast and main topmast backstay. "Employed clearing the wreck", reported the log (one imagines resignedly): but by 5 June the ship was ready and away again, this time bound on a 45-day voyage to the West Indies with dispatches "Express to Sir George".[96]

On 11 July, *Lively* anchored in Carlisle Bay, Barbadoes, for water, and set off again at once for Jamaica. It had been a reasonably uneventful voyage: an occasional sail sighted, a bustle once or twice clearing for possible action and the appearance of interesting sea-creatures—porpoises, dolphins, flying fish. On 23 June the captain had issued everyone with fishing lines, for occupation and for fresh food. At the end of June they crossed the Tropic of Cancer, where a year earlier Captain Thomas Pasley of HMS *Jupiter* had allowed his sailors "some fun; I did not admit of Ducking as the Ship went too fast—every other amusement I had no objection to. A Neptune or King of the Tropic with his attendants paid me a Visit before I had done dinner, with Drums, Fiddlers, and Bagpipes, and made me a thousand Speaches." Captain John Manley, on *Lively*, could have got away with no less, and this John Small probably had his first experience of what he was to know four more times in his life, though the fourth time would not be so jolly.[97]

From Barbadoes to Jamaica they were never far from land, the romantic small Caribbean islands John would have heard of in the chatter of Birmingham taverns and in the tales of old salts on the New York docks last year. Before the ship arrived at Jamaica, he saw the famed Martinico, St Lucia, Navassa, with routine jobs along the way like "scrubbing Hamoks", before anchoring in Port Royal harbour on 20 July. Only three days in port, for water and stores: and on 23 July she was off again in company with HMS *Montagu* and eight sail of the line, bound for New York.

On the 25th, David Butler ("marean") was in trouble, 24 lashes for theft. The fleet passed Navassa, Cape Tiberon at the west end of "Highspainyola", Cape Donnamaria further north, the Mole of St Nicolas to the west in the Windward Passage, and out past Mayaguana into the open ocean, passing the fleet that carried English troops from Georgia to Jamaica after the evacuation. On 5 August an exchange was made in mid-voyage: Captain Manley was ordered from *Lively* to *Montagu*, and Lieutenant Robert Cuthbert, by order of Lord Rodney, from *Montagu* to command *Lively*, parting company with the fleet on the 9th to head for New York with dispatches. After a series of "chaces" and several small prizes, releasing prisoners to a well-met flag of truce on the "Chisipick tack" (where the French and Americans were firmly in control), *Lively* was once again moored off the King's Wharf at New York on 24 August. A few seamen promptly deserted, and four days later John Squire was lost by drowning while the carpenter's crew was caulking the outside of the ship. Squire was an Exeter lad, aged 25 when he joined *Lively* on 1 November 1781, a familiar face now missing from the small complement.[98]

On 6 September another service was required of *Lively* by Admiral Digby (this time without Royalty), whose *Prince George* once again could not cross the bar to Sandy Hook and back again. And on 9 September, anchored off the Battery, New York, *Lively* received on board her new captain, Michael Stanhope, then aged about 31: that young midshipman who on *Eagle* in 1777 had watched Stephen Davenport's ship *Augusta* blow up in the Delaware.[99]

Captain Pasley of HMS *Jupiter* had a better opinion of the city than Prince William's first impressions. "New York is a very large Town, but Built with no Regularity. There are many Excellent Houses; it has, however, suffered greatly by Fire." It was a second visit for John Small, and perhaps he had opportunity to notice differences since the advent of Sir Guy Carleton some months earlier: Sir Guy had done much to restore law and order and to reduce much of the cruelty on the prison ships there.[100]

That month, *Lively* was sent north to Halifax, the log reporting a variety of "chaces" and successes: "An American Whale boat cutt a schoonar out from the foot of the Light house Sandey Hook Got under way and gave chace fired several guns but to no purpos she Got on Shore befor we could reach her with our shot. . . . Saw a sail . . . and gave Chace . . . and took her she was a whail fishing sloop from Nantuket put an officer and 4 men on Board for and sent her for newyork." At Halifax on the 21st, the master (David Swan) was sent to sick quarters, "being very bad in a feaver", where he subsequently died. John Small was losing companion voyagers who could ill be spared.[101]

Returning to New York, *Lively* took the *Charles* prize, laden with stock, off Rhode Island, and brought her in to New York on 6 October, her six American prisoners consigned to the notorious *Jersey* prison ship. Here Lieutenant Cuthbert went ashore on leave, and *Lively* received a new master, James Reilly, from *Namur*, to replace David Swan. When she sailed with Admiral Pigot's fleet from Sandy Hook on the 25th, *Lively* also had a new lieutenant, James Delancey Walton: unlucky Cuthbert had been held up by unfavourable winds from reaching the Sandy Hook anchorage in time.[102]

In Caribbean waters, another shipmate was missed, when 18-year-old James Nearne/Nairne of Newborough, Fife, was lost overboard. The pay due to him (£14.12s.) was on 16 September 1784 paid to William Balmain as attorney for the lad's father: though living in different Scottish counties, they were only about ten miles apart: Balmain and Nairne were evidently good friends.[103]

So the fleet continued to sail southwards, thirteen ships of the line, frigates and other vessels, under Admirals Pigot and Drake: and for *Lively*, and for Captain Stanhope, and for John Small, who had never missed a muster or been in any trouble, into disaster.

"On the 14th of November in my way from New York," wrote Admiral Hugh Pigot to Admiralty in January 1783, "I sent the Jupiter with the Lively with orders to proceed off the Havannah and gain the best Intelligence he could of the State of the Enemy's ships there." He was then to hasten to Lord Hood at the Caycos Islands with information, "and to send the Lively to me" at Barbadoes, where he had arrived with the fleet on the 21st.[104]

Jupiter, commanded by Captain Thomas Pasley and by far the larger vessel (some 1000 tons, a 4th rate of 50 guns with a complement of 350) recorded receiving two months' supplies from *Formidable* on the 14th, and with *Lively* in company, parted from the fleet in fair weather and light breezes, to make for the north coast of Cuba. On the 16th there was a "chace". The two ships kept company to anchorage at the south end of Abaco Island on the 22nd, and began dodging south among the shoals and small keys in the Exuma Channel. The 26th found them off Deadman's Keys, and about to enter the more open seas of the Great Bahama Bank, heading, as directed, for a cruise along the northern coast of Cuba as far as Havana, where strange sail abounded: sighted and identified and sent on their way, or chased in hope of capture, little *Lively* keeping about three leagues off.[105]

As far along the Cuban coast as Matanzas by the 28th, *Jupiter* swooped down on a group of merchantmen and found rich prize. "I saw a small Fleet . . . in the Night and captured by morning the American Ship Hero of Eighteen Guns with three hundred Boxes sugar having ten thousand Dollars on board, the Ship Le Nanethe French with about 90 Hogsheads of sugar some Cotton & Elephants teeth: The American Brig Dauphin with about two hundred Boxes of Sugar; The American Sloop Experiment with about 20 odd Boxes of Sugar and some Coffee, this last being trifling I took her Cargo on board and destroyed."[106]

Lively was engaged on her own account, her marines no doubt eagerly pitching in to some real action at last: she "captured the [American] Ship St Helena after an Action of some time, at last she struck to her on the

Jupiters coming up, she had on board above four hundred Boxes of Sugar & four thousand five hundred Dollars."[107]

There was every reason for *Lively* and her complement (it now numbered only 61), to feel satisfied with the result of their mission: an enemy ship captured, prisoners taken, valuable cargo in money and kind in her hands. As instructed, she went north in the night heading for Key Sal where she would rendezvous with *Jupiter*, where they could water and "the Prizes be put in proper Order to be dispatched". So, with 13 of her men on *St Helena* as a prize crew, and 44 American prisoners below hatches, *Lively* "stood to the NE as far as the Double Headed Shot Keys . . . and stood to the Leeward two or three days," wondering what had delayed *Jupiter*. Falling in with another ship, "our Water being nearly Expended got a temporary supply from her", Captain Stanhope learnt that unlucky *Jupiter* had gone aground on a rock in the Cuba Keys. Being in such need of water, *Lively* made her way at once to the Key Sal rendezvous.[108]

On 30 November, *Jupiter* had found herself "on Shore on the Shoals of Boca Nicholas on the Island of Cuba," a small rock about three feet below water that ran to depths of 18 feet on either side. Not more than four months earlier, Pasley had endorsed Admiral Pigot's disgust when several ships were grounded on rocks they would have seen "if they had only looked over the side". Pasley had added a comment in his journal: "This is too true to my knowledge." Now he found himself in the same predicament. By some miracle the hull was undamaged, "tho' beating on a bed of Rocks for Nine long Hours." But Pasley had the added mortification of seeing his best prize *Hero* seized by her prisoners (assisted, he feared, by the twelve men from *Jupiter* on board) "run off . . . to the Enemy at the Havannah" with her sugar and her ten thousand dollars. *Lively* had disappeared during the night, before the accident.[109]

Awaiting *Jupiter's* arrival at the rendezvous, Captain Stanhope sent a party of eleven men ashore for the much needed water. Thirteen more men were on board the prize, *St Helena*, including the mate, John Sibbett, James Fagan, midshipman, and three marines (two of whom, David Butler and William Drake, were from the original "serjeant's party"—12 privates and a serjeant—embarking at Plymouth in June 1781 with John Small). Only 37 men now remained on *Lively* from her depleted complement to guard the 44 prisoners.[110]

On 9 December, about 2 p.m., while Captain Stanhope was courteously dining in his cabin with *Lively's* master, James Reilly (who had just come off watch on deck), the captain of the *St Helena*, John Stillwell, and a passenger voyaging with him, he found his ship taken over by the rebel prisoners. "I was much alarmed when the prisoners attacked me in my Cabin . . . and we found it impossible to regain the Ship. . . . When I got hold of my Pistols and was attempting to go upon deck, the Captain held and prevented me, and seized my Pistols. At that time the Cabin was full of Prisoners armed, who asked me if I would surrender: as it was impossible to oppose them, I was compelled to submit."

The master, alarmed by the noise, "went immediately to my Cabin to get a case of Pistols out, the Lieutenant had then come down off the Quarter deck. On my attempting to go upon deck, I found two Centinals, with fixed Bayonets over the Companion; I went back to Captain Stanhope, who was preventing the Master and Supercargo from going upon deck. The Prisoners were now attempting to come down thro' the Skylight, and Captain Stanhope told the Supercargo he had surrendered."[111]

Lieutenant Walton, on watch with the carpenter Francis Floyd, seems to have been unarmed ("but I always went armed in the Night time"), and could do nothing to stop the onslaught. Of the crew, about eight were aloft; a quarter master was in the hold with three men stowing water casks, four or five men were on the bow-sprit with the boatswain, the rest "differently Employed about the Ship". At each of the two hatchways, one of the ten marines left on board (John Small among them) stood guard, armed with a cutlass.

It was generally agreed that only four persons were on the deck at the time: Walton, Floyd, and the two sentries. One prisoner only, according to Stanhope's orders, had been allowed up, a man named William Whitmore or Whipton.[112] At a given moment, he drew a cutlass from beneath his jacket and cried "Now; Now is your time": upon which the prisoners came in a rush from the main hatchway and overwhelmed the two marine sentinels and other members of the crew by their sheer numbers. William Green, the captain's cook, "in the Galley, sitting in my Berth unwell, saw the Lively's people knocked down . . . Edward Stoakes [carpenter's mate] was one, and several Marines." The prisoners, unarmed when they reached deck, made for the arms chests, one of which was unlocked, the lock having been taken off that morning "to put upon the Water cask, as we were at short allowance, and there was no spare lock on board". The sailors aloft had arms in the tops, but no ammunition, which Stanhope had ordered removed against the very event that was now happening. Floyd, who had actually been sitting on the unlocked arms chest, was cut on the arm. The boatswain, Thomas Muffin, attempting to oppose the rebels, was badly wounded in the shoulder by a tomahawk.

The master said afterwards he thought too many men were ashore for the watering. Stanhope was said to have received warnings a few days earlier, one from William Jenkins, boatswain's mate, and one from the master himself, that a rising was contemplated. In consequence, he had ordered all knives to be taken from the prisoners, and gave orders to arrange for putting them in irons. He later countermanded the order. "Do you know of a reason why the Prisoners were not confined?" the surgeon, Edward Bell, was asked at the subsequent court martial. "None, but Humanity", he replied: but Stanhope's humanity, it was generally agreed, was a mistake for which he paid dearly. "Had they been confined in Irons, it would have prevented it," said Lieutenant Walton, a fairly self-evident verdict repeated by most of the other witnesses.

Stanhope had given strict instructions for no communication between crew and prisoners, but three of them (one later found to be an American) were frequently seen to be talking with any who were on deck. These men—Joshua Oakes (carpenter's crew), George McCoy or Mackie (yeoman PR) and Thomas Hall (Ab) went down the hatch immediately it had been opened, and joined in with the rebels. It seems likely that these three had managed to loosen the hatch bars: almost all witnesses agreed that the gratings had been carefully secured and checked regularly.[113]

Poor Stanhope—his orders appear to have been sensible, given close personal attention, and to as great an extent as possible strictly carried out (though a certain amount of self-justification crept into the statements of the witnesses later)—was betrayed not only by three of his crew and by his "humanity" in leaving the prisoners unironed, but by a viper in his bosom, as it were. There had also been, it seemed, an enemy agent present—"a woman on board, that belonged to Captain Stanhope". Lieutenant Walton, the carpenter Francis Floyd, the surgeon Edward Bell, the purser William Bennicke, and the master, James Reilly, had all heard either directly or by hearsay that the rising had followed a rumour that the prisoners "were to have been put on Shore upon Key Sal; and that they had gained their Information from a woman ['Q: Of what country was she? A: America.'']."[114] Within not much more than an hour after the first attack, Matthew Noble, the gunner on shore with his party of seamen and boys who had been there since noon the previous day, was stunned "by seeing the English colours, hoisted under the American" on the ship he had served in since March 1780: and still carrying John Small on board, with his serjeant and the seven remaining privates, nursing a sore head or shoulder, probably handcuffed (there were enough handcuffs on board to have chained the 44 American prisoners two-and-two), and wondering about his future.

On 11 January 1783, the *Independent Gazetteer*, Philadelphia, printed a triumphant item of news. "On the 27th of November last, the ship Hero, of this port, from the Havannah, was captured by the British men of war Jupiter and Lively, who put a prize-master and 16 men on board to navigate her; but the Jupiter running aground soon after, the prize-master with four of his men, took the yawl, and went to her assistance. In this fortunate interval, Captain Douglas, Mr Gamble, the chief Mate, the Doctor, Carpenter, and two sick men, all of the Hero, rose upon the remaining twelve of the enemy, retook the vessel, after she had been 63 hours in their possession, and carried her safe into the Havannah.

"The ship St Helena, Captain Stillwell, was likewise taken by the above sloop of war Lively, the Commander of which, Mr Stanhope, of the Chesterfield family, ordered on board his own vessel, seizing a favourable moment, also rose, took possession of the Lively, and carried her into the Havannah.

"The Lively is a fine copper-bottomed brig, cutter built, mounting 12 eighteen pounders, carronades, and two long sixes, and, as a cruizer, will prove a most valuable acquisition. The St Helena, on her being captured, was ordered for Antigua. It is said, the six fortunate adventurers, who retook the Hero from double the number of the enemy, will share near 7000 dollars each."[115]

Part of a map of the City of Havana, Cuba, showing Morro fortress at entrance, middle top of plan.
Courtesy British Library.

9. PEACE AND RELEASE

The *Lively* may have been lost, but her prize, the *St Helena* was not. Her 13-man prize crew brought her safely to St John's Harbour, East Florida (held by and loyal to the British since 1763) where she arrived on 26 December 1782. *Lively's* men (except for three who promptly deserted) were taken aboard HMS *Belisarius,* from which John Small's two marine comrades, David Butler and William Drake, also tried (unsuccessfully) to escape. By May, *Belisarius* was at St Augustine, where most of *Lively's* men were discharged into HMS *Hound* under their former captain John Manley.[116]

The crew that had stayed on *Lively* were not so lucky. When *Lively,* entering Havana Harbour in December 1782, passed below the grim fortress of the Morro Castle, Michael Stanhope would be remembering, unhappily, an earlier encounter with those menacing guns. In June 1767, without warning, "the Morro Castle fired a Canon without Ball" at his first ship, HMS *Cygnet,* on which he had served as Ab for 18 months, as she attempted to bring dispatches to the governor. The captain, Philip Durell, explained his business and was told "to bring too and send a Boat on shore to the Morro", but was shocked by a second shot, this time with ball, directed at his masts, "and with the farther menace they would sink the ship if she did not put to sea."

Being now engaged in the difficult manoeuvres of anchoring, Durell said he would comply "when the ship was in a proper place of safety": whereupon the governor fired again. "The Ball (of 24 pounds) entered about six inches under the Larboard Whale, abaft the main chains, and lodged in the opposite side." Icy letters were exchanged between captain and governor, each regarding the affair as an insult to his respective monarch, the Kings of England and Spain. Passing under the Morro again in *Lively* at the end of 1782, Captain Michael Stanhope, now 15 years older than the young Ab (soon to be midshipman) of 1767, would have had vivid memories of that frightening day, though this time with no fear of being fired on.[117]

Apart from the apprehension for their careers that both Stanhope and Lieutenant Walton would be feeling, there was no suffering for any of the officers, who doubtless were received with the standard honours of war and released by cartel at an early date: at any rate, they are found in New York, having arrived at some date as yet undiscovered, and embarked on HMS *Vulture* on 22 June 1783 to return to Jamaica for the court-martial of the Captain, officers and company for the loss of *Lively*. The group "late Lively" included Stanhope, Walton, James Reilly (the master, with his servant George Harper), Edward Bell (surgeon), William Bennicke (purser), Matthew Noble (gunner), Francis Floyd (corporal), two of Stanhope's servants Thomas Langdon and James Johnson, and the captain's cook William Green.[118]

For the rest of the crew members, and the marines, including serjeant William Brown and private John Small, life in Havana for the four months they were held prisoner, would have been very different. Neither side in the war was noted for humanity to its prisoners. Reminiscences of Americans held in Plymouth's Mill prison (the superintendent, William Cowdry, would meet John Small some years later, if only briefly), and in the terrible prison hulks in New York, contain hair-raising anecdotes of brutality and lack of the most basic compassion. It would be no comfort to John and his companions, however, to know there might be others, among his nominal enemies, as badly or worse off. *Lively's* boatswain, Thomas Muffin, died on 14 March of the wounds he had received in the fight to defend the ship, and of those who were brought out when—mercifully—hostilities had ended within a few months, several were given a passage home by the navy, probably because they were not well enough to work their way.[119]

They may have been held in the dungeons of the Morro, or in "the Cavanna Castle near the Havannah" where an English merchant, Philip Allwood, spent several years in prison.[120] But the best account we can find for this period appeared in the *London Chronicle* for 1 November 1782, near enough to the time *Lively's* crew were taken into captivity.

"A gentleman just arrived in town from Havannah, in the island of Cuba, where he was confined upwards of a year, gives an account of the barbarous treatment he and others met with from the Spaniards: He says, that soon after they were carried into the Havannah, they were drove a few miles up the island, where they were stript of all their cloaths, except a shirt and a pair of trowsers, confined in a close yard four months without any shelter to keep them from the rain which fell at that time; that they lay upon the ground, and had not above an ounce and a half of meat allowed them per day, and their principal food was a coarse sort of bread with water, the latter they were obliged to buy out of their allowance; when they were permitted to wash, they were drove to a piece of water, and it was a favour to let them wash their shirts; but were not suffered to stay till they dried them, but obliged to put them on wet; afterwards they were put into a slaughter-house, where there were stocks, into which they were put every night, and locked down till the morning, and were obliged to lie on their backs upon the ground till the morning, through which hardships several of his fellow prisoners died; that they got a petition presented to the governor of the Havannah, setting forth the ill treatment they met with, and their having short allowance; to which the governor answered, he was sorry he had it not in his power to take off part of that. The captain of a cartel ship wanting hands, had the liberty of taking four out of the prisoners, and this gentleman was one; from thence went to Jamaica, and got a passage to England, in a ship that suffered much in the hurricane, and had seven feet of water in her hold when she arrived at Portsmouth; he is now at his father's, in so bad a condition with the rheumatism, that he cannot walk without help; he left many prisoners behind him in a most deplorable condition; amongst them were three captains of ships."[121]

Perhaps John and his companions would have heard rumours of the impending peace, which would have given them all much hope. Perhaps he was left to wonder, to the last moment, how many years he would have to stay in this miserable confinement. He certainly was unaware of the stately progress of the arrangements between Great Britain and the Most Christian King signed 20 January 1783 at Versailles, and between Great Britain and the Most Catholic King on the same day concerning prisoner exchange. Article 21 in the Treaty with the Most Christian King and Article 9 with the Most Catholic King agreed that the prisoners on each side "shall be restored reciprocally and *bona fide*, immediately after the ratification of the Definitive Treaty, without ransom, and on paying the debts they may have contracted during their captivity; and each Crown shall respectively reimburse the sums which have been advanced for the subsistence and maintenance of the prisoners by the Sovereign of the country where they shall have been detained, according to the receipts and attested accounts, and other authentick titles, which shall be produced on each side."[122]

Where are they now, those detailed, name-by-name "receipts and attested accounts, and other authentick titles"? It would have provided work for international accountants and translators for years to come. And how much more could we learn, could they be located!

With what cheer, then, would the bedraggled crew of *Lively* have heard of the arrival of HMS *Diamond* in Havana Harbour on 30 April 1783, carrying 38 Spanish prisoners to exchange for British sailors? *Diamond* left Port Royal, Jamaica, on 20 April, and came to under the Morro Castle on the 30th. No menacing shots this time, but a salute of 19 guns, which *Diamond* returned, exchanging another 19 with the Spanish admiral in his flagship in the harbour. *Diamond* then

"Wharp'd the ship up the Harbour" and discharged her prisoners, keeping a boat rowing around the ship to discourage deserters (tried by two sailors with dire results for both). Next day *Diamond* "Received on bd·from the Spanish prison [blank] Englishmen belonging to H. M. S Lively & 39 men belongš to Rattan." These included a few soldiers. One of *Diamond's* lieutenants, William Bowen, added "and 19 belonging to a merchantman from Jamaica." Another lieutenant, Benjamin Hickey, identified 27 prisoners as from HMS *Tickler,* the only other captured Royal Navy ship taken into Havana, captured on 10 February by the French 64-gun *La Triton.* Six other men were embarked on the 16th and 18th of May. One can almost hear the hearty cheering from John Small and his companions as their boats approached the British man of war, a cheer that would echo back to them from the decks of *Diamond:* probably there were tears of joy in many an eye.[123]

See John, then, walking free on the deck of a British ship once more, freshly clothed in navy slops, a supernumerary with no duties to perform as yet, watching with keen eyes the pencil-lines of many masts swaying against the sky, and the Spanish men-of-war at their stations in the harbour: looking with eager interest at the busy movements of shipping, too far up harbour to see the lowering Morro, no longer a threat, at the narrow entrance through which he had once passed in apprehension and would soon pass again, thankfully leaving his bad memories behind him.

Diamond stayed at Havana for 21 Days. What of the city could John Small see from her mooring? If he had been marched through it, he would have noticed what a grandson of his king, George III, saw some thirty years later when Sir Augustus d'Este spent a few days in Havana. Little would have changed. "The town appeared quite different from any accounts I had heretofore heard of Spanish cities, the houses appeared built of stucco, and painted, some with fantastic borders. . . . The Volante's . . . are a one horse chaise admirably adapted for the climate [the horse being a mule on which the driver sat] . . . the harness . . . covered with silver and the collar with little silver ball bells." The carriage itself was protected by an "apron" of cloth against rain, sun and dust. All the streets were narrow except for "The Paseo . . . a very fine broad road about a mile in length with a broad footpath on each side under the shade of trees, and a rivulet on each side." The "lots of pretty women" would catch the eye of *Lively's* sex-starved men, as they did the sex-starved Sir Augustus.[124]

Lively's marines remained as supernumeraries for victuals only until she reached Port Royal, when some were transferred to the ship's list and served as part of the complement (John from 16 June). The regular marine complement already serving on *Diamond* included, at Havana, Second Lieutenant Ralph Clark, who had entered her in July 1782 and would leave her for HMS *Preston* on 22 June 1783 in Jamaica.[125] One wonders if Clark was interested enough in the prison experiences of mere privates to question John or others—and did John recognize him in 1788 when encountered again in New South Wales?

Diamond's last *Tickler* prisoners were on board by the 18th. News of truce had percolated only slowly to the Caribbean: navy ships were still busily chalking up triumphs after the signing and before the captains could learn of it. This had been *Tickler's* fate: and as late as May a prize taken from the Marquis de Vaudreuil's squadron, loaded with £50,000-worth of masts, bowsprits, oak planks and timber, fell to Captain Pasley and *Jupiter*.[126]

Meanwhile, on 10 May, an event to stir loyal English blood (and perhaps especially John's, in the circumstances) had occurred with the arrival in port of the *Fortunee* carrying Prince William Henry on a brief visit to the city, accompanied by *Albemarle* under the command of Captain Horatio Nelson. Those of *Lively's* crew, like John, who had been on board at New York in September 1781 would have yarns to tell the *Diamond's* people (*ad infinitum, ad nauseam?*) as they watched the royal progress up the harbour:[127] ("He came on *our ship*", John Small might have said, "a lad of 16, then, fair-haired he was, and ruddy face, he came aboard from *Prince George* to cross the bar, little *Lively*, she could bounce over without a tide . . . I were that close to him. . . .". It was not an encounter quickly to be forgotten by the Birmingham boy.)

Once more the harbour rattled and banged with gunfire, saluting Lord Hood's main fleet hovering outside, and the prince. "Passed by the Harbour Lord Hood and his fleet," reported *Diamond's* captain, Bartholomew Samuel Rowley. "Passed by H. Royal Highness Prince William Henry, Mann'd ship & chear'd him and saluted him with 21: 12 Pdrs as Did the Spanish ships in the Harbour." The whole performance was repeated on the 11th when the prince departed: one sees and hears the sea-birds of the port rising in a great cloud and clamour of protest.[128]

The city council (as city councils the world over) had worried about "which department should supply the cost of the entertainments and welcome that this Illustrious Council offers to foreign Sovereigns or princes who pass through this City", but felt they should "show plainly the pleasure respect and courtesy due to his outstanding Royal Person." The council agreed that ". . . there shall be arranged a Ball and Public Banquet in the Colisseum with the greatest embellishment and magnificence . . . and that the Generals, Officials, and principal Aristocracy of both sexes be invited . . . requesting . . . there will be suitable illumination . . ."[129]

Two days later, *Diamond* sailed for Jamaica, arriving 14 June at Port Royal. From Jamaica (sailing 23 June) to Plymouth and home (anchoring in the Sound 8 August 1783) John Small was a working marine again, surely glad and relieved to slip back into a familiar routine.[130]

Left behind in Jamaica were the principals in the court martial held on HMS *Preston* on 27 August. The verdict went against Stanhope and his lieutenant, James Delancey Walton. "The Court . . . having maturely and deliberately considered [the evidence] Is of Opinion that . . . the necessary precautions were not taken to prevent His Majesty's sloop Lively from falling into the Hands of the Enemy, And . . . do therefore adjudge the . . . Captain . . . to be dismissed from His Majestys Service." A like verdict was recorded against Lieutenant Walton, who complained that persons who might have spoken on his behalf had been allowed to leave for England on *Diamond*.

Poor Stanhope indeed! He had lost a small (but undoubtedly useful) navy vessel, but he had taken good prizes for the benefit of Britain, and this as much as anything had left his own ship undermanned. He was also betrayed by some of his crew (three more "ran with the Rebels" on arrival in Havana).[131]

On 7 January 1784, Stanhope petitioned the Privy Council to be reinstated, that he might "once more [be useful] . . . in the profession to which he had devoted his life." Referred to the admiralty, his petition was refused on the 12th. He had served with some distinction in at least eleven navy vessels since 1765, ranging up and down the American coast, and having suffered serious burns and imprisonment after the encounter of *Serapis* with John Paul Jones off the English coast in 1779. It seems a pity that such service was discounted when other captains were acquitted on seemingly more serious grounds.[132]

Marine records show John Small (Newry) transferred (on paper) to 3 company Plymouth on 1 September 1783, John Small (Birmingham) to 64 company on the same date. Now we are in a position to decide which John Small embarked on HMS *Perseus* on 9 August 1783. Subsequent research had found Irish John sent from Portsmouth headquarters (after his release from Haslar hospital) to HMS *Edgar* on 2 December 1782, where he served on harbour duty until 14 March 1783. On the 15th of that month, he joined HMS *Standard* ("Recd from the Edgar a party of the Plymouth division to carry round to that port"), to do shore duty until needed at sea again.[133]

On 8 August 1783, *Diamond*, bringing home Birmingham John, anchored in Plymouth Sound, and on the next day a John Small from Plymouth headquarters embarked on *Perseus*. It would have been possible (barely, but unlikely) for *Diamond's* John Small to have been rowed across to *Perseus*, if *Perseus* were short of her marine complement. But John Small on *Perseus* attended his first muster on 15 August: and John Small on *Diamond* was attending a muster on that ship up to 21 August, to be discharged to Plymouth headquarters next day.[134]

Map shows Portsmouth and harbour, with the Mother Bank, Spithead and St Helen's, off the Isle of Wight.

Trial record of John Small and colleagues, Devon Circuit, March 1785.

Early drawing of a Woolwich hulk, n.d.

So it was Irish John who tossed and battled on a cruise up the Irish Sea in late 1783 and early 1784, in such terrible gales that the captain, George Palmer, wrote in November, "I have experienced a great share of blowing weather since I left the Sound;" and (off Liverpool on 7 January 1784) "I mean to stay untill the severe Winter Weather has in some measure abated and Days lengthened."[135]

Entering Liverpool, the ship ran aground. There was a great flurry to shore her up, but the sand was soft and the shoring timbers sank into it. To lighten her, beer and water kegs were thrown overboard as well as booms and spars, an urgent message brought a craft from Liverpool to take out her guns, and empty casks were lashed to the starboard side to right the ship, awaiting the next tide to float her off. The master, as a note of interest in this story, was John Fryer, who would encounter Captain William Bligh in HMS *Bounty* in August 1787.[136]

When *Perseus* was freed from her plight, the exertion and pitiless weather sent a dozen seamen to sick quarters. Irish John, declared "unserviceable", was discharged on 2 February 1784, and disappears from this narrative until pay records show his full wages as £3.7s.1d., which exactly equalled his stoppages. There is no record that payment was made. So one must assume that if he survived and was given a passage to his Plymouth headquarters for discharge, the 21-days' pay due for return to Newry (his place of enlistment) would be the only money with which he left the navy.[137]

As the news of peace reached the far-flung fleet, the ships began to come back to port. Talk of cutbacks in army and navy personnel was in the air. The *Whitehall Evening Post* on 14 February 1783 listed the ships to be laid up in ordinary—at Portsmouth 12, at Plymouth 11, ten at Chatham, two at Sheerness: masts and rigging and guns removed, decks covered in canvas against the weather, just as unused furniture is dustsheeted in unoccupied houses until needed again. Seamen began muttering, knowing they would be jobless, and small mutinies occurred.[138]

On 10 February 1783 a letter went to commanding officers at all marine headquarters to discharge, as they arrived home, "such . . . as shall appear to you from their age, size, or any other consideration unfit to be continued in the Marine service", under the proper regulations of paid up wages and arrears, and "paying them the usual bounty of twenty-one days' pay each to carry them to their homes." On 2 July an Order in Council demanded further drastic cuts, "it being still necessary that many others should also be discharged to reduce the said Forces to a number proportionable to the numbers of seamen, that will probably be employed in time of peace. . . ." The new establishment was to take effect from 1 September 1783: but on 28 December 1784 the number was still in excess, so that more discharges were ordered, retaining only the stoutest and fittest, "None to be discharged who are over five feet six inches in height and under forty years of age." This would reduce a force hitherto numbering 25,890 marines to a total of 4,480, and by order (if not earlier) John Small may have been caught, already paid up for his sea service.[139]

None of these four men who were to be tried at Exeter for highway robbery in March 1785 appear on any subsequent ship muster: it is clear that they were caught in the cutbacks, discharged at the time of the last pay received. John Small was the first of the four to return to Plymouth. He received £1.6d.1d neat wages for his service on *Diamond,* paid on 28 August, and on 16 December he received £8.10s.6d for his years on *Lively,* a total of £9.16s.7d. With his 21 days' pay on discharge, this was all the money he had to live on, apart from any odd jobs he might have managed to find, from mid-December 1783 until early in 1785.[140]

Stephen Davenport came home next, arriving on *Caton* on 4 November 1783. He was paid £2.8s.3½d for this service on 13 November 1783, and a further £9.1s.1½d on 17 February 1784 for his service on fire-destroyed *Nymph.* By that time he was probably in debt. Robert Ellwood's *Nemesis* had come to Portsmouth, her home port, on 24 April 1784, and he was landed at Plymouth, his own division, on 4 May by free passage on *Europe.* His *Nemesis* service earned him £8.13s.1d., paid on 15 June. John Herbert (if he is the right man in the robbery) had served on *Europe* for 2½ years as one of Arthur Phillip's servants, and was paid £15.16s.1d. on 26 July 1784. Our four principals thus seem to have been left, as so many others were, with their sea pay and their 21-days' discharge pay with which to return home, and with no further prospects of employment. Sea pay was 19s. a month: the 21-days' pay would be less than that.[141]

On 1 January 1785, 244 ships were reported laid up in ordinary, 209 more than reported in February 1783: 107 ships of the line, twelve 50-gun ships, 91 frigates and 34 sloops and cutters—a grim prospect for out-of-work seamen.[142] What of the intervening months and years for our four highway robbers?—John since the end of 1783, Ellwood and Herbert since April 1784 and Davenport since his last payment in mid-February 1784? Their 21-days' pay could have taken them to their home base: but perhaps they preferred to stay around Plymouth, hoping against hope for the work they knew and liked best, picking up the odd job here and there when money ran out, always hoping to be re-engaged. A full eleven months later (when it was far too late for our four), a correspondent to the *Morning Herald* of 10 December commented "that we live in times, when the voice, which he calls the Majesty of the people, is despised, when our brave soldier and sailors who have fought our battles, are neglected and left to beg in the streets," continuing with a long catalogue of the oppressions on the poor exercised by the rich and powerful.

Whatever the reason, all four were in Plymouth on that day late in 1784 or early in 1785, and all apparently in desperate need of money, when James and Rebecca Burt accused them of robbery "in the Kings Highway" and had them committed to the gaol at Exeter. For Ellwood it was to be the end of his life. For Davenport—who knows? He went back, perhaps, to his home base, wherever that was: for it was at this assizes that one merciful arrangement was adopted, "hinted at by the gentlemen of the grand jury, and adopted by Mr Justice Buller, of sending the several prisoners acquitted to their legal places of settlement; whereas when they were turned loose from the prison, without funds or money, and unable to procure employment, they frequently, either from the depravity of their inclination, or from real want, committed robberies and offences, which this salutary step may prevent."[143]

But for John Herbert and John Small, another fate lay ahead. Escaping death, they now had to face transportation "beyond the Seas for and during the respective Terms hereafter mentioned, Viz: . . . for and during the Term of Seven Years. . . ."[144]

10. *EXECUTIVE JUSTICE:* THE LENT ASSIZES, EXETER, 1785.

"I am at present at your bar friendless", said a spirited woman to the judge who sentenced her at the Old Bailey in December 1782 for the theft of a bundle of laundry, "and to a man who gets his money entirely by disposing of the lives of people that come before your Lordship, what have I to say?"[145]

The prisoners awaiting trial before the Assize Courts in the county towns of England were, in fact, the raw material, so to speak, from which hundreds of people, from the judges to the clerks who inscribed the documents, made their living. They were also the reason for a week of high festivity in all the county Assize towns, twice annually, when the circuit judges came riding in to hold the Lent and Summer Assizes: for the prisoners they were "lordly judges to frighten people with their bloody robes, state and pomp." For those unfortunate men chained in their filthy prison in the High Gaol at Exeter in March 1785 (John Small was there with his three companions in crime; Thomas Acres and John Smith on a similar highway robbery charge, and Robert Ruth; Samuel Lightfoot for burglary) the week was a period of shame, of miserable life and possibly painful death. For the merry-makers in the town it was a season of gaiety and enjoyment, with the entertainments of an Assize sermon at the Cathedral attended by splendidly attired judges and the cream of county gentry, and an Assize ball where the ladies could display their fine clothes and ogle the gentlemen—"The general festival out of prison, which, according to custom, takes place on the trial of the wretches within."[146]

Outside the gaol, preparations were being set in motion for the show being built around the prisoners. The first two weeks in March 1785 were busy ones for everyone in Exeter, especially the High Sheriff of Devonshire for that year, John Henry Southcote, newly appointed by his Majesty in Council at St James's on 7 February. Last year's Sheriff, Thomas Lane, would still be struggling in November 1785 to get recompense for the "Several Sums under Written for Money laid out and expended and for services done and perform'd for his Majesty during the

Year of his Sheriffalty", but he had had one more than the normal two annual Assizes, having had to arrange for the special commission in May 1784 to try the convicts who had escaped from the *Mercury* transport, and felt aggrieved at the delay in reimbursement.[147]

The Court had to be cleaned and fitted up, provided with cushions, fires, candles, "and other necessary things for the Judges" whose accommodation and upkeep (with their officers) had cost the Sheriff about £42 in 1784. The judges lodged at the Mayoralty House, "the Rooms being larger and more convenient," but not big enough to include the servants and cooks (sent to insure that no poison found its way into their Lordships' food), which added another £3.12s.6d. for separate lodgings. The bailiffs of the 34 Hundreds in the county had to be paid to proclaim the Assizes and summon the persons needed for the grand and petty juries. A messenger had to be dispatched to Dorchester to present the Judges with a Calendar and "a State of the Health of the Jail" (50 miles each way, £2.2s.), doubled in 1784 by the Special Commission in May to try the *Mercury* mutineers. The clerks (armed with the current edition of the *Crown Circuit Companion,* or its equivalent) were busily preparing their parchment, paper, pens and ink and looking forward to the pounds, shillings and pence they would be paid for the various documents to be inscribed: "for drawing every bill of indictment in felony, 2s. ... recording the appearance of every defendant, 5s.6d. ... copy of indictment or information, 8s.8d. ... recording every plea, 4s. ... for recording every acquittal, 13s.4d. ... drawing up every special verdict, per sheet, 1s. ... for engrossing same, per sheet, 1s. and copy thereof, 8d. ... for copy of the conviction of traitor, felon or murderer, £1.6s.8d. ... for every order of the Court, and copy, 4s. ... for copy of every jury impannelled, 3s.4d. ... for reading every exhibit offered in court as evidence (except charters and acts of parliament), 1s. ...."[148]

Flambeaux, trumpeters, bell-ringers and choristers would have to be provided (and paid) to take part in the ceremonies and festivities that were part of Assize week in the city. Throughout the neighbourhood the gentry, the attorneys who hoped for briefs, and anyone who could manage to be present were all in a high state of preparation and excitement. Assize week was a social highlight in the year's activities.

Baron Hotham and Mr Justice Buller had already held the Assizes at Winchester, Salisbury, Bodmin and Dorchester before arrival at Exeter. Though both would preside together, Hotham would try the civil causes on this occasion, Buller the criminal cases. Barristers and friends travelled with them, by coach and on horseback, and sometimes members of their own families; the entourage was met at the county boundary by the High Sheriff and all the dignitaries of the Court and the City, escorted by a cavalcade of trumpeters and "javelin men". "The judges," commented a French judge in 1822, "upon their approach to the town, are received by the sheriff, and often by a great part of the wealthiest inhabitants of the county; the latter come in person to meet them, or send their carriages, with their richest liveries, to serve as an escort, and increase the splendour of the occasion.[149]

"They enter the town with bells ringing and trumpets playing [an all-too audible cacophany to the hapless prisoners in the gaols], preceded by the sheriff's men, to the number of twelve or twenty, in full dress, armed with javelins. The trumpeters and javelin men remain in attendance on them during the time of their stay, and escort them every day to the assize-hall, and back again to their apartments." The splendid pageantry—"the well-staged theatre of an assize court"—was sturdily based in tradition that can be tracked through English legal history to mediaeval roots.[150]

A considerable procession thus entered Exeter, to be met by throngs of lesser folk eager to be awestruck, and to enjoy the feeling of fête. "When the Westminster judges on circuit arrived at a county town, all the local society came to meet them. A season of festivities began for the county, in which the trials were an afternoon diversion."[151]

Did Baron Hotham bring along with him one of his younger sons as he had done with his 16-year-old eldest when riding the Norfolk Circuit two years earlier? "I took Beaumont with me, as his holidays happened to fall just at the time; thinking that he was safer and better employed with me, than at home teazing his mother to let him do every thing that he pleased, which he is just of an age to do, and probably to succeed in. He was much amused, by Riding about the country during the mornings, and going into Court with me in the afternoon, unless a Ball happened to interfere." The anecdote could hardly add greater emphasis to the difference between the benefits of privilege and the wretched condition of "people . . . of the lower sort". Yet John Small, in his chains and apprehensions, behind the walls a young Beaumont may have passed with cheerful thoughtlessness on his way to the drama of the afternoon court, probably accepted it as the natural order of things.[152]

Upon arrival in the city, the judges would proceed at once to the Cathedral for the Assize sermon; splended in scarlet robe and mantle, amid a congregation equally finely attired. The sermons, with obsequious compliments to the goodness of the monarch, were preached on suitable texts. "If thou do that which is evil, be afraid: for he beareth not the sword in vain: for he is the minister of God, a revenger to execute wrath upon him that doeth evil", thundering on about "the Iniquity of the Times, and the general Depravity of Manners . . . the flagrant Impiety of our Days, the excessive Corruption of these Dregs of time": or "Righteousness exalteth a nation: but sin is a reproach to any people." These sentiments were expressed in the early part of the century, but in

January 1785 the press was (as usual) deploring "The alarming increase of crime, depravity and dissipation, among persons of both sexes, as well as of almost all ranks, classes, and ages, [which] calls aloud for the attention of the legislator, the moralist, and the divine." Perhaps more wisely (as the Reverend Sydney Smith did in 1824), some preachers exhorted the judge. "His words should be weighed, because they entail no evil upon himself, and much evil upon others. . . . When magistrates, under the mask of law . . . are more studious of inflicting pain than repressing error or crime, the office suffers as much as the judge. . . ."[153]

The trials did not begin until the second day, the first being given up to reading the Commission, empanelling grand and petty juries, and other legal niceties. When the actual trials began, the Court was crowded. "The judge permits his Bench to be invaded by a throng of spectators, and thus finds himself surrounded by the prettiest women of the county—the sisters, wives or daughters of grand jurors. . . . They are attired in the most elegant neglige; and it is a spectacle not a little curious to see the judge's venerable head, loaded with a large wig, peering among the youthful female heads."[154]

The Reverend Martin Madan, barrister and clergyman, writing as *A Sincere Well-wisher to the Public*, deplored, in 1785, "the noise, crowd, and confusion which . . . seldom cost the *Judge* less than almost an hour, before the court can be brought in to any kind of order." The court sessions offered the macabre thrill of seeing the victims shambling in who soon might be dead, and when sentenced, watching their reaction to their fate: often chained, dirty and ill-dressed men and women, their unkempt appearance damning them even more as immoral and licentious (sometimes their tatters were masked by "a dress like a carter's frock", a new-fangled idea criticised by *Sincere Well-wisher* as disguising a villain's true villainy, though the intention was—as the traditional flowers on the Bench were—to reduce the risk of infectious disease entering the Court). When the sentences were announced at the end of the session, John Small, John Herbert, Robert Ellwood and Stephen Davenport were among the 16 felons against whose names the dread sign of Death would be inscribed.[155]

From all through the county, witnesses, attorneys and sightseers were arriving. James Burt and Rebecca his wife (likely enough with feelings of some importance as prime witnesses) came up from St Budeaux to give their evidence against our four highwaymen. From Modbury, near Plymouth, attorney John Andrews started his journey to Exeter on Monday 14 March, prepared to look for briefs and join in the gaiety. He arrived at Exeter in time for breakfast on Tuesday, the first day of real business, after the legal niceties in preparation for the trials had been completed. He spent the days in court and the evenings in pleasure: on Wednesday night, the entertainment of "Robin Hood with the female

West Indian", and a musical evening at the Choir on Thursday. He did not mention the Assize ball: perhaps he was not sufficiently grand to attend, or too elderly, or perhaps more squeamish than most. "It is rather too much to see the ladies putting on their bonnets in the morning, to look at the judges, and hear the prisoners condemned to death; and then take them off again, to prepare for the dance at night," commented an observer. "One would not expect that they should return home to eat no dinner, but, without incurring the charge of any mawkish sentimentality, one may be permitted to feel something revolting in the very name of an *assize-ball*."[156]

In 1820, Mrs Offley of Dorchester, in verse that was not the less compassionate for its banal expression, caught the same feeling, taking as her epigraph some lines from the poet James Thomson: "Ah! little think they, while they dance along, How many feel this very moment death, And all the sad variety of pain." She tried to compare the two scenes in the long poem that followed.

"Sad contrast! in that dismal mansion near,
There are, who through the night's long doleful gloom,
Wake but to shed the unavailing tear,
And meditate the horrors of their doom.
"Each in his solitary cell confin'd—
For justice sternly now asserts her claim.
And each to death or exile has consign'd—
Death ignominious, or a life of shame."

No transcript of the trials of John Small and his companions has survived, only the indictment and conviction written in the Devon Gaol Book and sundry papers recording his reprieve and eventual pardon and transportation. The four men would have appeared in the dock on the one charge, and according to procedure (very carefully set forth step by step in a Western District treatise in 1807), the Clerk of Arraigns would charge them with the Indictment in the following manner. . . .[157]

"A.B. [and C.D., E.F. and G.H., in this case] hold up your Hand[s]— You stand Indicted by the name[s] of A.B. [and C.D., E.F., and G.H.], Labourer[s] [marines and seaman?]—for that you on &c (reading through the whole Indictment) how say you are you Guilty of this *Felony, and Murder* (or Burglary as the case may be) whereof you stand Indicted or not Guilty? The prisoner[s] generally pleads 'Not Guilty'—The Clerk of Arraigns then says '*Cul-prist*—How will you be tried?' To which [they] answer[s] 'By God and my Country'—and the Clerk of Arraigns Replies—'God send you a good Deliverance'—and as they plead Not Guilty, he must write '*po-se*' (or 'puts himself') over every prisoner's Name upon the Indictment."

The scene that faced John Small in court on 14 March 1785 has been described generally by *Sincere Well-Wisher to the Public*. There is little doubt that John Small would nod agreement—"yes, that's the way it was"—with the picture drawn in the year of his trial.

"The very appearance of the *Judges* at the assizes, if we include the attendance of the high-sheriff, his under-sheriff, and other officers—The first gentlemen in the county forming the constitutional bulwark, the *grand jury*—that other excellent institution, the *petty jury*, who are to pass between the crown and the prisoners, on the trials of their several lives and deaths:—add to this, the vast concourse of people flocking from every part of the county, and assembling in multitudes to hear the solemn determinations of punitave justice . . .—the Judge's solemn appearance in his robes, when seated in the place of judgment . . . strike a terror . . . not easily forgotten. . . .

"Methinks I see him, with a countenance of solemn sorrow, adjusting the cap of judgment on his head—while the crier proclaims—'O yes! O yes! O yes!—My lords, the king's justices, strictly charge and command all manner of persons to keep silence, while sentence of death is passing on the prisoners at the bar, on pain of imprisonment'. . . .

"His lordship then, deeply affected by the melancholy part of his office . . . addresses, in the most pathetic terms, the consciences of the trembling criminals. . . . Tells them how best to employ the little time left, the necessity of speedy repentance. . . .

"The dreadful sentence is now pronounced—every heart shakes with terror—the almost fainting criminals are taken from the bar—the crowd retires—each to his several home, and carries the mournful story to his friends and neighbours;—the day of execution arrives—the wretches are led forth to suffer, and exhibit a spectacle to the beholders, too awful and solemn for description. . . ."[158]

Robert Ellwood would be all too aware of the terror so emotionally depicted by *Sincere Well-Wisher*, when he was taken on 1 April, with the five other condemned men who had not been pardoned, almost two miles outside the city to Heavitree Gallows, and there hanged, to be buried in the "small inclosed spot of land for the interment of those unfortunates who suffered." A thrilled crowd of beholders would watch keenly to see how they behaved—"with that Decency that became their untimely end", or, refusing to acquiesce humbly in their own demise, "behaving in a very hardened and audacious manner." The Exeter victims "died penitent", the *Exeter Flying Post* assured its readers.[159]

"Before the Judges left town, eleven convicts were reprieved, and six left for execution." Among the eleven were John Small, John Herbert and Stephen Davenport; Thomas Acres and John Smith; and Edward Smith. *Sincere Well-Wisher* did not at all approve of the increasing tendency to reprieve "before the Judge left town." He was also dubious of the value of transportation, and was against the exercise of too much mercy. "A Judge's *Oath* respects the laws *as they are*—not as he may think they *ought to be* . . . Nay, I once heard a *Judge*, in his charge to the grand-jury, say to this effect, that, 'Where men robbed on the highway, and did not use violence, or do any mischief to the persons they robbed, he thought them proper to be recommended as objects of mercy'." Mr Justice Buller would have earned *Sincere Well-Wisher's* strong disapproval, but John Small and his companions bore him heartfelt gratitude.[160]

Reprieves were only temporary respites until confirmed after formal application to the king, made by Mr Justice Buller on 26 March. Until then, all the capital convicts remained in the High Gaol, with only hope to sustain them. All those pardoned were recommended to seven years' transportation beyond the seas, except Stephen Davenport, for whom a Free Pardon was requested. And not until 5 April did a letter go off from Lord Sydney to the Justices of Assize for the Western Circuit announcing that "His Majesty has . . . been graciously pleased to extend His Royal Mercy unto them . . . that you may give the necessary Directions accordingly". For nearly a month the noose of death had hung over their heads. Davenport's free pardon was confirmed in a letter from Lord Sydney on the same date.[161]

So, justice was done. James Burt and his wife Rebecca could return to their St Budeaux tavern with their expenses and the £40 bounty paid for prosecution resulting in conviction. John Andrews, attorney, had left Exeter for Modbury on Friday 18 March, by way of Totnes, after visits with friends en route, satisfying days in court, and evenings of pleasant discourse and entertainment. The judges went on their way to hold the last of the Lent Assizes in Somerset. Ellwood was dead: was he the instigator of the attack, and the one who actually assaulted Burt and his wife "in the King's Highway," relieving them of the small fruits of the robbery? No doubt Davenport won his freedom on the basis of an honourable career in the marine corps: and John Small's months as prisoner-of-war were probably also taken into account, and his trouble-free service for at least two years in the marine corps. Perhaps all three were little more than accessories to the robbery, part of the group with Ellwood as instigator, when the attack took place. Authority to arrange the transportation "with any Person or Persons for the Performance of the Transportation" was given to two local magistrates: but the government had as yet no place to which they might be sent. John Small, with John Herbert, Thomas Acres, John Smith and Edward Smith, and the three who had received transportation sentences only—Robert Ruth, John Bryant and Samuel Lightfoot—would remain in Exeter High Gaol until 30 January 1786, when, with others convicted later, they were loaded into a waggon for Plymouth, to be held on the *Dunkirk* prison ship. It would be seven more months before they would know where they were going.[162]

11. THE DUNKIRK PRISON SHIP

The *Dunkirk* prison ship was moored in that loop of the Hamoaze known as Millbrook Lake, near enough to the Cornwall border to be described as being "in the River Tamer in our county of Cornwall". She was an old 60-gun ship, ordered sold in February 1783 "unless adviseable to keep [her] for a Hulk", and in October that year ordered by the Navy Board to remain at Plymouth "till we decide what to do with her." Built in 1754, a vessel of 1,246 tons, she had been employed in harbour service since 1778, latterly as the port admiral's flagship. When Exeter gaols found themselves overrun by convicts escaped from the *Mercury* transport in April 1784, she was handily empty and unused, and hastily established as an emergency prison "for the reception of the Convicts in Exeter Goal & for those who were in some of the Western Countries." From June 1784 to 28 October 1786, when by Order in Council she was struck off the Royal Navy list, the *Dunkirk* was not in the regular prison-hulk service, but was simply a holding place for the *Mercury* convicts until it could be decided where to send them.[163]

The overseer during this period was William Cowdry, former superintendent of the Mill Prison at Plymouth where prisoners-of-war were held in the recent war with America. He lost the hulk appointment (his anguished pleas and protests unavailing) on the incorporation of the *Dunkirk* into the prison-hulk system, when a contract was signed on 10 March 1786 with Henry Bradley. Bradley's brother James was chief clerk (and later secretary) to the India Board established in 1784, and a friend of Evan Nepean: thus does influence rear its ugly head. The *Dunkirk* was now open to receive convicts regularly from Western District gaols.[164]

On 30 January, John Small, with 19 other Exeter convicts, was conveyed in a waggon from the High Gaol to Plymouth (a journey that cost the county treasurer the sum of £30.0s.4d.) and there put on board the hulk. Within days, 15 convicts arrived from Shropshire: and the *Fortunee* (another old navy ship of 40 guns and some 950 tons) established as a prison hulk at the same time at Portsmouth began receiving convicts from all over the kingdom.[165]

Duncan Campbell, by now an experienced superintendent of the Thames hulks since 1776, had been sent to Portsmouth in September to inspect and advise on the fitting of the *Fortunee* for the convicts. James Hill had been working as overseer since early December, receiving his warrant on 4 January 1786, but 100 convicts had been sent down in a rush from Newgate on 8 December 1785, at a cost of £93.18s. plus £40.5s.6d. for victualling and security, before the hulk was ready (and another 100 on 2 February 1786), and had to be accommodated on the *Firme*, another old navy vessel, until 20 February. Only two months earlier, in September 1785, the distinguished physician Sir Charles Blagden had written to Sir Joseph Banks about similar haste and confusion on the part of government when trying to find a distant destination for the convicts. "The whole is the usual ridiculous hurrying of office, which will spoil the business without answering any purpose whatever." The convict victims of this haste were ill and dying on the *Firme*. "They have nothing but the ships decks to lay on and when wet weather is imposible to keep them dry for want of tarpolings." The decks could not be kept clean, "as wee have no place to remove the sick out of the way of washing." The weather had been particularly bitter: "The Thames was already frozen [early in January] even so low as Kew", with the thermometer 15 and 16 degrees below freezing.[166]

On the *Dunkirk*, John Small encountered the 84 *Mercury* convicts who still remained for transportation, and nine others sent there to relieve Western District gaols of their "transports", the only other prisoners received on board since the hulk had been readied to receive *Mercury* mutineers in June 1784. A gale that had lashed Plymouth three weeks before John Small arrived there would have left the unhappy people on the *Dunkirk* even more unhappy. "At three o'clock [a.m.] the gale increased to a hurricane, accompanied with such a heavy rolling sea as we never but twice before have seen in this port . . . Near 40 sail of brigs, sloops, barges, trawl boats and passage boats, were driven by the impetuosity of the sea, all together . . . Several got on shore, some sunk at their anchors, others staved in heads and sterns. The howling of the wind, the raging of the sea, the crash of the different ships, driving against each other, the dismal cries of those on board, formed a scene too dreadful to dwell on." Even if by then she was moored in the more sheltered Millbrook Lake, the *Dunkirk* could not have escaped the heavy movement of tide, wind and waves in stormy weather.[167]

Of the *Mercury* people still on *Dunkirk*, three would die within the year (Morgan Williams, John Anderson and William Vowler). Three would be pardoned and released: Ann Taunton, on receipt of security for seven years' good behaviour; Luke Hoyle, thoroughly penitent, because "he has been the means in a great measure by his exemplary behaviour of reclaiming the other convicts"; and Charles Keeling (who had been a mutineer on the earlier *Swift* transport fiasco and escaped the death sentence then too, though scathingly condemned by the judge as a ringleader) because he was "a genteel young fellow", after pathetic petitions from himself and his mother. His brother, John Herbert (usually known as Herbert Keeling), some eight years younger and also a *Swift* mutineer, had not been on the *Mercury*, and would go as a First Fleeter from the *Censor* hulk to the *Scarborough* transport in 1787.[168]

Three *Mercury* mutineers would be held back among the 19 convicts left on board after First Fleet embarkation in March 1787, and of these, two would die before the expiration of their sentence (Richard Wingate and Michael Lyon). Only one, Francis Liddy, probably unable to go with the Fleet in March 1787 through illness, served his full seven years on board the *Dunkirk*, to be released on 14 January 1791, by then aged 28, with a guinea in money, and "A Coat, Waistcoat & Breeches, Shirt, Shoes, Stockings, Hat, Hankerchief & Buckles the Value of £1.13s.6d." His signature was on the receipt.[169]

The 84 *Mercury* mutineers and six of the nine other convicts had already been held on board for 19 months, the other three since March and August 1785 respectively. For the *Mercury* people the first months on board had been noted for disgraceful treatment received from the marines acting as guards. Cowdry's shocked protests against the use of the eight women, who were systematically and cynically brutalized and humiliated by the marine officers, were shrugged off from one authority to the next until a proper code of orders was issued at the end of November 1784 and the marines replaced by soldiers. Cowdry, who had been insulted by the marines, and helpless to oppose them, was given extra staff and greater authority.[170]

It is hard to discover just what form the "fitting" of the *Dunkirk* for the convicts took at this stage, beyond keeping them locked up, and an Admiralty order in July 1784 that the convicts should be supplied with "unserviceable beds and the troops . . . with such as have been repaired". After the institution of the code of orders some elementary improvements seem to have been made; the port admiral wrote on 19 November 1784 that "since she has been fitted in a proper manner with different Cells and Hospitals, and the men and women kept separate, and two persons to act as Turnkeys," there had been no complaint (though on the *Fortunee*, overseer James Hill would write in January 1786, "We find the soldiers much greater thieves than the convicts").[171]

No care had been taken to protect the convicts against the winter cold, however, and it was not until after John Bastard, MP for Devonshire, acidly reminded Lord Sydney in November ("I suppose your Lordship cannot be ignorant that many of the prisoners are nearly if not quite naked") that authority was given to spend a guinea per man on clothing. Prisoners' clothing had been noted by an observer in 1776 on the first hulk in the Thames to consist of two brown linen shirts, one pair of stockings, a thick woollen cap, a jacket and a pair of breeches, at a total cost then of 10s.[172] An order had been issued to allow the labour of convicts on hulks at both Portsmouth and Plymouth to be used on the construction of fortifications, but there is no evidence that this was ever done at Plymouth, though men from the *Fortunee* (and later the *Lion*) at Portsmouth were kept busily engaged in this work under the Duke of Richmond, Master of the Ordnance.[173] No occupation was provided in county gaols even for prisoners held for several years, and there is no reason, lacking evidence to the contrary, to be surprised that work may also not have been provided for the convicts on the *Dunkirk*. It is probable that all John Small and his fellow prisoners ever saw again of the city where he had served at marine headquarters when on shore duty, was the distant, unchanging view from the deck of the ship (when allowed up from below), except for the busy coming and going of naval vessels at the dockyard across the water, and the seasonal changes of wind, snow, rain and sun.

In 1776, when the first hulk began operations at Woolwich, William Smith, a London doctor, went to see for himself "the Present State of the Convicts sentenced to Hard Labour on Board the Justitia". He found the men chained two and two: a very few well-behaved prisoners had had their chains removed. They ate in messes, as in the Navy (John would find this a familiar routine), six convicts to each mess, receiving every 24 hours half a bullock's head (very occasionally hearts and shins of beef), which it was estimated would amount to between three and eight ounces of meat for each man daily. This was supplemented by four pounds of biscuit and broth thickened with bread and oatmeal. Only water was available to drink, and Dr Smith noted that "the water was muddy & saltish . . . the flesh-meat green with rottenness . . . the bread . . . very unwholesome . . . their broth at times tastes strongly of the verdigrease. . . . Heat, moisture, nastiness, & bad air from the putrid effluvia of bodies, joined with unwholesome food," Dr Smith felt, would create contagion and kill. Perhaps, after all, not very different from what John Small and those of his fellows who had been seamen had been used to in the navy, though less in quantity by a third.[174]

Now he would hear from the *dramatis personae* themselves, as it were, their own account of the melodrama that had been excitedly reviewed in Plymouth streets and taverns when, in April 1784, they had taken over the *Mercury* transport en route to America and run her into Torbay some fifty miles to the east as the crow flies. Twelve leagues beyond the Scillies, they would tell him, some of the convicts "rose suddenly upon

Deck" and overwhelmed the crew. High on wine and excitement, they ransacked the ship for valuables "riffled" the steward George Holt "of all [his] Property", and steered first for Ireland, "but the Wind coming to the Northward, they then steered for Spain, & on the 11 April a Gale of wind took place". Some of the crew had to be released to control what was by then "the distress'd ship", and ordered to steer for Torbay.[175]

Francis Garland, who had actually got as far as Plymouth Dock [Devonport] before being recaptured, had spent nearly a year on a Thames hulk, one of six men capitally convicted at Winchester who had attacked and robbed a wayfarer of 12 yards of muslin and £5.13s. in money (a bigger "take" than John Small and his companions had made). Two of his partners in crime were here with him on the *Dunkirk*, Joseph Morley and Henry Roach, both caught scrambling down the side of the ship in Torbay Harbour. One other, John Leary, had been left on the *Censor* hulk in London: him they would meet again. One had not got free from the *Mercury* and was now—where?—at Honduras, it was whispered, after America had refused admittance.[176]

Thomas Barrett, his first crime (in London) the theft of a silver watch and some clothing, might have told with dramatic effect how he had avoided the gallows a second time because of the humanitarian impulse that had saved the throat of the *Mercury's* steward from being cut, and the captain's ear—"the scissars were put to his head". Robert Sidaway might have been something of a hero among his fellows, so vigorously involved in the deck fighting that he had suffered a severely wounded shoulder from the surgeon's gun. He had, nevertheless, got as far as Totnes, so weak when re-taken that a chaise was needed to bring him to Exeter, where he had remained in hospital until mid-June. He had earlier served three years on a Thames hulk at hard labour from 1778 to 1781 for a crime he denied, implying a "frame" for the informer's bounty ("They got the keys somewhere on purpose to get £40 by us"), and was sentenced to seven years' transportation the following year on suspicion of another crime, running to escape down a narrow lane "with such a force that he came into the full street before he could turn . . . he had like to run over the post." Through an opportune hole in the passage when being returned from the Old Bailey to Newgate, he made an impulsive escape: retaken within a few days, disguised in woman's clothes, he had been reprieved from death to life transportation.[177]

Most of these men had escaped the gallows twice, and yet were ready to take more chances. "A general Escape had been attempted and very nearly effected more than once" before overseer Cowdry had been granted enough turnkeys to keep proper watch in the early makeshift arrangements on the *Dunkirk*. John Small would probably have heard gleeful stories of the two who had got away at Ivybridge, Richard O'Brien and Thomas King, while being taken from Exeter to Plymouth, and "have not since been heard of". O'Brien got clean away: Thomas King they would meet again in Sydney Cove when he arrived on the *Scarborough* transport's second voyage in June 1790.[178]

One convict our John did *not* meet on the *Dunkirk* was James Ruse. Capitally convicted in July 1782 at Bodmin for the theft of two silver watches and other goods, he was sent after reprieve to London's Wood Street Compter on 7 December 1783 (many months before the *Dunkirk* was established), where he required a good deal of medication—pills, purges, liniment—to help him survive the dank and dismal dungeons, before dispatch to the *Ceres* hulk when abortive preparations were in hand to send the convicts to Africa. He was transferred to the *Censor* hulk on 1 June 1786, whence he embarked on the *Scarborough* transport at Portsmouth in February 1787.[179]

Their ultimate destination would have been an endless source of speculation. At the very time of John Small's conviction in March 1785, government was already well advanced in the plan to make Lemain Island, a fever-ridden swamp 400 miles up the Gambia River in West Africa, the new destination for the convicts who were no longer accepted by an independent America. On 29 December 1784, Evan Nepean had written to the mayor of Plymouth, "that circumstances have . . . changed with respect to the removal or detention of the convicts on board the Dunkirk. . . . It is at last determined that they shall forthwith be removed, with some others . . . to the coast of Africa . . . which you know in the routine of Punishment is considered as next in degree to that of Death. . . . Be so good as to look upon this letter as a Private one, for it would be likely to create trouble were the intentions of Government known with respect to the destination of the Convicts."[180]

Whatever the intentions of government, the secret was leaked. As early as 5 February 1785 the *Bristol Journal* had reported that "Government have contracted with the African Company to transport 150 felons to the coast of Africa". But Nepean's fear of trouble was well-justified, and a hot debate in the House of Commons, followed by a Commons inquiry that revealed the deadly nature of the climate, killed the plan. "To Africa!" Judge Willes had cried in 1783. "I would rather hang him." And convicts on the Thames had been riotous when the possibility of Africa hung over their heads. For the same reason, insurrection broke out on the *Fortunee* hulk at Portsmouth in March 1786.[181]

A young *Mercury* mutineer on the *Dunkirk*, Thomas Limpus, could tell John of the horrors of Africa. With Samuel Woodham, John Ruglas, and some 36 other convicts, he had been transported to Africa on the *Den Keyser* in November 1782, and managed to survive to find his way back to England (as Woodham and Ruglas did too, both now held on the *Ceres* hulk at Woolwich: John Martin escaped the African horror by illness, actually embarked on *Den Keyser* but sent back to Newgate, to languish

British Museum, Great Russell Street, London, Duke Street (now Coptic Street) where Mary Parker lived and worked, opens from left.

A VIEW of DEPTFORD.

Deptford 1779, on the Thames, past which Mary Parker and women from Newgate were rowed to the *Lady Penrhyn* at Gallions Reach, downstream from Woolwich.

on the *Ceres* hulk until he became a First Fleeter in 1787). Limpus could also tell John Small what to expect on a prison hulk: when only fifteen he had been sent for three years of hard labour in London, from October 1777. Released at the end of 1780, he had been convicted in September 1782 for theft of a handkerchief, and transportation to Africa had followed at once.[182]

The 19 convicts from the group who were landed at Goree from the "Benkiasa" [*Den Keyser*], Limpus among them, were lined up and told they would have to do the best they could for themselves, as no provision had been made for them (the governor of Cape Coast Castle, receiving some of the rest of them, protested to government: "They are landed as it were naked and diseased on the sandy shore . . . these poor Wretches are to be seen dying upon the Rocks, or upon the sandy Beach, under the scorching heat of the sun"). Limpus stayed on a ship in the bay, going ashore a few times to do work for the governor, and returned to England planning to ship out again in the same vessel. He was unlucky: retaken in Seven Dials, he was sentenced to death, reprieved to transportation for life, and sent to the *Mercury* from Newgate. He was one of those retaken in Devon, and one of the 24 tried and sentenced by Mr Justice Heath at the Special Commission Assizes at Exeter: Limpus received another death sentence and was reprieved again to life transportation. Sixty-six of the other recaptured convicts were not tried at all, but remanded to their former orders: two, tried at the Assizes, were unaccountably acquitted and released.[183]

In the weeks and months to come, 12 more *Mercury* escapers (apart from Thomas King, already mentioned), were caught. There may have been others who never came to light at all. Of the 12, four went to New South Wales: (two of them, Charles Peat and John Harris (who had both reached London and were tried there) as First Fleeters, the other two—Mary Potten and Michael Nowland—on later transports: and three were hanged, unlucky perhaps in the judges who tried them, except for the one who had committed another crime while free.[184]

The fear of Africa in their minds, and the long-drawn-out uncertainty about their destination, was an additional torment to be borne in these years of confinement. Who knew what further horrors they might have to face? Government had received many suggestions from members of the public, some of them with signatures, some anonymous. Among the more sensible plans was one for establishing a herring fishery (but the author wanted a "Patent Right" before disclosing details). "Were Greenland to be purchased," wrote another, "and made a receptacle for convicts . . . they might all be made useful in a profitable fishery". Sir Watkin Lewes offered to employ 600 convicts in the Woolwich rope yard, and gave careful details about personnel and cost. "Of the more than ten thousand [ships] that sail out of the ports of Great Britain", suggested one gentleman, "one in ten might take a single convict, who might be obliged to do all the dirtiest work of the ship . . . and the crew would have before them a constant memorial of the danger that attended vicious practices." The same writer had also suggested "transporting the convicts to the remotest part of the coast of *Labrador,* and leaving them on shore upon the main, with provision for twelve months, at *half* allowance, so as to make labour and industry necessary, and supplying them at the same time with hatchets, saws, and *intrenching* tools, so that they might dig caves in the earth, to defend them from the extremity of the winter season, and with fishing tackle. . . . Their numbers would, I presume, be considerably reduced by the severity of the climate even in one winter but I fear recruits would be never very scarce."[185]

There was also that gentleman who sent twelve foolscap pages of Biblical severity. "In Holy Writ we are informed that the Deity ordained, as a Just Punishment for Sinners the consigning them to Eternal Darkness—Now Sir, I dont know of any punishment . . . similar . . . to send the Convicts 50, or 100, Fathoms, under ground to work for their Relief in the Coal Mines, for a certain Number of Years, without Ever coming up, till the Expiration of their Sentence . . . where they will sigh in Perpetual Darkness, and the whole Length of their Slavery, will be One Mournfull Alternative, of insinsibility and Labour, where not even the smalest hope of Escape can ever Reach them. . . ." It would be cheap, too. "One man at the Top, or mouth of the Mine, can command Ten Thousand in this Deep Prison:" and profitable—"Besides Government would have all those great Profits, which arise to the present Proprietors"—or they could "tender the Convicts, free of all costs, to the Different Proprietors (who are very *numerous,* of the Coal, Lead, Tin, and other Mines)."[186]

In the early part of 1786, government had sent a naval vessel to investigate the possibilities of another part of the West African coast, the Das Voltas region (now Namibia). Only when a devastating report revealed the aridity and uninhabitable nature of the area (there had been some thought that it might prove useful for American loyalists in exile) did the Home Secretary, Lord Sydney, announce with great suddenness on 18 August 1786 that Botany Bay, discovered in April 1770 by Captain James Cook, had finally been chosen as the destination for the convicts now swelling British gaols and prison hulks.[187]

It could have brought nothing but relief to John Small and most of the convicts sentenced to transportation, though some bemoaned the formidable distance from their homeland, giving them little chance of ever returning to it when they had worked out their sentences. It was rumoured that several wives wanted to go with their convict husbands, but were refused. Botany Bay offered the possibility of a better climate, and brought at least a sense that something was about to happen to relieve the monotonous discomfort after years of miserable confinement. The tremors many of them may have felt contemplating the long sea journey would hardly have shaken ex-marine John Small: he might in fact have welcomed the prospect, especially if he could have foretold that on this first convict voyage the prisoners would be treated as humanely as possible, and left unchained for most of the eight months it would take to get there. Almost like the old navy days: as a man used to life on a navy ship, John Small—though he was indicated by superintendent Henry Bradley as among those "troublesome at times"[188]—probably took his 13 months on the *Dunkirk* philosophically, used to a degree of discomfort. A lot better, doubtless, than what he had endured in his four months as prisoner-of-war in Havana: he could tell tales of adventure with the best of them.

At the time of Lord Sydney's official letter of 18 August 1786, the *Dunkirk* was carrying some 200-odd convicts, all male except for the seven *Mercury* women, two others from Exeter (Jane Meach and Elizabeth Cole) and later three more from the same gaol, Mary Braund, Catherine Fryer/Prior and Mary Haydon/Shepherd; this in spite of Nepean's later statement that "The Act of Parliament does not justify the Removal of women to the temporary places of Confinement, nor is there any vessel appointed for their reception, could it be legally done." Nevertheless, as soon as the Botany Bay decision had been made, letters were sent far and wide from mid-October to dispatch women transports at once to the *Dunkirk*. They began arriving from the end of October 1786: Mary McCormack from Liverpool, Susannah Huffnell from Worcester, Elizabeth Clarke from Derby, Margaret Jones from New Sarum, Mary Cleaver from Bristol—31 women in all, the last one, Mary Bond, received on 30 January 1787. Ann Smith and Hannah Smith from Winchester each brought a child, 12 months and three months old respectively. The small son of Susannah Holmes and Henry Cable, born of a love-match in prison, arrived with his father from Norwich on 16 November, his mother having preceded him by 11 days. The child of Jane Parkinson/Partridge/Ann Marsden had presented Henry Bradley with a problem. "Jane Parkinson . . . brought with her a male child about nine months old; the Gaoler who delivered these people assured me, that every means, except that of force, were used in vain, to prevent the child being brought here, the mother declaring that she would destroy herself if seperated from her Infant. Pray Sir inform me whether this little one is to accompany its mother to Botany Bay, or be returned to Lancaster." Permission was granted.[189]

Just before Christmas 1786 the transport *Friendship* arrived at Plymouth, and on 7 January moved into Hamoaze where the *Charlotte* had just come to anchor. For two months both vessels took on stores, made certain alterations "for the greater security of the marines and convicts", painted and cleaned ship; took on crew to make up the complement, repaired and stowed sails, and on 10 March took on board the marines and their baggage.[190]

On Saturday, 10 March, strong gales with hail and rain had lashed Plymouth harbour, but on Sunday the 11th the weather was moderate and cloudy, to the great relief, one imagines, of the 223 Dunkirk convicts (especially the women with children) who went down the side of their prison ship and into the *Friendship* and *Charlotte* transports. Of the *Dunkirk's* total convict complement (244) as known in London from the latest returns at the end of December, Bradley had been ordered to send 80 male and 22 female convicts to *Friendship*, 99 males and 22 females to *Charlotte*, making a total of 223. Any beyond that number were to go on *Charlotte* to be allocated to other transports at Portsmouth: Bradley was to use his own discretion about those who might be too ill to go. *Charlotte's* log records receipt of 107 males (these included 15 of the *Mercury* mutineers) and 20 females. *Friendship* received 75 males (49 were *Mercury* mutineers) and 21 females (including all seven remaining *Mercury* women) "all secured in irons, except the women." The 95 males recorded in her log was either a slip of the pen or failure to make a head count: the difference of 20 is accounted for by the 18 too ill to go, the one who had died since London's orders, and Charles Keeling, released from custody on the 8th, by an order barely in time to save him.[191]

It had been intended to discharge the *Dunkirk* as soon as the Fleet had sailed, and the totals allotted to each transport had been meant to clear the ship. However, the *Dunkirk* operated until March 1791, when the 86 convicts then on board were sent to the *Lion* hulk at Portsmouth by the ship *Peggy Success*. Between 1787 and 1791, *Dunkirk's* convict population fluctuated between 300 and 450. And on board, for almost three years from 30 January 1787, one of the convicts left behind, too ill to be embarked for the Fleet, remained confined until embarked on the *Neptune* transport in October 1789—Mary Bond, *the only woman among upwards at any one time of 350 men.*[192]

John Small went on board *Charlotte* from the *Dunkirk* on 11 March 1787, with 18 of the 20 who had left Exeter High Gaol together in January 1786 (one had died on the hulk). Next day, *Charlotte* and *Friendship* got under sail for Portsmouth, where all the other ships of the Fleet had already gathered: the three storeships, *Borrowdale*, *Fishburn* and *Golden Grove:* the two navy escorts, HMS *Sirius* and HMS *Supply:* and the other convict transports, *Alexander, Prince of Wales, Scarborough* and *Lady Penrhyn*, the latter chartered to carry out the female convicts.[193]

The *Alexander* had taken 184 male convicts from Newgate at Woolwich on 6 January, by warrant 3 January to the Superintendent of the hulks, Duncan Campbell, and on the same day, "on Saturday morning early, 56 women felons, under sentence of transportation in Newgate, were conveyed from the said prison on board the hulk lying at Woolwich, in order for their transportation to Botany Bay." The hulk was in fact the transport *Lady Penrhyn*, Captain William Cropton Sever. On 9 January six more women, three with young children, were embarked on the transport, and on the 26th, sixteen more, with one child. On the 31st, by then at Gravesend, the *Lady Penrhyn* received 22 more women, brought down by waggon from London, where they had been gathered together from country gaols and held with Southwark prisoners in the New Prison in the Borough.[194]

Later (18 March) Governor Phillip would write, "The situation in which the magistrates sent the women on board the Lady Penrhyn, stamps them with infamy—tho' almost naked, & so very filthy, that nothing but cloathing them could have prevented them from perishing, and which could not be done in time to prevent a fever, that is still on board that ship, & where there are many with Venereal complaints that must spread in spite of every precaution I may take hereafter, and will be fatal to thousands—there is a necessity for doing something for the young man who is on board that ship as surgeon, or I fear that we shall lose him, & then a hundred women will be left without any assistance, several of them with child."[195]

Among the first 56 sent to the *Lady Penrhyn* down the Thames in open boats in the bitter January weather was Mary Parker, whose life would be joined to John Small's in New South Wales, and whose story it seems fitting to introduce at this point.[196]

12. MARY PARKER

The house in which Mary Parker lived and worked in London in the 1780s was on the west side of Duke Street, Bloomsbury, now renamed Coptic Street. The site, and even the fabric of the house, may still exist: of the thirteen houses then standing between Woburn Court and Castle Street, at least half a dozen, at the north end, probably survived the slash of New Oxford Street when it cut through the area in 1847. The street opened, and still opens, onto Great Russell Street almost opposite the west boundary of the British Museum, with The Fox tavern then at the corner. A block away to the east, on what is today New Oxford Street, the parish church of St George's, Bloomsbury (divided from its parent parish of St Giles in January 1731) raised and still raises its spire to the sky, capped by the odd and incongruous statue of George I draped in a Roman toga.[197]

The tenants of the fourth house south of Woburn Court, John Hickman and his wife Mary, paid their rent to an absentee landlord, the lowest rung in a ladder of landlords whose rent ultimately reached the owner of the estate, the Duke of Bedford. Here Mary Parker worked as a domestic servant, helping Mary Hickman with what cleaning was done, perhaps running errands, and almost certainly doing some of the washing Mrs Hickman took in as an additional source of income to that received from her lodgers and whatever her husband earned from whatever his employment. The house accommodated, with the overcrowding and discomfort typical of the area and the times, lodgers uncertain as to number but certain to have been more than decency allowed. Some twenty years earlier the High Constable of Holborn was complaining "that in the parish of St Giles's, there were great numbers of idle persons and vagabonds, who have their lodging there for two pence a night. That in the above parish and in St George's Bloomsbury, one woman alone occupies seven of these houses, all properly accommodated with miserable beds, from the cellar to the garret, for such twopenny lodgers. That in these beds, several of which are in the same room, men and women, often strangers to each other, lie promiscuously, the price of a double bed being no more than three pence, as an encouragement for them to lie together."[198]

Perhaps Duke Street was slightly better than the area around Dyott street a few blocks west, notorious for its massive human misery, a bolt-hole for the hopeless, inhabited by the wretchedly poor and the outcasts of society. Newspapers at the end of 1784 complained of the criminal behaviour in Dyott street, where "a gang of housebreakers, foot pads, and other disorderly persons assembled together in a house," and, except for six taken by peace officers, "got clear off". Parish registers record the pitiful unknowns—"a poor woman . . . a little boy"—found dead and unmourned in the stinking rooms.[199]

Only a few blocks further south and west lay the rookeries of St Giles, whose squalid horrors have been preserved pictorially by Hogarth and verbally by such horrified observers as Robert Willan, a Scottish physician practising in London in the 1780s. "It will scarcely appear credible, though it is precisely true, that persons of the lowest class do not put clean sheets on their beds three times a year," wrote the good doctor from his own comfortable background of clean sheets and airy rooms, perhaps equating the lack of cleanliness in his patients with some moral insensitivity (fortunately absent from the character of their betters) rather than with the sheer lack of sheets to change. "Even where no sheets are used, they never wash or scour their blankets or coverlets [no soap?] nor renew them until they are no longer tenable [no money?] . . . curtains, if unfortunately there should be any, are never cleansed but suffered to continue in the same state till they fall to pieces; lastly . . . from three to eight individuals of different ages often sleep in the same bed; there being in general but one room and one bed for each family. . . .

"The room occupied is either a deep cellar, almost inaccessible to the light, and admitting of no change of air; or a garret with a low roof and small windows, the passage to which is close, kept dark, and filled not only with bad air, but with putrid excremental effluvia from a vault at the bottom of the staircase. Washing of linen, or some other disagreeable business, is carried on, while infants are left dozing and children more advanced kept at play whole days on the tainted bed: some unsavory victuals are from time to time cooked: in many instances, idleness, in others the cumbrous furniture or utensils of trade, with which the apartments are clogged, prevent the salutary operation of the broom and whitewashing brush"—even, one is tempted to suggest, if the occupier could afford possession of such broom and brush and whitewash—"and favour the accumulation of a heterogeneous filth.

"The above account is not exaggerated; for the truth of it I appeal to the medical practitioners whose situation or humanity has led them to be acquainted with the wretched inhabitants of some streets in St Giles parish . . ."[200]

These comments come from a notably concerned and kindly man, at a time when an earning labourer in the south of England, with 4-5 children, had an estimated budget of £41.17s. a year, leaving him short of his needs by £6.10s. Small wonder curtains were not renewed nor luxuries like brooms bought.[201]

Perhaps Duke Street, nearer to the fashionable areas of Bloomsbury Square and Montague House, may have been less squalid. John Hickman was, perhaps, a respectable householder: he had occupied the house for several years, and the name occurs many times in parish registers, indicating that the family had lived in the district for a long time. His neighbour five doors down the street was John Vinn, constable, whose name appears proudly on the List of Freeholders, Copyholders, and Leaseholders of St George's Bloomsbury, 1st Division. Whatever his trade, Hickman and his wife eked out their income from rooms let to lodgers at an average rent of up to two shillings a week, or twopence and threepence a night, as was the custom of the day.[202]

"In a large proportion of the dwellings of the poor," wrote another concerned doctor, T. A. Murray, in 1801, "a house contains as many families as rooms: on the ground floor resides almost universally the master of the house with his family, which, if pretty numerous, sometimes occupies the whole of that floor, if not, the back room is occupied by another family. This apartment is in many instances of a size scarcely more than sufficient to admit of a bed, with space for a person to pass it, and so much as is necessary for a fireplace. The rooms which are in the front part of the house are usually large but they are often occupied by families more than proportionally numerous.

"But although the accommodations in the middle and upper part of the house are extremely uncomfortable, they are in every respect preferable to those in the lowest apartment or cellar, where darkness, dirt and stagnant air combine to augment all the evils resulting from such a situation. . . . Many of the windows cannot be opened without admitting air apparently more noxious, certainly not less offensive, than that already contained in the room; in other instances, the sashes have frequently been rendered by age or accident immovable; wood or paper has been substituted for broken panes or glass; every crevice is so carefully stuffed by woollen rags or some other filthy substance, that as a means of admitting fresh air the windows are often totally useless."[203]

In such conditions in her early twenties Mary Parker passed her drab and toil-filled days, paid as likely as not only in food and lodging, with not a penny in cash. If she was that child Mary born to John and Esther Parker and baptized in the parish of St George's, Bloomsbury, on 9 December 1759, she would have been 25 when she found herself caught for the first time in the toils of the law. A John Parker was buried from Duke Street in May 1767, an Esther from Broad Street in the parish in

December 1780: it seems logical that a girl who knew and was known in the Duke Street neighbourhood might find work there when it became necessary.[204]

On the other hand, she said in April 1786, when asked if she could produce friends or witnesses, "I have none in London," and her age on one record is given as 25 in 1786, so it is very possible that she was not a London-born girl at all, but one come in from the country to find a livelihood. Parkers abound in Birmingham registers: is it illogical to wonder. . . .? But we may never know more of Mary Parker than from the moment when on that April Friday in 1785 she was first seized for stealing two of Mrs Hickman's tablecloths, value 5s.[205]

What turned her to theft? It has been suggested, in the light of subsequent events, that she may have been wrongly accused. Or did she fall victim to a moment of irresistible temptation, in the hope of gaining a few pennies of her very own, by the sale or pawning of these two items?—pennies with which she who was without possessions might buy some coveted article forever out of her reach by any other means? She was held in the New Prison, Clerkenwell, for six months before standing trial, an abnormally long period for which there seems to be no explanation. The trial by a Middlesex jury before Mr Baron Hotham on 21 September 1785 caused no stir, and was only cursorily reported in the Old Bailey Sessions Papers. Mary Hickman and Henry Baker, as witnesses, were paid fifteen shillings and ten shillings and sixpence respectively. Mary Parker was sentenced to be confined in the House of Correction at Clerkenwell, and was delivered there from Newgate on 24 September.[206]

Mary Parker was an infant, or perhaps not yet born, when another inmate of the Clerkenwell Bridewell was publishing his own experiences as a prisoner within its walls. After completing a three-year sentence for a publication condemned as blasphemous, Jacob Ilive, a London printer and author, prepared a pamphlet in 1759 describing conditions and routine within the Bridewell and offering some sensible suggestions for reform. His account, though dispassionate, reeks with the offensive stench of 18th-century prisons: the tiny cells only six feet wide that were night accommodation for up to 11 people: the bare beds, sometimes with smuggled blankets that the keeper burnt if he discovered them: the "dark ward" kept for those who had not paid the ward dues, or for punishment: the cells with two beds used for "bawdy houses" at the whim of the keeper: the two wards for women prisoners at night, 7½ feet square in which "I have seen sixty-five to seventy women, suffering bad health in consequence".[207]

Perhaps Mary Parker suffered less than some of her fellow-prisoners because she was employed as a prison nurse during her six-months' stay. Was she therefore exempt from the task of hemp-picking, which demanded eight "punnies" a day (each a 2-3 lb. skein of hemp) from the women, with punishment of heavy leg-irons and hands cuffed behind the back for failing to meet the quota? Three times during her imprisonment, Mary Parker was called as witness during inquests on prison deaths. On 17 December she gave evidence when one John Edwards died of dropsy: she had put him to bed and given him every care and attention before he died. On 20 January 1786, she explained what she had tried to do for 70-year-old Mary Patmore "who died of a quick decay occasioned by Old Age by the Visitation of God and not otherwise to the knowledge of this Deponent": seven days later she endorsed the attention the apothecary had given to Isabella Hall, a consumptive who had been in her care for a fortnight before she died.[208]

Mary's term of six months would have ended on 24 March 1786. What she did three weeks later had its origin in either a total stupidity, a total innocence, or a furious and festering resentment.

At about 10.30 on the night of 19 April 1786, Mary Hickman, in her house on Duke-street, was informed by some excited tenants "that a Thief was in the House."[209] When she went to investigate, whom should she find "coming down very deliberately" but Mary Parker, "who was formerly her servant and who had been convicted for Robbing her House." Making sure the intruder was secured, Mrs Hickman went on up to the garret, "and the first thing she saw was a great number of shirts which were wet lying on the Garret stairs". Then she found that the garret door had been broken open, "and a large Quantity Linnen and wearing apparell which were hanging on lines in the Garret to dry packed up with intention to be taken away."

Reporting the outrage to the magistrate next day, she was supported by one of her lodgers, William Headland. Headland had been told of the intrusion by "a little boy who also lodges in the said House," who said he had heard somebody going up the stairs. Headland went up at once, and found the linen on the stairs and on the garret floor: and in the garret he found Mary Parker "who had her shoes off when he assisted in securing her."

Her trial on 26 April followed the offence more promptly and was reported more fully than the earlier one, in the Old Bailey Sessions Papers. The property she was accused of stealing this time consisted of "two muslin gowns and coats, value 40s. a cotton gown, value 10s. three cotton frocks value 4s. a callico bed-gown value 2s. four pairs of cotton pockets, value 4s. eleven shirts, value £3, one shift, value 2s. and one diaper clout, value 6d., the property of John Hickman".

In court Mary Hickman gave an excited account of the incident. She had been washing until ten o'clock, when she hung the clothes in the garret. Not yet in bed, she heard the commotion—"an alarm of Thieves,

I ran up in my hurry, and another witness, who is here, and his lodger, he run up also." On the upper stairs she met Headland and Mary Parker, and continued up to the garret "to see how my things were . . . the clothes of different people that I wash for". She then went out to fetch a constable.

Headland amplified his original statement. "This little boy had been in to my wife to light a candle, I came in about half past ten, the little boy run down to me, and said, there was somebody in the garret." At the bottom of the garret stairs he called up twice, but received no answer. In the garret, after noticing the clothes lying about, he found Mary Parker standing in one corner. "I knew her, she had lived with Mr. Hickman before." She made no reply when he asked her what she was doing: "I said to her, Molly, what do you mean to come here to rob your mistress again, and I said, come bundle out of the room; she set off to come out of the room, and she stooped to put her shoes on. . . . I stood by the door and caught hold of her gown tail, and she asked me in the passage to let her go out, I told her no."

An exchange then occurred between the Court [the Judge] and Mrs Hickman about the lock on the garret door, a strong lock that had been found broken.

"Had you fastened your garret-door? . . . .

"Oh yes! I locked it myself, and hung the key in my parlour; when I came up, the door was standing wide open; it was wrenched open. . . .

"Perhaps it was flipped back, and an old lock?

"No, no, no, no! I am too well used to it for that, it is not a bad lock."

The bolt of the lock shut "into a great iron staple". The bolt had been slid back out of the staple, pushed back, according to Mrs. Hickman, "by two great nails" which she said she had seen in Mary Parker's hands when she came down the stairs. "And when she put on her shoes, she dropped them beside her shoes in the passage."

It transpired that Mrs Hickman had not seen her drop the nails. The person said to have been the actual witness, her servant Nanny, was not in court.

"How do you know that she did this with these two nails?" asked the Court. She could not do it with any thing else, Mrs Hickman surmised, not even with a false key. "Oh no, no."

Mary Parker denied all the accusations. She was not in the garret, she said. "I went to speak to the gentlewoman that lodged in the two pair of stairs, to ask a person to give me a character; she was not at home." As for the nails, "I never saw the nails till they were fetched out of the parlour from Mr Hickman to give to the constable."

There were discrepancies in the evidence. William Headland seemed to imply that she had put her shoes on in the garret: Mary Hickman that she had stopped at the bottom of the stairs to do so. And if Headland had secured her in the garret, how was it that Mrs Hickman noted that she came down the stairs "very deliberately"?

Perhaps, however, the evidence most favourable to the prisoner was Mrs Hickman's statement at the beginning of her report to the Court. When she met Mary Parker coming down the stairs with Headland, "she had no property about her." Evidence proved only that there was clothing lying about: not that Mary Parker was the one responsible for putting it there, or that she had had any intention of removing it. Headland said he saw clothing lying about, but not in Mary's hands. At no time did any of the witnesses find any of the clothing in her actual possession.

Nor was there any evidence that the broken lock was her doing. If, in fact, she did have the two large nails in her hand (Headland did not mention seeing them), had she perhaps, when she arrived on the garret stairs looking for the gentlewoman she had hoped to find at home, wondered about the clothing that lay around, and about the door that was wrenched open? Simple curiosity would have impelled her to pick up the nails (if in fact she did), and look into the garret. Much was made of her shoes being off. But when climbing the stairs late at night in a house full of people likely to be sleeping, silence may well have been an act of thoughtfulness—and in any case, the last person she would have wished to rouse was Mary Hickman, whose evidence had brought her what amounted to a full year's incarceration on the earlier charge.

She urgently needed "a character" if she was to find future employment. Where more likely to obtain one than in a house where one lodger at least might be counted on to be friendly? It has been suggested that if she was in fact innocent of the first charge, she may have scattered the recently washed articles onto a dusty floor as a small revenge for the year of imprisonment unjustly suffered: but the risk would have been enormous in relation to the momentary satisfaction. It has also been suggested that she may have been seeking only what was hers—her own clothing vindictively held back by her former mistress. Whether innocent or guilty, she was acquitted of burglary—she had not entered the house forcibly, and the jury seemed unconvinced that she was responsible for breaking into the garret. She was, however, convicted of stealing.

"Have you any friends or witnesses?" asked the Court. She replied: "I have none in London." The goods she was convicted of stealing were valued at £6.2s.6d. The witnesses against her received payment of 5s.6d. each. Mary Parker was sentenced with 60 other men and women "to be transported to parts beyond the seas for 7 years", and for the next eight months and ten days she would be held in Newgate prison.

On 6 January 1787, she was embarked, in a group of 56 women, on the *Lady Penrhyn* transport for Botany Bay. It could have been worse. It could have been the west coast of Africa.

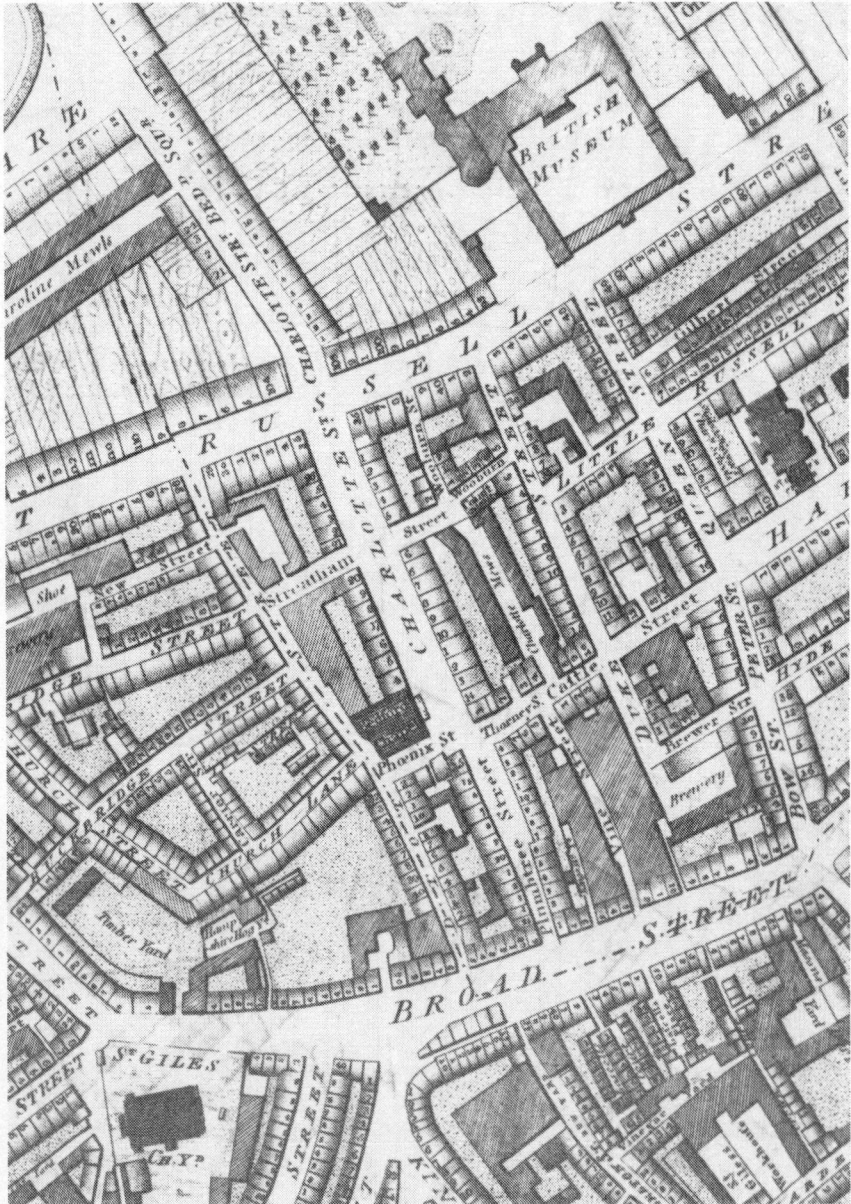

Part of a map of London showing Duke Street, the home of Mary Parker.
Courtesy London Topographical Society.

13. POLE STAR TO SOUTHERN CROSS

When John Small arrived at Portsmouth on *Charlotte* on 13 March 1787, the day after *Friendship* (*Charlotte* was to prove a heavy sailer), he found all the Fleet already anchored at the Motherbank. The *Lady Penrhyn* had arrived on 11 February after a rough Channel passage: *Sirius, Supply* and *Alexander* had been held in the Downs for 15 days "to ride out a Gale of wind" and did not arrive until the 22nd. John Easty, private marine on *Scarborough*, noted the arrivals in his journal "Arrived the Sirous & Suply men of w... and the Alexander Scarbrough Lady Penariean and Prince of wailes Transports att mother Bank." The *Prince of Wales* came in next day and began taking on her marines: from 14 March she began receiving her convicts, mostly in twos and threes as turnkeys from Chester, Lincoln, Lancaster and other country gaols arrived with women convicts and children. A batch of 37 women from Newgate went on board on 3 May.[210]

No selection at all, according to age or skills, was made in sending out the First Fleet convicts. "The ships which are to proceed to Botany Bay ... are intended to convey all the convicts now in the hulks to that settlement", Nepean wrote in October 1786. After the cruel failure of the scheme for an African destination in 1783, the governor of Cape Coast Castle had written in disgust, "The grand consideration seems to be, *to get them out of Europe at all Events.*" No attention was paid to James Matra's sensible suggestion in 1783 for an advance group to choose a site, erect buildings and establish gardens before the arrival of any settlers, nor to Phillip's own 1786 advice. It was his ultimately futile attempt to arrive at least a week or two ahead of the Fleet that led him to move to *Supply* and make a dash with the three fastest transports on 25 November: a move frustrated by the speed with which the others followed him. In April 1790 surgeon John White would write to a friend in London: "In the name of Heaven, what has the Ministry been about? ... How a business of this kind (the expence of which must be great) could first be thought of without sending to examine the country, as was Capt. Thomson's errand to the coast of Africa, is to every person here a matter of great surprize."[211]

On 4 October, 1786, Nepean had written, "I expect that the ships which are to proceed to Botany Bay will be ready in the course of the month." On the 24th, Treasury told the navy that the ships "would be ready to proceed from Gravesend in about a month at furthest". The newspapers published rumours of sailing dates "within a week" right up to 12 April 1787, when the *St James's Chronicle* wrote, "Strange as it may appear, we are credibly informed of the Fact, that the Transports for Botany Bay have not as yet sailed." By the actual date of sailing, 13 May 1787, Mary Parker had been on board *Lady Penrhyn* a full five months, John Small on *Charlotte* for two. Some shuffling of convicts from ship to ship (19 Cornwall convicts were moved from *Charlotte* to *Scarborough* on 6 April, two women from *Friendship* to *Lady Penrhyn* the day before, and two more *Charlotte* men to *Scarborough* on the 12th) may have brought a little light to the general gloom with the arrival of fresh faces, with perhaps a few new snippets of grapevine news.[212]

Of the 184 convicts received by *Alexander* in January, 52 came from the *Justitia* hulk, 31 from the *Censor,* and 101 from the *Ceres.* The warrant to Duncan Campbell dated 3 January contained 202 names, copied directly, unchanged in order except where a death had since intervened, from the Orders in Council that had legally changed the destination originally named in each sentence. In 1785, when Africa had been proposed for the *Mercury* mutineers on the *Dunkirk* hulk, Nepean had been concerned to discover only names, ages, where and when convicted, the sentence, and how much of it remained to be served. There was never a request for information about occupation or skills.[213]

On 20 January a warrant to deliver a further 25 male convicts to *Alexander* was given to Duncan Campbell, but these were not embarked in the Thames: they were added to those in a further list of 191 names on a warrant dated 24 February. A total of 209 from these two warrants was sent off on 27 February to be embarked on *Scarborough* (184) and *Alexander* (25) at Portsmouth. Of these, 29 came from the *Justitia,* 149 from the *Censor,* and 31 from the *Ceres* hulks. The only sign of interest in the skills possibly valuable to the settlement is found in a letter to Admiralty from the senior officer (Portsmouth) Captain Marshall, with an account of the many seamen volunteering to serve on *Sirius* in place of those discharged unfit. "I had forborn to complete her Complement 'till Captain Phillip came down that He might furnish himself with those whose occupations He might stand most in need of." This bore no application to the skills of convicts: only of the seamen.

On 25 May, when the Fleet had traversed the Bay of Biscay and had reached the northernmost coast of Spain, Phillip sent to each transport to try to discover what his 750-odd convicts were capable of and experienced in, and might contribute to the new community: a bit late in the day to find out that no one had asked before. Any list that may have been made up was certainly no longer available to him on arrival in New South Wales, and the departure of the transports carried off all the papers for each individual convict. This was a lack of information he found himself sadly in need of in the following years, especially when terms of servitude had been completed.[214]

As soon as the hulks were thus partially cleared into the transport ships, orders flew to county gaols for sending some of their male prisoners to fill up the empty places. Only the women, plucked from the lists requested by Nepean, were ordered to the Fleet, except for two men in Surrey (James Squires and James Bloodsworth), one in Gloucester (Edward Pugh), and three others believed to be husbands of women convicts.[215]

The 209 convicts from London arrived at Portsmouth on 2 March, in such dreadful weather that they could not be immediately sent to the transports. In anticipation, HMS *Gorgon* in Portsmouth Harbour, had been hastily supplied with guards, provisions and security measures. "I am sorry", wrote Captain Marshall, ". . . that the Weather continuing so bad, I have been obliged to Embark them on board the said ship . . . I have three Sailing Lighters laying at the Buoys, which will be ready to carry them off to the Scarborough when the Weather moderates:" which it did on 4 March.[216]

Many years later, a seaman recalled youthful memories of the convicts' arrival at Portsmouth. "I recollect perfectly all the shop-windows and doors of Portsmouth being closed on this occasion, and the streets were lined with troops, while the waggons, I think 30 in number, passed to Point Beach, where the boats were ready to receive them: as soon as they were embarked, they gave three tremendous cheers, and were rowed off to the transport ready for the reception at Spithead." The cheers were probably the only form of bravado and irony possible for the men in their chains.[217]

By 13 March there had already been seven deaths on board *Alexander*. Now this transport was struck by a "malignant disease" which carried off six more men before the Fleet sailed (she remained an unhealthy ship: 15 more would die on board before arrival at Botany Bay). She was whitewashed and "smoked", and this seems to have satisfied the surgeon general, John White—though he recommended fresh provisions "and a little wine for those who were ill"—who indignantly refused to believe that there was in fact a malignant disease on board. *"Their complaints are neither malignant nor dangerous,"* he assured the worried men, and told an equally worried Portsmouth surgeon "that there was not the least appearance of malignity in the disease under which the convicts laboured, but that it wholly proceeded from the cold; and was nearly similar to a complaint then prevalent, even among the

better sort of people, in and about Portsmouth." It may well have been:
but it proved deadly on *Alexander*.[218]

The authorities were having difficulty in making up the proper lists of
those intended to go and those actually on board. The contractor,
William Richards Jr., noted that Jacob Messiah was not on board
Scarborough at 31 March, but failed to recognize him as the John
Mathias already received, under which name he had been convicted.
Elizabeth Lee and Elizabeth Lee/Lees, convicted at the Old Bailey on
different dates and for different crimes, were both marked in Prison
Commission records as having been sent from Newgate to *Lady
Penrhyn*: only one of these women appears in any First Fleet list. Did the
women wonder among themselves what had happened to the other one?
Richards thought he had received Daniel Williams from Presteign on
Friendship, but Williams remained behind and was discharged in due
course from the *Stanislaus* hulk on 1 July 1792. The *Prince of Wales*, the
last transport to be chartered, received her convicts in small parties,
shepherded from country gaols by the turnkeys: two women from
Chester on 14 March, four women and a child from Lincoln on the 25th,
three women from Lancaster on 9 April, one from Flint on the 12th.
Thirty-two women, including Esther Abrahams with the daughter born
in Newgate on 18 March, arrived on 3 May from London: and one
imagines some frantic rowing (perhaps also praying) as the turnkey
from Lancaster with three more women convicts and one man watched
the wind fill the sails of the Fleet on 13 May.[219]

John Small, like his male companions, was for some of the time at
Spithead chained, but probably allowed on deck with a few of his fellows
for a brief period daily, closely watched by the marine guard, as he had
once, to no avail, watched prisoners on *Lively*. Did he bitterly regret the
moment of weakness that had brought him to this pass?—and resent the
freedom of the marines, a freedom he had once enjoyed? Did they know
he had once been one of them?—or did shame keep him silent about his
former service? At least the sea sounds and sea sights would bring a sense
of familiarity, reviving happier memories. The women were always freer
than the men to come up on deck to "behold a city upon inconstant
billows dancing, for so appears this fleet majestical". Would someone
have told Mary Parker on *Lady Penrhyn* about the tragic sinking of the
Royal George whose wreck she would see still lying half-submerged in
the Spithead waters?—drowning Admiral Richard Kempenfeldt, with
hundreds of men, women and children, when the old ship keeled over in
August 1782? The rolling waters on which Mary Parker unwillingly
tossed would be as full in 1787 as at the time of the 1782 disaster of the
forests of great masts rising around the transports in this naval haven,
the chequered castles of the guardships and men of war heaving at
anchor, the busy scatter of caterpillar-oared lighters; jolly boats,

admirals' polished barges, wherries bring stores, goods for sale, visitors (wives and children) to ship-bound sailors: a city indeed.[220]

Perhaps the women would have been frightened by the crash of a 13-gun salute from *Sirius* on 7 April when Lord Hood hoisted his flag on HMS *Triumph* in Portsmouth Harbour. John Small on *Charlotte* would know what it meant, if not its specific purpose on that day, and suffer an ache of nostalgia, no longer one of the proud marines who dressed ship for the occasion. In what words would he have told his stories to his companions on *Charlotte*? "That day at Havana when Prince William Henry came into harbour on *Fortunee*, *Albemarle* came in too, with Captain Nelson . . . The Spaniards and us fired salutes, 21 guns, 19 . . . 17 . . . 21 . . . 19 again . . . should have heard the echoes, like to burst an eardrum." There was much time to while away, and many a tale to be told by the prisoners thus brought together. Surely John's would have been an oft-told tale. "And did I tell you about the time the Prince came on board *our* ship in New York?"[221]

Arthur Bowes Smyth, the surgeon on *Lady Penrhyn* who cared for convicts as well as crew when the convicts' surgeon was ill, came down to Portsmouth and boarded the transport on 22 March, and noticed other, less pleasant sights. A corpse, "sew'd up in a Hammock floated along side our Ship" on 19 April, and another on the 26th, in "Rainey & squally" weather that grew worse, so that "The Women very sick wt. the motion of the Ship", and on the 30th "it encreased to a perfect Hurricane with hail & rain." Not only the women would have suffered the discomforts of mal de mer: there were plenty of landlubbers among the men.[222]

Birth and death and pain accompanied the *Lady Penrhyn*, as in life anywhere. Mary Parker, prison nurse, could be counted on to use her experience as well as her compassion. Her recorded appearances as a prison-nurse witness at Clerkenwell Bridewell concerned only the deaths of elderly convicts, but there had to have been many unrecorded occasions for her presence to minister to the sick and the pregnant as well as to the dying. One-year-old William Green had died on *Lady Penrhyn* just before the transport reached Portsmouth: his mother Ann had shared a few months in Newgate with Mary, her crime the theft of 19 china plates (7s.6d.) and a china bowl (6d.) from a Marylebone china-mender.[223]

Ann Wright, who had said "the devil was very busy with her, she was in liquor" when she stole clothing and money from her mistress, died on 4 April: elderly, bewildered, 70-year-old Elizabeth Beckford, "taken instantly with the [12-lb. Gloucester] cheese" she had tried to carry off from a London shop, died on 12 July, surviving about five months of the voyage after having been bundled aboard 16 days after her conviction on 10 January 1787: and poor, consumptive Jane Parkinson from

Altrincham, Cheshire, who had so desperately refused to leave her child behind, died on 18 November, transferred from *Friendship*. She had been held in confinement since the end of July 1785 for the theft of a few yards of cloth. The orphaned child, three-year-old Edward, was one of three who became public charges for education and care, the produce of a Norfolk Island plot of ground assigned to cover the costs. He left the island on 30 March 1793 by the *Chesterfield:* could he have been the 14-year-old servant to HMS *Buffalo's* master, William Raven (whom he had doubtless met on the latter's many calls at Norfolk Island and Sydney), shipping back to Australia, who fell overboard to his death on 3 August 1798 somewhere in the South Atlantic?[224]

Mary Tilley's son William ("who is likely to do very well," wrote Bowes Smyth) was born on 13 April (but he died in Sydney just over a year later, followed in two months by his mother). Isabella Rosson/Lawson had a daughter on 31 May, two days before the Fleet reached Teneriffe. In July, Elizabeth Colley's stillborn child was delivered. On 23 October, at the anchorage in Table Bay, Jane Langley gave birth to a daughter, Henrietta, whom Bowes Smyth entered in his journal as a boy named Philip, his mind evidently on the name of the supposed father Philip Skirving/Scriven, a seaman on *Lady Penrhyn:* and on 16 November, the last child born on *Lady Penrhyn*, a son Joshua, was born to Ann Morton (or Mary Moulton). Mary Parker's experience probably included midwifery, and she would in these cases have been of great help: but she had not been midwife to the birth of Esther Abrahams' child, as a later convict, James Sheedy, asserted, Mary having been on board *Lady Penrhyn* for ten weeks when this child was born in Newgate. There may have been, however, a warmth and friendship for the 20-year-old girl (already two months pregnant when she was sent to Newgate) from the heart of which a grain of truth could grow into such an assertion. It is possible that the birth to which Mary may have been midwife was that of the son Esther bore to Captain-Lieutenant George Johnston, baptised 4 March 1790.[225]

The Fleet sailed comfortably down Channel after departure on 13 May, Arthur Phillip as captain of *Sirius*, John Hunter as second captain, Philip Gidley King as second lieutenant, who would go to Norfolk Island as soon as possible after arrival at Botany Bay. King would become lieutenant governor of the island in 1789, and later governor of New South Wales. Hunter, too, would serve as one of the colony's first governors. The *Supply* was commanded by Lt. Henry Lidgbird Ball, who would have an interesting life ahead of him, though not in Australia after 1792, and would be a rear-admiral of the Blue when he died in 1818. The last sight of England for all of them was the Lizard on the 15th, a day that brought a windfall—"a great many Casks of Geneva [gin] floating on the water of which the fishburn pick'd up 35 & the

Scarborough 25". Probably no convict chained below saw the St Agnes light winking from Scilly at 1 a.m. on the 16th, the last signal many of them would receive from their homeland.[226]

On *Charlotte,* life was much more comfortable for John Small and his fellows from 20 May after release from irons (though surgeon Bowes Smyth reported some dangerous illness on board, and on the 28th Ishmael Coleman—"worn out by lowness of spirits and debility, brought on by long and close confinement, resigned his breath without a pang").

There were a few moments of ironic cheer for the convicts: on the 15th, Corporal William Baker had managed to shoot himself through the foot with his musquet, and rumours reached them of an incipient mutiny on *Scarborough* that had earned the ringleaders, Philip Farrell and Thomas Griffiths, 24 lashes each on *Sirius* and transfer to *Prince of Wales.*[227]

The little Fleet said farewell to the escorting frigate *Hyaena* on the 20th and bowled over the water in fair weather, pushed to Teneriffe by trade winds, but "with a heavy rolling sea", and John was surrounded once more with the sounds he had known so well, slap of waves, clap of ropes, snap of sails, the ship's bells calling the time, and the smell of tar, vinegar and whitewash.[228]

To the convicts, Phillip was a name, a shortish figure appearing in a momentary flurry of piping, saluting, and flourish of musquets when he came aboard to inspect their quarters. The careful sailing instructions by which he manoeuvered his charges over the oceans meant nothing to the convicts. The "proper day and night signals . . . established for the regulation of his convoy, and every necessary instruction . . . given to the masters to guard against separation," were beyond their ken, though "'' e conspicuous light in the main-top" carried by *Sirius* at night may have been a comforting star in the darkness to those convicts on deck at night. The men were interested in possibilities of escape and avoidance of restrictions, the women in what gifts the sailors might bring them from shore leave. The trivia of the voyage were their main sources of interest and excitement: the strange birds and sea-creatures, the gossip of goings-on between women and crew (and sometimes officers), the misadventures of their fellows, and the ever-present vagaries of the weather.[229]

In the week at Teneriffe, where the Fleet anchored on 3 June, fresh provisions came aboard, and a thrill of excitement was provided by the escape and recapture of John Power from *Scarborough:* also (doubtless heard with some glee) an account of "an Affray . . . on Shore between the Sailors of [a large Dutch East Indiaman] & the Sailors of the Sirius, attended wt. no other ill consequences than some broken pates & bloody noses." The convicts would see the fishing boats with lights flitting through the Fleet at night, and the snow on the high Peak of the island.

But John Small, and others who had been seamen, would have wondered that the obligatory naval salute failed to occur here, leaving unhonoured His Majesty's birthday on 4 June, unaware of a special arrangement between Phillip and the Santa Cruz governor to omit firing salutes.[230] The Fleet left Teneriffe on 10 June and passed the Canaries and the Cape Verde Islands during the following week. If someone pointed out to John Small the Island of Sal about four leagues off at 9 a.m. on 19 June, what memories the name would bring of an earlier Sal in his life at almost the same latitude on the other side of the Atlantic![231]

On 14 July they "Cross'd the Equinoxial Line exactly at 12 o'Clock this night", when a rather disapproving Lieutenant David Collins remarked that "such persons as had never before crossed the Line were compelled to undergo the ridiculous ceremonies which those who were privileged were allowed to perform on them." The ceremonies would have dribbled into the 15th, a Sunday: the officers of the Fleet were not so circumspect as Captain Pasley of *Jupiter*, who, while enjoying the fun "on crossing the Tropick" in 1782, had postponed the ceremony to the following day, "altho' we crossed Yesterday, as I did not choose to admit these Amusements on Sunday."[232]

Surgeon White pointedly wrote that no one on *Charlotte* seemed interested in holding such a ceremony. Master's mate Daniel Southwell described very fully what he clearly had enjoyed on *Sirius* held over until the following day (though not from the religious scruples that had made Captain Pasley delay the fun, which he seems to have enjoyed as long as they were not held on the Sabbath, but because of the late hour of crossing'. "Some of the Tars dress themselves out in the most frightful and extrordinary manner," wrote young Southwell to his mother . . . "one of these . . . is supposed to be Neptune and the rest . . . his Train they get over the ships side unobserved and then come on b^d as 'tho out of the sea and others of the old stagers are ready to welcome him." These high-jinks are not mentioned in the log of *Lady Penrhyn* (neither are they in that of *Sirius*), so one may wonder whether the sailors on the women's transport may have tried to amuse their female passengers with this kind of entertainment too. Mary Parker and her friends would have found it all a welcome break in the monotony.[233]

"A number of small yellow birds . . . perchg. upon the rigg[ing], & on the Decks" on *Lady Penrhyn* doubtless intrigued the women as they did surgeon Bowes. There were thunderstorms: some sharks shot by the sailors: luminous bodies covering the sea "wh. gave a most beautiful appearance": porpoises: "a very large Whale . . . blow'd the water very high wt. a great noise" (the first whale surgeon Bowes Smyth had seen and as much a curiosity to most of the convicts): Mother Carey's Chickens, and a Booby, and landfall on 3 August, "the peak of Rio abt. 8 leagues off . . . The appearance of the Country . . . is beautiful, consisting of Lofty Mountains & verdent Vallies, the one cover'd wt. lofty Trees &ca. & the other wt. Oranges, Lemons, Limes &ca. Sugar Canes also grow here in great abundance."[234]

This was a city (Rio de Janeiro, the capital of Brazil) in which Arthur Phillip felt quite at home, speaking Portuguese after his four-year service in the Portuguese navy (1774-78): unlike Ralph Clark, who issued a breakfast invitation on *Friendship* to a Portuguese guard-boat officer who could "neither speak English or French So we . . . Satt like Posts."[235]

They stayed at Rio for a month, effecting repairs and taking on stores. Here the master of *Sirius*, Micah Morton, had to be invalided home due to a rupture, and James Keltie, a former navy master serving as first mate on *Friendship*, was sent to take his place. Many of the exotic fruits were enjoyed by the convicts. Canoes paddled by naked negroes flocked around the ships with oranges to sell, and fish, and from the market the officers returned "wt. a large quantity of the finest cabages I ever saw, also Yams, Bananas, Guavas, Limes, Lettices, Barangoles & Oranges, also some very tollerable Beef." The officers saw a grand procession on 15 August, with bands of music, choirs, elegantly attired ladies: probably denied to the convicts, many of whom yet may have been allowed on deck at night to see "a grand display of fireworks off the top of one of the Churches."[236]

The Fleet left Rio on 4 September, this time with the crash of gun salutes, for the five-week voyage across the South Atlantic to the Cape of Good Hope. Two days later, "the Goat Mr Collins brot. at Teneriffe died" on the *Lady Penrhyn*, and on the 8th, in a violent storm, "Capt. Campbell's Kid broke its thigh by the Chicken coops falling on it, by the Ship's rolling." On the 14th, "a pidgeon went overboard & lost." The women suffered too: the weather was for the most part "Very wet wt. frequent Squalls of wind." On the 13th the sea had run in through the lee portholes, and on the 24th "there were many heavy squalls the Ship roll'd so very much that everything in the Cabin gave way. . . . Many of the Women also recd. hurts & bruises from falls."[237]

On September 19, John Small had lost one of his *Dunkirk* colleagues, William Brown, a *Mercury* mutineer originally convicted at Winchester in July 1783: "a very well-behaved convict" on *Charlotte*, who fell overboard "bringing some clothing from the bowsprit end, where he had hung them to dry." He was lost, in spite of immediate launching of boats from *Supply* and *Charlotte*. "The people on the forecastle . . . say that the ship went directly over him."[238]

Bowes reported much squally weather during September; on the 24th he "cd. get no sleep all night the roll of the Ship was so great." Mary Parker was suffering with the rest. "Many of the Women also recd. hurts & bruises from falls." Not much chance to enjoy the sight of the "many

Albatrosses & Pintado Birds astern," or perhaps even to notice (though Bowes did) the "Many Birds & Porpuses abt. . . . 5 very large Sperma Caeti Whales very near" *Lady Penrhyn* early in October. The Reverend Mr Johnson came from the *Golden Grove* storeship on 7 October to deliver some "great & small Tooth Combs" for the women. On the 13th the Fleet came to at anchor in Table Bay, South Africa, about half the voyage completed.[239]

Cape Town, Table Mountain. *Sirius* and Convoy in Table Bay, November 1787. Drawn by Lieutenant William Bradley RN from his Journal *A Voyage to New South Wales*.
Courtesy State Library of New South Wales.

Table Bay was probably the noisiest port the Fleet had visited. Every ship of the Netherlands exchanged a 13-gun salute with the fort on entering, as did *Sirius*. It was probably the busiest, not only for the number of ships coming and going, but for the Fleet because of the provisions that had to be taken on here—the last port of call before Botany Bay. It was a time, too, for discovering more about what had been happening on the other transports. On 14 October, Surgeon Bowes heard from Surgeon White that "upwards of 30 had been very ill wt. a putrid fever & Dysentery onboard the Charlotte & that he expected the death of 3 of them this day." Now the news flew from ship to ship of another attempt at convict mutiny, this time on *Alexander*. From the time of embarkation on the Thames, her convicts had been "very troublesome and could take their hands out of irons": a boat had had to be rowed continually around the ship in the River to prevent escapes.[240]

At Rio, they had used threats to the officers. Aided by three dissident seamen, some of them had been "provided . . . with instruments for breaking into the fore-hold of the ship (which had been done, and some provisions stolen thereout)." The seamen were exchanged for three from *Sirius*, and "Some of the Convicts concerned were chain'd to the decks." One was John Power, thwarted in his earlier escape attempt at Teneriffe.[241]

Lieutenant Ralph Clark of the marines had been having a wretched time with his noisy, obstreperous women on *Friendship*, so infinitely less worthy in every way compared—unfavourably—with his pampered wife Betsey. He had been utterly dismayed by the loss of six of his "best" women to *Charlotte* at Rio and receipt of the six worst in exchange on 11 August. "I dont know what I shall doe now . . . the[y] are the only women that can wash amonst them." Like Bowes, he had a poor opinion of the convicts, especially the women ("Ther wair never a greater number of D....d B......s in one place as ther is in this Ship"), never once making any allowance for the conditions in which their lives had been led, the strictures of abject poverty, the utter humiliations suffered all their lives, and the present lack of any way to make themselves attractive. The spitting furies Clark encountered never gave an inch to authority, and the obscenities with which they met every punishment were the only gauntlets they could hurl in the face of their fate. Bowes said of his *Lady Penrhyn* women that "there was never a more abandon'd set of wretches collected in one place at any period," though he had the grace to admit on arrival at Sydney Cove that they were "dress'd in general very clean & some few amongst them might be sd. to be well dress'd." How far Mary Parker was included in this acid generalisation (she was never mentioned in any journal yet discovered) we do not know. Not even the six who had "uniformly behaved well", of whom five from *Lady Penrhyn* would go to Norfolk Island with the first group in February 1788, were exempted at this time of speaking. Ann Inett and Ann Yates later caught the eye of influential "husbands", and fared well. Olive Gascoigne made a respectable marriage to a convict, Nathaniel Lucas, who also did well. Elizabeth Lee and Elizabeth Colley did not prove immune from punishments on Norfolk Island. There were others—Esther Abrahams, Hannah Mullins, Ann George, Mary Marshall, Maria Hamilton, Mary Parker herself—whose lives, given the opportunities for respectability, would largely rebut these criticisms.[242]

The damnation by Bowes of the *Lady Penrhyn* women included their "base Ingratitude" to sailors "who have at every Port . . . spent almost the whole of [their] wages . . . in purchasing different Articles of wearing apparel & other things" for the women, and for the latters' "plundering the Sailors . . . of their necessary cloaths & cutting them up for some purpose of their own". Possibly this was for the needs of feminine hygiene. It was always difficult to keep seamen and women apart—five of them had been found with crew members at Portsmouth in mid-April (one of them with the second mate)—but in these encounters it was almost always the women who were the "abandon'd wretches". Clark on *Friendship* at least once was prepared to admit that "never was ther a Set of greater rascals together than [the seamen] are . . . ten thousand times wors than the convicts."[243]

The gifts from sailors would in any case have gone only to a few of their favourites: and Bowes should also have remembered that the Fleet had sailed without "a great part of the clothing supplies for the women." What they did have, Phillip wrote from Rio, "was made of very slight materials, much too small, and in general came to pieces in a few weeks." He had bought 100 sacks of Casada (cassava) for the convicts against a shortage of bread supplies, with the thoughtful intention of using the "strong Russia" of the sacks for clothing the people, "many of whom are nearly naked". The women had a rough time on the voyage, scorned for their acceptance with less than docility of the discomfort and distress of cold, fear, nakedness, illness and overcrowding, and for taking advantage of what any man could offer of momentary pleasure and perquisites in a sex bargain—something they had had to live by for most of their lives.[244]

Meanwhile, in the great amphitheatre of Table Bay, there was plenty of activity to watch, leaning over the deck rails, as the Fleet replenished its supplies of water and wood, and loaded as much meat, fruit, flour, wine, spirits, as it could accommodate. Short sharp squalls sent many of the women to their quarters from time to time, suffering the miseries of mal de mer: but in calm weather they could come up to watch the arrival of large foreign ships that called forth huzzas from their own. There had been much cause for chatter on 1 November when Phebe Norton fell overboard from the head and was luckily fished out by the prompt action of two sailors, who jumped overboard and got her into the *Lady Penrhyn's* pinnace fastened to the stern. She was luckier than Patrick Vallance from Leith, aged about 40, quarter master from *Sirius* sent to *Friendship* in August as second mate, who had drowned three days before, largely due to intoxication.[245]

As well as provisions, the Fleet took on animals, as many as could be crammed into the vessels, both for government and as private stock for some of the officers. On 5 November, *Lady Penrhyn* women were able to watch perspiring sailors manhandle on board a stallion, three mares and three colts, which would travel in canvas slings 'tween decks: to care for them, Thomas Kelly, a convict from *Alexander*, had been sent across two days earlier. "Were you to take a View of [*Sirius*], below," wrote young Daniel Southwell, master's mate, to his mother on 11 November, "you would be apt to take it for a Livery stable of Note for there are a number of partitions all along the Between Decks, and racks for the Provender, nor do we want pig sties, Hog-troughts and all the necessary Apparatus. Among the stock are many of the featherd kind; and also plants of various sorts: these all together will take up much room and the ship is lumber'd." It was a pity, after all the effort, that most of the stock died, and the plants and seeds spoiled and rotted.[246]

On 28 October, Lieutenant Ralph Clark had thankfully got rid of his women, when they were transferred to the *Prince of Wales* (13), *Charlotte* (4) and *Lady Penrhyn* (4), and their quarters adapted for 30 sheep. "I think we will find much more Agreable Shipmates than they were." The consideration he showed for the sheep as they died one by one is touching.[247]

So, ocean-bound again on 13 November: and next day, on *Charlotte*, Catherine Prior gave birth to a son, probably by John Arscott, whom she married later, having been on the *Dunkirk* prison ship, as he had, since mid-1786. There were no cigars to pass round: but perhaps John Small, and Arscott's friends, drank some purloined rum to the health of the newborn child.[248]

Contrary winds drove the Fleet south and west when they wanted to go north and east to round the Cape, until the 21st: *Prince of Wales* lost a Scandinavian seaman from the main top-sail yard on the 22nd, and on *Charlotte* a marine private, Daniel Cresswell, died of dysentery. On the 16th, Phillip had decided to go ahead with part of the Fleet, to get some kind of settlement established before the rest arrived. On the 25th he moved into *Supply* with Lieutenants Philip Gidley King and William Dawes from *Sirius*, and some artificers—carpenters, sawyers, blacksmiths—taking with him *Scarborough* (Lieutenant Governor Major Robert Ross on board), *Friendship*, and *Alexander*, under Lieutenant Shortland's command: and the Fleet separated, leaving *Sirius* to follow with the three storeships and the transports *Prince of Wales*, the sluggish *Charlotte* with John Small on board, and the unsteady *Lady Penrhyn* carrying Mary Parker. Bowes thought Phillip's move "a mere abortion of the Brain, a Whim which struck him at the time," unaware that he had had permission for this move when he judged it right, before leaving England. Within two days "the flying squadron" was out of sight.[249]

Bowes thought the convicts had been well provided for by government. "I believe few Marines or Soldiers going out on a foreign Service under Government were ever better, if so well provided for as these Convicts are." But Lieutenant Ralph Clark wrote on 1 December "I never lived So poor Since I was born", and Captain Watkin Tench wished he could congratulate government on the "unhoped for success" of the voyage, "but . . . some of the necessary articles allowed to ships on a common passage to West Indies, were withheld from us: . . . portable soup, wheat, and pickled vegetables were not allowed; and . . . an inadequate quantity of essence of malt was the only antiscorbutic supplied." It would soon be apparent, from letters by Phillip (who had had some portable soup but had unavailingly demanded more) and the Surgeon General John White, how lamentably far Bowes's view fell short of reality.[250]

In the frequent squalls and storms that alternated with some calmer weather, various mishaps occurred on *Lady Penrhyn*. In the gales on 29 November, Bowes was providentially saved from losing his legs, nearly crushed between two large chests that rolled across the cabin. Later in the day "a Shark . . . seiz'd a pr. of white Trowzers of mine wh. were towing astern & snapt a new chord as big as my little finger in pieces . . . in a few minutes after saw the Trowsers come up again & float astern & the Shark followg. them." It is not difficult to imagine the ribald laughter in the women's quarters.[251]

There were accidents from time to time. Margaret Burn, "scallded her Leg in a dreadful manner," on 1 December, and on the 2nd the stable-lad Thomas Kelly was found to have got at a puncheon of rum, which he shared with several of the women in a drinking spree. On the 4th, "the last Hen Pidgeon fell overboard & drown'd." And on the 18th, Mary Davis fell down the hatchway onto her head ("well defended by false hair, rolls, &ca. &ca.").[252]

Religious feeling was not entirely absent from among the convicts. When Elizabeth Mason's baby son Thomas died on *Friendship* (she would be a near neighbour of Mary Parker in days to come as the wife of Richard Hawkes), Henry Lavell (another *Mercury* mutineer) said a prayer as the tiny body was committed to the deep. On *Scarborough* on 16 December, in the midst of a storm that kept the hatches closed, "Herbert Kealing read A Sermon to the Convicts Down in there own Burths", though in this case one suspects some hyprocrisy and an assertion of his educational superiority. He had been a *Swift* mutineer singled out for scathing condemnation as a ringleader, would ingratiate himself with Major Ross at Sydney Cove, and would, in the end, be hanged for forgery in 1806.[253]

In gales and heat and thunderstorms the last few weeks of the voyage were passed. The existence of Bass Strait then unknown, the ships went south to round Van Diemen's Land, first sighted by *Prince of Wales* in the second contingent on 7 January. The very hot weather for the week past may have been a godsend for the women, a chance to dry out; many of them, on the last day of 1787, "were wash'd out of their Births by the Seas we ship'd—The water was brot. out from between Decks with Buckets . . . the Sea was mountains high, sometimes it seem'd as if the Ship was going over." The first day of 1788 Mary Parker and her women colleagues spent clapped under closed hatches, "otherwise the Ship wd. have been in danger of being sunk." Frightful thunderstorms ("the Lightening was the most forked & vivid" Bowes had ever seen) had the women "down on their knees at prayers," but Bowes found them "uttering the most horrid Oaths & imprecations" as soon as it cleared: rather the reaction of the mother who punishes the thoughtless child barely saved from death after some accident.[254]

Relief felt on arrival at the long-famed Botany Bay on 10 January and discovery that "the 4 Racers" had safely survived (they had anchored only one and two days earlier) was quickly tempered by the realization that no time had been saved to allow advance preparations to be made; that in fact, this large, flat, unsheltered, shallow and inhospitable bay was not the expected haven and journey's end, and that more days (even weeks) might have to be spent on board the wretched transports. Moreover, something of a scare had been caused by the arrival off shore on the 24th, of two strange sail, held by adverse winds from entering Botany Bay until the 26th. These proved to be no threat, after all, but the *Bussole* and *Astrolabe*, under the command of the French navigator and explorer M. de la Perouse: their arrival immediately raised hopes (sadly to be dashed) in some convict breasts for a chance to enlist and escape.[255]

On the 21st, three open boats took Phillip northwards, with Captain Hunter, Lieutenant Collins, James Keltie (master of *Sirius*), a lieutenant and a party of marines, to look for a better site. They were amazed and gratified, after the "unpromising appearance" of the entrance to the harbour Cook had named Port Jackson without entering it, to discover what would immediately be claimed by everyone as "one of the finest harbours in the world." Two days of examining the harbour and its surroundings assured Phillip that he had found the proper site for the settlement. Returned to Botany Bay, he proposed going ahead in *Supply*, to get as many preparations as possible made before the arrival of the full Fleet.[256]

On the morning of the 24th, while the Fleet was preparing to leave Botany Bay, everyone was electrified to see the "two large ships plying hard in the offing to get into the bay." With what emotions must John Small have learnt "that they had French colours flying"—colours that during the whole of his time at sea had meant danger and apprehensions. On 26 January the Fleet moved against a strong head wind from Botany Bay to its final location, passing the astonished French visitors with little time to offer the barest naval courtesies of assistance in entering the Bay. The commander of the two vessels of exploration M. de la Perouse, had been astounded "to find our fleet abandoning the harbour at the time he was preparing to enter it."[257]

The departure from Botany Bay on 26 January was fraught with danger, and earned much criticism from Bowes on *Lady Penrhyn* and Ralph Clark on *Friendship*, and some heart-in-mouth emotion from John Small and his fellows on *Charlotte* as he saw first the *Prince of Wales* run against *Friendship* and carry away the jib boom, and then, far worse, felt the shock of his own ship in a tangle with *Friendship*. "I was more frightened than I was When the prince of Wales was foul of use," wrote Clark, "—if it had not being by the greatest good luck we Should have been both on Shore on the rocks and the Ships must must [sic] have been all lost and the greater part if not the whole on board drownd for we Should have gone to pieces in less than a half of an hour." To have ended the eight-month voyage in death amid the furious waves crashing at the base of Port Jackson's menacing cliffs would have been a bitter fate for John Small. As it was, the collision "carried away a great deal of the Carv'd work for her (the Charlotte's) Stern, & it was wt. the greatest difficulty our Ship avoided the same fate", wrote Bowes: Mary Parker and the women on *Lady Penrhyn* had had their moment of terror, too, all the small ships beating against the wind to pass through the narrow rock-bound entrance.[258]

At 7 p.m. on the 26th, without further difficulty, both *Lady Penrhyn* and *Charlotte* were anchored at Port Jackson "at a small snug cove on the southern side" about six miles from the entrance, where the destinies of John Small and Mary Parker would meet and run together for the rest of their lives. "Port Jackson would afford sufficient and safe anchorage for all the navies of Europe," wrote John White. "A port superior, in extent and excellency, to all we had seen before," wrote Watkin Tench. "This noble and capacious harbour, equal if not superior to any yet known in the world," wrote David Collins. "It abound with many capacious Bays & Coves for many miles up the Country & all these surrounded wt. rocks of Stone . . ." wrote Bowes: ". . . The Water close to the sides of these rocks in all the Coves is deep enough for a Line of Battle Ship to lye close." "I never saw any like it," wrote Clark, ". . . this Said port Jackson is the most beautiful place . . . here we make the Ships fast to the Trees on Shore both sides of Governours Cove." "None", wrote surgeon Worgan, ". . . equals it in Spaciousness and Safety."259

As *Sirius* made her way up harbour to the site Phillip named Sydney Cove, young Daniel Southwell let his imagination run free. "The White sides of the stony Eminences with very little help from Fancy, have at Distance the App[earanc]e of grand Seats, superb Palaces and *Sumptuous Pavillions.*" The grand seats and superb palaces would become reality. But now there was no sound from these magnificent structures, no busy docks and wharves, no thronging of vessels moving busily over the water as there had been at all the previous ports of call. Until they came to the anchorage and the sounds and shouts of the Fleet reached them, and perhaps some of the natives *Fishburn's* captain Robert Brown remarked "as we came in to Port Jackson . . . who hallow'd to us Saying walla Walla wha or something to that effect, and Brandish'd there spears as if vex'd at our approach," the harbour John Small and Mary Parker had now entered greeted them in silence: the land covered with silent uninterrupted forest, the untrammelled waters silent except for sea-sounds, waiting for the white man to turn it into the reality of a great port and city beyond the imagination of those who first saw it.260

Yet there was one prophetic voice.
  "*There* shall broad streets their stately walls extend,
  The circus widen, and the crescent bend;
  There, ray'd from cities o'er the cultur'd land,
  Shall bright canals, and solid roads expand.—
  There the proud arch, Colossus-like, bestride
  Yon glittering streams, and bound the chafing tide;
  Embellish'd villas crown the landscape-scene,
  Farms wave with gold, and orchards blush between.—
  There shall tall spires, and dome-capt towers ascend,

And piers and quays their massy structures blend;
While with each breeze approaching vessels glide,
And northern treasures dance on every tide!''[261]

Part of the map of the Settlement of Sydney Cove, 16 April 1788, attributed to Francis Fowkes.
(Reproduced in full on the dust jacket).

Courtesy National Library of Australia, Rex Nan Kivell Collection

Governor Phillip wasted no time in getting the settlement established: he had little time to waste, with nothing prepared ahead of arrival in which to keep stores safely and accommodate the marines and convicts. On 25 January he went on *Supply* with a small detachment of the Port Jackson marines, some artificer seamen from *Sirius*, and 40 convicts, and left Botany Bay to return to Sydney Cove in the evening. The next day was put to valuable use clearing enough ground to encamp the officers' guard and the convicts. Arriving at Port Jackson on the evening of 26 January, John Small on *Charlotte* and Mary Parker on *Lady Penrhyn* could note the British flag planted on the foreshore the previous evening, a brave spot of colour around which the Governor and officers drank the first toasts to the health of his Majesty and of the new colony, while the marines fired several "vollies" to add to the· ceremonial effect.[262]

There was no silence within the cove itself. "The stillness . . . for the first time since the creation, [had] been interrupted by the rude sound of the labourer's axe, and the downfall of its ancient inhabitants." Next day 100 convicts from *Scarborough* were landed ("every man stepped from the boat literally into a wood") to continue the urgently needed work, "carrying with them the necessary utensils for clearing the Ground and felling the Trees."[263]

The marines were landed, and most of the male convicts, by 28 January. More tents went up, more trees were felled, more roots were grubbed out, and the smell of woodsmoke drifted over the water. All the ships had begun at once unloading as fast as possible, and the small boats came and went, scurrying like the enormous ants everyone soon found to be an irritating problem. "I never Sleept worse . . . than I did [last] night," wrote Ralph Clark on 1 February, "—what with the hard cold ground Spiders ants and every vermin that you can think of was crauling over me." The shore was piled with bales, boxes, casks full of axes, nails, cooper's tools; and forges, anvils (one lost overboard from *Scarborough*), cross-cut saws, smith's tools, splitting wedges, a pair of

Mr Justice Buller (later Sir Francis), the judge who presided at John Small's trial, Exeter, March 1785. Artist, M. Brown.
Courtesy National Portrait Gallery, London.

Dramatic view of the entrance to Port Jackson, N.S.W. through which the First Fleet entered in January 1788. (c1820).
Courtesy British Library.

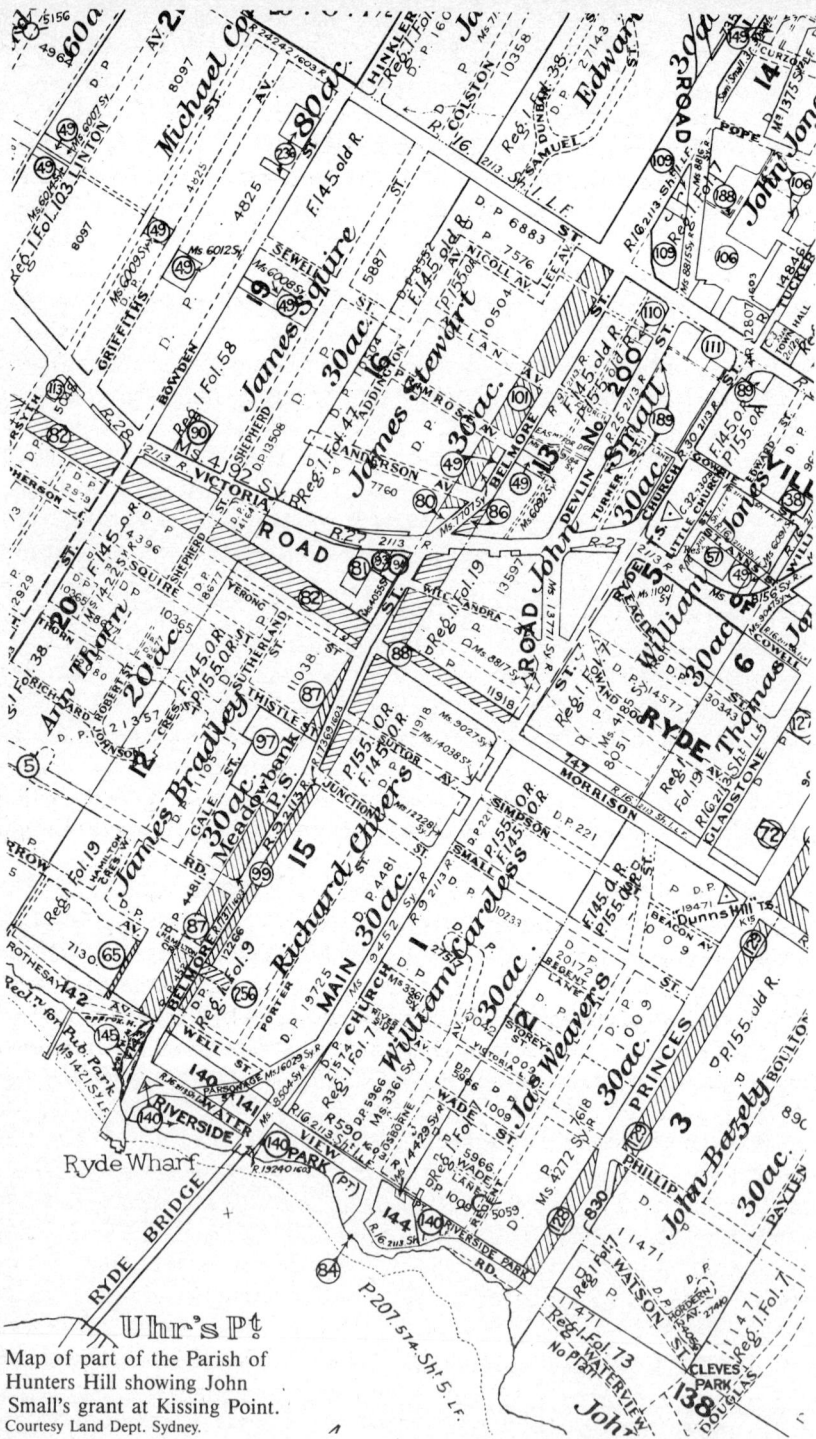

Uhr's Pt

Map of part of the Parish of
Hunters Hill showing John
Small's grant at Kissing Point.
Courtesy Land Dept. Sydney.

bellows, spades, two carts, two wheelbarrows, two grindstones, tents and more tents with their poles and pins.[264]

Mr Smith of Knightsbridge had made up to the Governor's specifications a portable canvas house and sent out packed flat, "45 feet long 17 ft 6 ins wide 8 under the Walls and to be packed in the Floor with five Windows of a side 3 ft 9 by 3 ft for the sum of £130, "and this had been sent ashore and set up on the east side of the stream that ran down the middle of the camp (though in May, Phillip would write "the Canvas House I am under [is] neither Wind nor water proof"). An enclosure had been built to hold what livestock had survived: the Governor's 23 sheep and five lambs were landed on 30 January, and what had survived of the government stock and privately owned animals were also landed as soon as possible, as food for them on board was running dangerously short. "I am Surprize that any of the Sheep are alive for The[y] have had nothing for these Several days past but water and flouer," Clark had noted on *Friendship* on 18 January. One of the first tasks for the seamen in Botany Bay had been to cut grass for the animals. At Sydney Cove, *Lady Penrhyn's* horses were landed on 30 January: with the one bull, four cows and one bull-calf, they were located at the eastern point of the cove (near the site of today's Opera House) until they had cropped all the pasturage, when they were moved to the small farm cleared at the head of the adjoining cove (Farm Cove).[265]

The women had had to wait on board the transports until some kind of temporary accommodation was prepared for them, and all were landed on 6 February. *Lady Penrhyn*, carrying 103 women at the time of arrival, discharged 98 of these, with ten children, on 6 February. Five were retained on board, chosen by Bowes from some of those "who behaviour on board during the Voyage had been the least exceptionable" to go with the first group to settle Norfolk Island. These five—Elizabeth Lee, Elizabeth Hipsley, Elizabeth Colley, Olive Gascoigne and Ann Inett—remained on board and were discharged from *Lady Penrhyn* into *Supply* when she sailed on 14 February. The sixth woman who went was Susannah Garth, a *Mercury* mutineer who had arrived on *Charlotte*.[266]

The behaviour in the camp on the night the women landed from the transports shocked Bowes. "The Men Convicts got to them very soon after they landed, & it is beyond my abilities to give a just discription of the Scene of Debauchery & Riot that ensued during the night." The reunion was evidently in no way affected by "the most violent storm of thunder, lighteng. & rain I ever saw." A more tolerant Tench wrote that "a candid and humane mind [will not] fail to consider and allow for the situation these unfortunate beings so peculiarly stood in ... when landed, their separation became impracticable, and would have been, perhaps, wrong." One could hardly be surprised that these sex-starved men and women fell joyfully into each others' arms, and renewed associations with old acquaintances from *Dunkirk* and Newgate days, separated for months on the different transports. Bowes tells of the sailors on *Lady Penrhyn* celebrating the departure of the delinquent women with a scene of dissipation that matched what he deplored in the convicts. They had "requested to have some Grog to make merry wt. upon the Women quitting the Ship . . . The Scene wh. presented itself at this time & during the greater part of the night, beggars every discription; some swearing, others quarrelling others singing, not in the least regarding the Tempest . . . almost all drunk & incapable of rendering much assistance had an accident happen'd & the heat was almost suffocating." On the same night, lightning struck a large tree in the centre of the camp, splitting it from top to bottom and killing all five of Major Ross's sheep and a pig belonging to one of the lieutenants. It was a fitting introduction to a genuine Australian summer.[267]

Charlotte's convicts, except for 11 who were sick, got ashore on the 28th. The scene was all bustle. "In one place, a party cutting down the woods; a second, setting up a blacksmith's forge; a third, dragging along a load of stones or provisions; here an officer pitching his marquee, with a detachment of troops parading on one side of him, and a cook's fire blazing on the other." John Small probably went straight to work at the hospital, the service to which we know he was assigned. This was almost certainly the source of the family legend of the "ship's apothecary" (it seems a probability that John had also had some occasion to be useful to the surgeon in *Charlotte's* sick bay, if not long before on board *Lively*). Perhaps he helped erect the laboratory tent and the two tents for the sick ("soon filled with patients afflicted with the true camp dysentery and the scurvy. More pitiable objects were perhaps never seen. Not a comfort or convenience could be got for them, besides the very few we had with us.") All the hospital necessaries would have had to be transported from the shore by John and his fellow hospital workers, on their backs or rolled or hauled along the rough ground, largely uphill: the medicine chests, the sick kettles, barrels of provisions, and tools and gardening implements for the hospital garden, already laid out to provide the vegetables they would need, though it would be a long time before any of these sprouted. Construction of a more permanent hospital building next to the tents, in the Rocks area on the west side of the Cove, had already begun even in these early days: and people from *Sirius* had begun on 30 January to clear ground for the observatory above the hospital, where Lieutenant Dawes would carry out his astronomical studies.[268]

There is no record of the service in the colony to which Mary Parker was assigned. Her name appears on no surviving document, not even as a witness to any of the trials held in subsequent days, nor even in the narrative of other witnesses who frequently mentioned seeing so-and-so who lived nearby, or who was passing at the time, or who shared a hut. Bowes records on 5 February that "5 of the women, who supported the best Characters on board were this day landed on the Governor's side of the Encampment, & had Tents pitch'd for them not far from the Governor's house." (These were perhaps, not the five destined for Norfolk, as they were marked in *Lady Penrhyn's* log as being discharged into *Supply* on the 14th unless they had remained as "undischarged" while being victualled from the transport). If Mary Parker was among *this* group of five, and assigned to domestic service in the Governor's household, it would lend credence to a family legend that the first child of her marriage to John Small was born at Government House on 22 September 1789. This information was reported in *The Daily Telegraph* on 23 January 1888 by John and Mary's son William, who seems to have believed it.[269]

On the other hand, Mary's prison-nurse experience might well have sent her to work in one of the hospital tents, in which case she would have become acquainted with John Small through his duties in the laboratory tent. In the absence of any record of her work in the colony, either suggestion could be valid.[270]

Next day, 7 February (Phillip having wisely ignored the night's dissipation) the opening ceremony, as it were, for the new colony was held. The convicts were gathered in a large cleared area before the table on which lay two red sealed boxes and around which the governor, his officers and gentlemen were grouped. The legalistic language of the governor's commission and the courts to be established by which the colony was to be governed went largly over the heads of the men and women sitting on the ground in the broiling sun, probably more than a little bored, and it may have found John Small at the lowest point of his life, no longer a free person but an almost nameless nonentity with the title *convict:* watching with sour and critical eye the marching of the marines in a drill he knew so well and might have been a part of, as with colours flying and music playing the guard came from the site of their barracks and were reviewed by the governor. He was now liable to arrest and punishment by former fellow marines for any action that might be considered insubordinate or insolent.[271]

After the reading of the legal documents, the governor made an encouraging speech to the prisoners, and retired with his officials to a large tent erected near the site of the marine barracks, where a cold collation was enjoyed and toasts drunk, from some of the 34 dozen of wine glasses order in November 1786. The convicts were dispersed to their own tent homes, and to the endless work of sorting order from chaos. The masters of the transports, who had taken the trouble to come ashore for the ceremony were not included among the officers and gentlemen, nor, it seems, was Bowes, who was highly offended.[272]

It was now that the deficiencies of this hastily arranged and poorly organized expedition became appallingly apparent. Phillip found he had no record of the convicts' crimes, sentences or date of conviction. Among the hundreds of men sent out there were only 12 convicts who could be considered carpenters: those that could be spared from the ships (16) had to be hired to build the store to house the provisions and utensils, and the huts that became increasingly needed as colder weather arrived. The supplies from *Charlotte*, *Scarborough* and *Lady Penrhyn* had to be transferred to the storeships until proper houses to hold them were built, and in any case Phillip had no proper person to issue the stores and rations to the people. "The convicts who are proper for this, are those who have some little education, and they are the greatest villains we have." No overseers had been sent to supervise the work of the convicts ("naturally indolent") and Phillip was forced to use men "drawn from amongst themselves, and who fear to exert any authority [which] makes this work go on very slowly." The marines had refused to undertake any of this supervision. "Most of them have declined any interference with the Convicts, except when they are employed for their own particular service . . . and [say] that they were not sent out to do more than the Duty of soldiers . . . the saying of a few words to encourage the diligent . . . and pointing out the Idle, when they could do it without going out of their way, was all that was desired." This refusal to co-operate marked the beginning of obstruction by Major Ross that ran through the whole of Phillip's term in New South Wales.[273]

"Most of the Tools were as bad as ever were sent out for Barter on the Coast of Guinea," wrote Phillip (a sad confession in its own right). The women's clothing continued to be a problem: not enough of it, of poor quality, and not even thread to mend it. Warm clothing would be needed as winter approached. Shoes lasted hardly a month, and there was no leather to replace the soles. The list of articles most needed accompanying Phillip's letter of 9 July was eloquent: house carpenter's axes, stone mason's tools ("none sent out"), wheelbarrows, felling axes, crosscut saws, pit saws, files for crosscut and pit saws ("a considerable number as they soon wear out"), gimlets, augers, chizels and gouges, iron pots to hold three, four and five gallons ("much wanted at this time"): scythes, reap hooks, nails and more nails, spikes and brads: bolts of canvas for sails (in April *Sirius* found 320 yards of canvas, parts of sails, boat covers and other items so rotten that they were thrown overboard): twine, sail needles, trowels for bricklayers (some bricks, at least were available, 5000 having been sent out, and a good source for making them had now been found—though the lack of lime for mortar was to be a long-term problem): armourer's tools ("none sent out", and—the Fleet having found itself on its way without ammunition for the musquets—"Gun Powder, Musquet Balls, and paper for the use of the Garrison, none sent out"). The "great southern port" and the "development of a flax industry for naval use" dreamed up by recent writers as the reason for the settlement rather than for the disposal of unwanted convicts seem to have been somewhat negated by this sorry account of inadequate supplies of even the most elementary equipment.[274]

The hospital was sadly without "necessaries" such as nourishing, easily digested food, and medicines. In July 36 marines and 66 convicts were under medical treatment, and a further 52 convicts were unfit from infirmity or old age. In July surgeon White sent Phillip a list of the most-needed items, including "Blankets & Sheets for the Hospital none of which are in the Colony, altho' they are essential and absolutely necessary—the want of them makes that Observance and attention to Cleanliness . . . utterly impossible." By September, White was writing that scurvy "still prevails with great violence, nor can we at present find any remedy against it." In July 1788, Phillip had written to London, "Many [convicts] from old Age, and disorders which are incurable, and with which they were sent from England, are incapable of any kind of Work".[275]

Very little edible vegetable food had been found, though Collins wrote optimistically of the "wild celery, spinach and parsley" growing abundantly about the settlement. He also indicated that plants from Rio and the Cape were growing satisfactorily in the garden near the Governor's house, but surgeon George Worgan was sadly disappointed in the results. "Whether from any unfriendly, deleterious Quality of the Soil or the Season, nothing seems to flourish vigorously long, but they shoot up suddenly . . . look green & luxuriant for a little Time, blossom early, fructify slowly & weakly . . . many of the Plants wither long ere they arrive at these Periods of Growth."[276]

The spectre of starvation hung over the colony from the very beginning, and almost the only phrases Phillip underlined in his letters home were those "as to provisions". All seed wheat and the greatest part of the grains and seeds from England "had been heated on the long passage . . . very little of which, when sown, ever vegetated." The seed wheat put on Sirius at Table Bay had been destroyed by weevils, leaving not enough to sow a single acre. Most of the stock from the Cape was dead by July, and a careless attendant had let the cattle escape (they were not found until November 1795, a fat, healthy and greatly increased herd in the Cow Pastures). The horses, at least, were doing well.[277]

A week's ration per man on arrival was seven pounds of bread or flour, seven pounds beef or four pounds pork, three pints of peas, six ounces of butter, and one pound of flour or half a pound of rice. The women received two-thirds of this allowance, children a half. The meat brought from England was salted, of course, and there were too few live animals in the area to provide fresh meat. By July the flour ration appears to have been eight pounds per week. By September each man's weekly flour ration was reduced by one pound, the women's in proportion, and in October *Sirius* was urgently dispatched to the Cape to take on a 12-months' supply of provisions for her own company, and "as much flour . . . as she could stow". To make room for more, eight of her guns were taken out. In retrospect, the governor shuddered at the possibility that any of the three storeships might have been lost, advising care in staggering the dispatch of future storeships with the provisions he appealed for with growing urgency as the months—and years—passed.[278]

. . . And for more women. The gap in numbers between male and female in this new world was pitifully out of proportion. Not only were the male convicts more than double in number, but the sailors on the ships, and the marines, competed for female attention: and robberies not only for food and clothing for themselves but of other items that could be bartered for more food or clothing and for sexual favours, could hardly have been unexpected in a community both deprived and composed largely of persons accustomed to living by theft. Lord Sydney's original idea for women from the Friendly Islands to be sent for to fill the gap did not win Phillip's approval. He could not see "bringing them to pine away a few years in misery."[279]

So the convicts (without proper supervision) wandered into the woods with any willing female and got into the women's tents whenever they could ("the whore camp—I would call it by the Name of Sodem for ther is more Sin committed in it than in any other part of the world", wrote Clark): quarrelled and fought with each other and the sailors over the women, and got drunk on the spirits the seamen were strictly forbidden to bring ashore. It was impossible to keep the convicts from straggling away from their work, intent on finding some small treasure for themselves that might be sold as souvenirs to the sailors—animals, birds, shells, and (worst of all because of the animosity it aroused) artifacts left by the natives—spears, shields, fishing lines they had hitherto had no reason to hide. Moreover, they became adept at "losing" their tools, hindering the progress that was slow enough without the loss of such precious goods.[280]

They also quickly found a way through the bush to visit the French ships, many seeing them as a way of escape from their exile. It is quite possible that John Small may also have made the trek to Botany Bay: he could offer his shipboard experience as an inducement to be taken on, the French having lost many men on their voyages in America and Samoa. But the French honourably refused to accept would-be escapers, and as far as is known none was found on board when the two vessels left in mid March. As it happened, any such hopefuls had a narrow escape:

both ships vanished from history until the discovery of wreckage near the New Hebrides in 1828.[281]

Early in July, John Small had his only other known fall from grace.[282] When on the 3rd, Surgeon White was aroused from his bed in the small hours by the sound of vomiting, he found Joshua Peck, one of the hospital servants, fully dressed and noticeably staggering outside the surgeon's tent. The sentinel and the corporal of the guard, Martin Conner, were called, and in Peck's tent a tea-kettle was found holding a pint of red wine. Nine bottles had been filled that day from a cask in the store tent, and placed in a locked chest in the laboratory tent, where John Small and Samuel Lightfoot both slept. An extra bottle had been drawn (surreptitiously, it would seem) in the absence of the surgeon's usual supervision.

The cask was then found to have an open kettle standing beneath a spike hole to catch any possible drops. Surgeon White, with the two senior surgeons William Balmain and Thomas Arndell, then went to the laboratory tent, where they found John Small "laying [on one of the chests] in a state of beastly Drunkenness . . . so drunk that he could not speak." Another hospital servant, Thomas Chadwick, who was on night duty to provide wine that might be needed by a very sick patient, John Ball, was also found to be far from sober: both he and Peck were sent to the guardhouse, but "Small was so drunk he could not be removed," and was left where he was until morning.

At the trial on the 16th, the sentinel, who had gone into the laboratory tent to escape bad weather (and seemed to have been a fairly willing collaborator) then said that Lightfoot, who held the key to the chest, had gone to bed about nine, having also been drinking earlier, and had suggested that John Small take the key and get a bottle out for the rest of them. John not acting at once, Chadwick had taken the key from Lightfoot's pocket, opened the chest and removed two bottles, from which they all drank except the now-retired Lightfoot. The bottles were then refilled from the kettle, which had presumably caught some of the wine dripping from the cask.

All the stories seemed to tally at the trial. John Small, in his defence, said nothing more than that "he was prevailed upon by Chadwick, & Peck to drink"—in other words, to join the party. Chadwick was given an excellent character by Captain Shea of the marines—"[he] behaved very well on the Passage, & was particularly attentive to the Sick under the Surgeon": a testimonial endorsed by surgeons White and Balmain. White spoke strongly for Peck—"his Conduct appeared so good he took him for his servant; & says he had an equal Confidence & good opinion of the Prisoner Small." For both Peck and John Small, Captain Tench of the marines said that both had come out with him in the same ship—"that he never heard of any Act of Dishonesty in Peck, who he had an Opportunity of knowing much of, & had a good opinion of him. Small he did not know so much of, but never heard any Complaints of him."

No comment at all on the case was made at the time by David Collins, Judge Advocate, or by the persons present at the trial (Captain John Hunter, Lieut. William Bradley, Captain John Shea, Captain Lieutenant James Meredith, First Lieutenant John Creswell and Second Lieutenant William Faddy). The verdict was simply "Acquitted, all and each of them." Nevertheless, Collins wrote privately about the case. "Wine was stolen from the hospital, and some of those who had the care of it were taken upon suspicion and tried, but for want of sufficient evidence were acquitted. There was such a tenderness in these people to each other's guilt, such an acquaintance with vice and the different degrees of it, that unless they were detected in the fact, it was generally next to impossible to bring an offence home to them. As there was, however, little doubt, though no positive proof of their guilt, they were removed from the hospital, and placed under the direction of the officer who was then employed in constructing a small redoubt on the east side."[283]

Any severity would have been for the theft, and not the drunkenness (Faddy himself was notorious for heavy drinking), but the double standards are implied. Convicts get beastly drunk on liquor when they can obtain it, officers (who don't need to steal it, having a regular allowance) merely get intoxicated: convicts stick together in lies, officers tell the truth. Convicts, it seemed, were not supposed to want, need, or receive any wine, a belief in the need of which—"the allowance of liquor is a great support to nature"—had caused some trouble among marines at Portsmouth before the Fleet sailed, when they thought there would be no provision of wine and spirits for them after arrival at Botany Bay.

Joshua Peck and Samuel Lightfoot had both been on *Dunkirk* with John Small, Lightfoot tried on the same day at Exeter, Peck a year later. John Ball, the sick convict, was also a *Dunkirk* prisoner, and also from Exeter, capitally convicted for the theft of a sheep, value 10s. He was over 50, and died early in October. Chadwick, who had ravaged a London garden in July 1784 and was caught with a bag full of cucumbers, said he came from the West Indies. All of them, hospital patient and hospital servants, had many subjects in common with which they could while away conversational hours.[284]

16.   FREE BY SERVITUDE

On 12 October 1788, John Small and Mary Parker were married, properly and decently, by banns, in a ceremony performed by the Reverend Richard Johnson and witnessed by his servant Samuel Barnes and John's friend from Exeter High Gaol, the *Dunkirk* prison ship, and the *Charlotte* transport, Thomas Acres, the bride and groom signing by mark. Johnson had no church until 1793, and then it was built at his own expense (£76.12s.11½d, not repaid until 1797) and against the wishes of the Lieutenant Governor Francis Grose. It was burned down in October 1798. He performed his services for the first years of the colony under a tree, or in a storehouse. The wedding of John Small and Mary Parker may have taken place in the open air, with friends and passers-by gathering around, or perhaps, like that of Martha Eaton, who married Edward Jones as Martha Beddingfield in March 1788, it took place in a marquee, with some kind of festive party to celebrate. Weddings at all times are occasions for rejoicing, and there were many of Mary's friends from Clerkenwell and Newgate and *Lady Penrhyn* days to wish her well in her new partnership. It was to be one of the stable marriages made in those early days.[285]

So many questions!—and all we can do is use imagination against the background of the few known facts and the great rocky bones of the land around today's harbour. Yet there could have been answers, some at least, had opportunities not been lost. John Small's granddaughter, this writer's great-grandmother, was 22 when the old man died. I was 14 when *she* died, and had lived in the same house for five years. His hand had clasped hers, hers has clasped mine. One life only separates me from the convict who landed in Sydney from the First Fleet that January evening in 1788, so close we are in time. But at fourteen and younger, who has the wisdom to ask the questions?—or even know that they are important, and might have had important answers? From the old man his granddaughter must surely have discovered more about his own background, and that of his wife Mary Parker, her grandmother: more

111

about what they did in that first year, how they met, what the marriage day was like.

Here we must digress for a moment to look at the way Mary Parker lived in those first months of 1788 between landing and marriage. The government had no plans for the men—witness the random collection sent out, chosen in almost exact sequence from the hulk returns without regard for age, or health, or skills—except to get rid of them (one hears again the despairing echo of Governor Miles at Cape Coast Castle in Africa, ". . . *get them out of Europe at all Events*"). They were a "lump" from which could be drawn labourers to put to clearing ground and supply unskilled work erecting buildings. But for the women there was even less of a plan. The use the women were to serve was implicit in the government's suggestion that women from the Pacific islands might be brought to the Colony as a sexual outlet for the men, to level in some way the disparity in numbers between men and women, while at the same time considering those who went with the Fleet as public nuisances. Even Phillip said they were "most of them very abandoned Wretches," and almost all the officers who kept journals referred to the women's encampment as the whore tents. Yet nothing else was offered to them as occupation. "The female convicts have hitherto lived in a state of total idleness," wrote Watkin Tench in July 1788, "except a few who are kept at work in making pegs for tiles, and picking up shells for burning into lime."[286]

On that ceremonial 7th of February, Phillip had recommended marriage, "assuring [the convicts] that an indiscriminate and illegal intercourse would be punished with the greatest severity and rigour."[287] Such cynicism is almost beyond belief. What did he expect, in a community of 750-odd convicts, of whom only about 200 were women?—to say nothing of the more than 100 marines without wives, the sailors on the transports and navy vessels, and the officers themselves, who took care, when they needed women for themselves, to select according to their own choice—? with no need to go into the woods to lie with them. The batch of young shoplifters and prostitutes tried at the Old Bailey in February 1787 and rushed to the Fleet at the end of April may have been meant to bring the balance up between male and female, but what use to males, or to the work of the colony were, for instance, Jane Field (almost 60), Elizabeth Beckford (70) and Dorothy Handland (age given as 80)?

If Mary Parker was not employed in hospital work, or in the domestic establishment of the Governor's house, how then did she spend her time in this settlement where there was no employment for women? Eventually, women convicts were employed making up material into "slops"—wearable clothing for the men, but this was not until later, when the second wave of transports arrived in mid-1790 with the supplies of cloth, thread and needles (all too few, even at that) that should have gone out with the First Fleet.[288]

If there is no record of Mary's service during her term of sentence, and if she left no memoirs, we can see her only against a background of what other people wrote about life in the community during these years. Such an account would have to consist of questions—*did she . . .? . . . would she have? . . . how often must she . . .?*—or of suppositions: *perhaps she . . . she may have . . . she would have*—thus drawing a picture by conjecture and analogy. Or could we pretend—basing our assumptions on information available in contemporary documents and on what would have been known to Mary's granddaughter Eliza Hughes Small (and on what she might have preferred to gloss over)—that a wiser 14-year-old in the 1920s asked questions of her great-grandmother, then in her 90s and her memory by then with gaps in it? She could hardly have failed to know that her grandfather, old John, was an emancipist, as her father Mathew Hughes was: a writer in 1843 commented that "a strong line of demarcation is in most instances observed between [emancipists] and the free emigrants and settlers".[289] It seems unlikely she would have made this knowledge known to her own children, by then remote from intimate knowledge of the colony's past history. Certainly in the family legends their ancestors were never seen as having been convicts. Great-grandmother Eliza Small, wife of her cousin Robert Small, would have been careful to omit any implication of convict ancestry. Why should she not?—her cousin George Oakes had been a respected member of the legislature, her cousin Lucy Armstrong had married James Reading Fairfax, her own father had been for nearly 50 years, since 1799, a school teacher, her own husband a customs clerk in the service of government. Her daughter, my grandmother, honestly believed John Small had been a free man and a "ship's apothecary." Let us then lend imagination to basic facts.

"Yes, my grandfather worked in the hospital, he had been a ship's apothecary, I believe, but he got into some kind of trouble (only once, though!) and he never told us what it was. Afterwards, with his fellow culprits he was moved to help build a redoubt—defensive earthworks—on the east side of the cove, under Lieutenant Dawes. Dawes was an astronomer, and also in charge of artillery and engineers. The rules were so strict then that hardly anyone escaped getting into trouble, especially at first when the work was rough and the provisions in such short supply. One of the fishermen, grandfather told me, William Boggis, was charged with gambling with cards—he said he'd hoped to win a knife. And even Mr Squire—he had a lot of property near grandfather's, and became a very rich and respected brewer—he got 300 lashes at the end of 1789 for stealing some medicine and pepper from surgeon White and the hospital stores:

grandfather wasn't the only one who made a mistake like that. Until the British government sent out fresh supplies, theft of food was punished very severely."[290]

"How did he meet Mary Parker?—she didn't come out on the same ship?"

"She died three and a half years before I was born, so I only know what grandfather could remember, and he often forgot things like that. It was a long time ago. She might have worked at the hospital too, grandfather said she had been helping sick convicts in a London prison some years earlier.

"Just like Elizabeth Fry?"

"Perhaps—I don't know. I've also heard she was working in the governor's house, perhaps in the kitchen, perhaps doing washing. My uncle William told me that: he was my father-in-law, too, because I married his son Robert, one of my first cousins. She lived in a tent at first, all the women did, and there were some tents for the women on the east side—she might have met grandfather when he was moved to that part of the cove."

"Couldn't she have done washing and mending for the marines?"

"Perhaps. But the officers had marine privates as servants who mostly did those things. And there was no thread, and no proper needles."

"What about her own clothes?"

"They were pretty much in tatters. The officers in London sent them off without proper clothing, and there weren't enough new ones sent to replace those that wore out. And after a while I don't think she had any shoes at all until the Second Fleet arrived: even the marines were going around barefoot, there wasn't any leather to repair the soles. And the ground was rough and stony—you know the way it is even today in the country."[291]

"What did she do then? Wasn't there *any* work for the women?

"Precious little. A few of them made wooden pegs that held the shingles on the roofs of the hospital and storehouses as they got built, and some collected shells to burn for lime. They had bricks and good stone to make buildings, but until they found lime they couldn't make the mortar to hold them together."

"Did she live in a tent for very long?"

"Probably until the governor got carpenters from the ships to help build huts for the women some time in May—the weather begins to get pretty cold then, as you know."

"What was it like living in the huts?"

"Still pretty cold, I'd imagine. The sides were made of the wood from gum trees, and it was rough, and split easily, and warped to let cracks between the planks. They made the roofs of thatch—men were sent out to cut rushes and reeds for this.[292] I expect they had to spend a lot of time trying to stuff leaves and twigs into the cracks, and there was no glass for windows. Perhaps they hung some bits of canvas over the window spaces, or made wooden shutters. But canvas was in short supply—they might have got some from the sailors, for favours."

"What kind of favours?"

"Well . . . anyway, if they had a fire in the hut there'd be a hole in the roof, or perhaps they kept the cooking fire going between the huts outside, and sat by it at night. But the governor wouldn't allow chimneys while the roofs were thatched, too many of them burned down."[293]

"Did she live alone in the hut?"

"Probably she shared with two or three of her friends, a lot of the women lived together. I'd think they shared the work, too—taking turns to cook the dampers from their flour allowance and roasting their bits of dreadful old salt meat. And they would have to search the woods to find any kind of vegetable that might be edible, though they'd be afraid to wander too far in case they got lost. There was always lots of bracken in the woods, they could gather it for putting on the dirt floor, or even to stuff their bedding, what there was of it. My grandmother might even have had scurvy, which spread very quickly, too much salt meat and flour and not enough fresh food and greens. She might have met grandfather in the hospital if she had been a patient there in the early days."

"I've heard about the way some of the women used to go with the men into the woods, and . . . and that they stole things from each other . . ."

"Not my grandmother, I'd say. They tell me there isn't a single mention of her in any of the old papers and records, and there were plenty of stories of some of the other women always getting into trouble. Grandfather said they were a pretty rough lot, many of the women. They'd go to the shore to be with the sailors—even though the sailors weren't supposed to be on shore after sunset—and get liquor to drink. Drink made you forget a lot of your miseries. Mary Davis (she came out in the same ship with grandmother) hit one of the sailors with a bottle when he called her a bitch.[294] The governor made strict rules—they all had to attend church services on Sundays, and no gambling. No one had much of anything, and there must have been a great temptation to pick up something left lying around, if no one was looking. But if my grandmother ever took anything, she was not caught at it. I think she was a quiet girl, who simply got on with making the best of things and kept out of trouble."

"There weren't any churches then—where did she and John Small get married?"

"Could have been under a big tree. That's where the minister, Mr Johnson, held his church services on Sundays and all the convicts had to go to them. The government sent only one chaplain for all those people, even though some Catholic priests offered to go out at their own expense. Everyone was afraid of "Papists" in those days, poor souls—they often had to die without religious comfort. My grandparents may have been married in a tent, or a marquee. But they were married properly, by banns, by Mr Johnson, on 12 October 1788, and the witnesses were Mr Johnson's servant Samuel Barnes and grandfather's old friend Thomas Acres, whom he knew in Exeter, and they came out to Sydney together in the Charlotte. He had been a marine, you know, and I believe he served with Mr Acres on a ship called the Dunkirk [*thus can family legends grow twisted!*].

"My grandmother couldn't have had much of a wedding dress, but one of her friends might have let her borrow something special, like Frances William did when Anthony Rope married Elizabeth Powley [Pulley] in May. Frances Williams wasn't a London friend—she came down from somewhere up in Wales, and probably brought some better clothes with her.[295]

"Maybe my grandmother borrowed a bit of ribbon, or a scarf. Or she might have put flowers in her hair, or carried a bouquet gathered in the woods. It was a very bright, windy day, grandfather said. Perhaps they had a party like the Ropes did: the Ropes had a sea-pie: Grandfather might have trapped a bird for roasting, or perhaps he went down to the wharf and persuaded William Bryant, who was in charge of the fishing boats, to sell him some fresh fish, though he wasn't supposed to sell government fish. You remember the story of William Bryant?—how he and his wife Mary Braund left the colony in a small boat with their children and some convicts early in 1791?"

"Were William Bryant and Mary Braund *convicts*?"

"I'm not sure—they may have been. Grandfather knew them both: she came out on the same ship. Sydney was a pretty rough place to live in those days, and a lot of people wanted to leave. Perhaps they were homesick—and of course all the ones who were convicts naturally wanted to escape. Grandfather didn't talk much about those days."[296]

"What did Mary Parker look like?"

"I don't really know. Grandfather didn't talk much about things like that, and he never really told me, whether she was fair with rosy cheeks, or had dark hair like his own used to be, though I only knew him when he'd gone grey. He looked sad when he talked about her: not often. She might have been dark-eyed: grandfather had hazel eyes, but a lot of us now have black eyes, or very dark brown."

"Did they have a house together when they were married?"

"I'd be surprised if they didn't, and probably by October the houses were a bit stronger. Grandfather would make a little garden around it and try to grow potatoes and cabbages in his free time, but there were a lot of animals running wild in the settlement, people's pigs and goats, not properly penned, and sheep, and they often did damage to the gardens.

"No, I don't know what he did when the redoubt was finished at the end of the year. They put some guns in it and a flagstaff. When the Second Fleet arrived in the middle of 1790, so many of the convicts were sick that they needed extra tents for the hospital even though a portable one had been sent out. Grandfather might have been sent back to work there again—I really don't know."

This is one way of seeing Mary Parker and the way life was for her and John Small, but dimly because personal records are lacking. Everything my great-grandmother could have told about those days, from the lips of one who was there, and about John Small and his family in those first years, is gone forever. The five blank years, until they had served their terms of transportation, in which nothing is on record except marriage, that petty theft, and the births of children—the more that might have been learned beyond what can be gleaned from the journals and official papers that have survived—will never now be filled in, the questions never asked when the opportunity was there.

Of course she could have given me much more than I have been able to conjure up in this imaginary conversation. She was married two years before old John died, to her cousin Robert Small, whose father William, John's second son, would recall such vivid memories, even forty years later, of those early days. It is inconceivable that she would not have heard, over and over again, his tales of a boyhood in Birmingham, of his courtship of her grandmother Mary Parker, the salty tales of his days at sea, his months as prisoner-of-war in Havana: those *specific* anecdotes that have not survived, of persons and events in the early years of a life he had actually lived in the founding of New South Wales: and stories going further back still, of his English ancestors and the way life was in the England of the last half of the 18th century.[297]

Rebecca, the first child of John and Mary Small, was born on 22 October 1789, named for his mother (and how lovingly he would have told Mary about his Birmingham boyhood! It would be nice to think he was able in time to send a message back by some friend, to tell his family there of his own family and his new life in the growing colony). Their second child, another daughter, was born on 13 December 1791 and named Mary, for her mother Mary Parker and John's eldest sister (at least the one he could best remember).

In the early months of their courtship, John and Mary would have walked the shores of the cove, and stared at the odd-looking natives that haunted the woods and paddled past in fishing canoes; at first with curiosity and then with apprehension as fellow-convicts fell victim to their spears. Captain Robert Brown of *Fishburn* had scribbled in his log some comments on the native population as he first saw them. "I went down ye Harbour with ye Long Bt, and Landed at ye Bottom of it where I saw 9 or 10 Women, who were quite Familiar. I tied A handkerchief, an old Stock, & some other things I had Round 4 of their heads which they were quite pleas'd with. They were stark Naked & did not show ye least Signs of shame. They likewise Eat some Beef & Cheese But the Bread they hove away. Two of the Women had each a Child, which they always carry upon their Back, the Childns Heads were ornamented with Fish Bone. there was 16 Men Close by them but were quite inoffensive. at our Departure in the Long Boat Two of the Ladies oblig'd us with a Dance in which they threw there Limbs in odd postures, they are Form'd exactly like Uropian Women but they Bend a good deal Forward & there Breast's slabby of course."[298]

But this was in February, before friendly relations began to fray. In May, four convicts were attacked, only one of whom, William Ayres, escaped, though badly wounded: with Peter Burn he had been allowed out as a convalescent from the hospital to gather the sweet tea herb. At the end of the month, William Okey and Samuel Davis, gathering rushes for thatch, were horribly mutilated by spears and a hatchet. Early in October, Cooper Handy had strayed away from the armed marine guard on the path to Botany Bay and was killed in a group attack, the shouts of the affray clearly heard by the helpless marines ahead. Ayres and Handy had both been on *Dunkirk*, both *Mercury* mutineers. Some of them had brought their fate on themselves by stealing native spears and fish-hooks.[299]

So John and Mary saw the town grow around them: the tents became huts, the huts brick buildings, the governor's portable hut turned into a solid two-storey building. Roads were built, though they turned into almost impassable muddy quagmires in the heavy rains ("my God how it did thunder and Lighting . . . I never Saw that I Recollect it Rain harder": Clark's comment, but threaded through the journals of all the other officers). A public cellar was dug on the west side by marine and convict labour, to hold the spirits till then stored on *Fishburn*. In August *Supply's* carpenter began putting together 8-oared and 16-oared boats brought out in frame: the smaller one was in the water by August. A road was built to the west side wharf, making easier the work of rolling provisions to the large storehouse completed in May. More and more huts appeared among the trees (and often burned down, either from cooking fires or lightning).[300]

In December the carpenter from *Sirius*, Robinson Reid, built a boathouse for constructing a launch to transport supplies 16 miles up-

William, 1st Baron Downes, sentencing judge at Downpatrick, trial of Mathew Hughes in July 1796.
Courtesy National Portrait Gallery, London.

Main street of Loughbrickland, Ireland, where Mathew Hughes, with the Westmeath militia, was stationed in 1796 (c1929).

View of Kissing Point, New South Wales, (c1820). John Small's land grant lay at the top of the hill overlooking the Parramatta River.
Courtesy British Library.

Detail of headstone showing incorrect information. It should be: John Small died 2nd October 1850 aged 88.
Courtesy John Pollock.

Tombstone of John Small in St Anne's churchyard, Ryde, N.S.W., before removal to Field of Mars cemetery.
Courtesy Dr James Woolnough.

river to the farm, Rose Hill [Parramatta] that had been established in November.[301] In March 1789 the marine detachment took over the completed barracks, and a brick house for the commissary was begun on the west side.

But progress was slow. When in June 1790 Captain William Hill of the New South Wales Corps arrived in the Second Fleet, he was aghast at what he found, not fully realizing the tremendous odds Phillip had faced, with shortage of equipment and food, unwilling and lazy convict workmen, and not enough marines to guard the new settlements he was only too eager to establish.[302] Hill criticised the lack of inland exploration, suggesting that Phillip might have set up advance posts at each point reached, as stepping stones to the next expedition: a criticism that did not take into account the inability to spare supplies for storage from the rapidly worsening food shortages in the colony, and the lack of military personnel to guard them from depredations by the natives, could they have been established.

But Hill also found too little progress in building, again underestimating the facilities available to Phillip. "All here, the officer, soldier, sailor and convict have the same ration allowed by the Governor [this had been a frequent complaint by marine officers, with little realization that starved convicts could not work properly] and to enter no farther into the detail of our miserable existence, I will give you a just account how I am situated, which is preferable to many by my being second Captain in the Regiment consequently entitled to a second choice of quarters," wrote Captain Hill to a London friend eight months after his arrival in *Surprize*. "Here I am living in a miserable thatched Hut, without a Kitchen, without a garden, with an acrimonious blood by my having been nearly six months at sea . . . not a mouthful of fresh meat to be obtained, and if, rarely, such a thing should present itself, not to be purchased but at an exorbitant price . . . Fish is by no means plenty, at least, they are not caught in abundance, not enough to supply the sick. . . ." The price of soap, "bad Irish salt butter", sugar and flour ("when any can be bought") were all too dear for an officer's pocket. How much more so for convict or ex-convict!

What appeared as a hardship to an officer and gentleman, however, seems to justify Phillip's even-handed rationing: what convict, freed or still prisoner, could have hoped to afford such additions to his daily rations? And it remains a terrible commentary on the government in Britain, who sent too many people with too few supplies to a place about which almost nothing was known, and left them unsupplied with any more for two years . . . and then with more mouths to feed as the transports came out with yet more helpless and incompetent convicts.

The lives of Mary and John Small were confined within the community, finding sources of interest in the gossip about their fellows:

the time Elizabeth Needham was beaten by marine Thomas Bramwell ("a most infamous hussy," Bowes called her, but she was beaten for *refusing* to go and lie with him in the woods): the way Sarah Bellamy made fools of James Keltie, master of *Sirius*, and Captain Meredith of the marines, when they tried to break into her house in drunken conviviality—Sarah, who would be a loyal helpmeet to James Bloodsworth in later years, he then in charge of the brickfield about a mile outside the town, and an acquaintance of John's from *Charlotte*: the fun of seeing the disgraced young sailor, caught in the women's tents, drummed out of the town dressed in a petticoat.[303]

There was the macabre horror from time to time of public executions: Thomas Barrett ex-*Mercury* mutineer and acquaintance of John's from *Dunkirk* days: young John Bennett, another *Dunkirk* prisoner: Edward Corbett, who had tried to abscond, and returned, terrified and starving after 19 days to be hanged in mid-June, as if his ordeal had not been punishment enough. They would not forget the terrible day in March 1789, when six marine privates died together in public ignominy, after systematically stealing liquor and food from the stores they had been guarding for months past (though there may have been some satisfaction in seeing justice done to marines as well as to convicts): and the death of Ann Davis, tried at the same Old Bailey sessions as Mary in April 1786, sent to *Lady Penrhyn* on the same day in January 1787, and hanged in November 1788 for theft of clothing from Robert Sidaway's house. She pleaded pregnancy, but a jury of "twelve of the discreetest women among the convicts, all of whom had been mothers" denied the claim: perhaps Mary Small was one of the twelve, her first child born only two months earlier. Robert Sidaway was himself a convict, with a long criminal record, a *Mercury* mutineer and known to John on *Dunkirk:* like John, he would redeem himself as a worthy and respected citizen in later years.[304]

How did Mary manage when baby Rebecca was born, without the childbed linen Phillip had urgently requested in 1791? And who was midwife in the difficult circumstances of childbirth in that spartan pioneer life?—one or other of the "discreetest women"? Hannah Mullens, perhaps, sentenced to death for fraud at the Old Bailey on Mary's trial date, who had sat in the condemned cell until pardoned in January 1787, and whose daughter, now nearly five years old, was soon to have a brother from Hannah's marriage to Charles Peat in February 1788? Ann Sandlin, or Ann Green, whose baby sons had both died on *Lady Penrhyn* on the voyage? Jane Langley, or Isabella Rosson, whom Mary may have helped when their own children were born on the voyage?[305]

There was the blessed freedom of Saturdays, when all except working convicts had the day to themselves, to work their own garden plots, strengthen huts, search for vegetables. One wonders if Mary tried to decorate the hut with shells, feathers dropped from the bright birds, or flowers: even perhaps kept a parrot as a pet. There were occasional special days to celebrate royal birthdays, with extra freedom, bonfires around which to dance and sing (many of the convicts former sailors with a repertoire of sea-shanties and hornpipe dances), and time to walk out to the brickfield or watch the ship movements in the harbour (the coming and going of *Sirius* and *Supply* until the former was tragically lost at Norfolk Island in March 1790)[306] and the little fishing boats: and in the evenings, the beautiful white clouds that always hang low around the circle of Sydney's horizon, and the stars that fill southern skies with a diamond glitter more sharply clear than ever are seen in northern heavens.

John's term of servitude was completed in March 1792, Mary's not until April 1793. It is possible that John could have asked to have his wife assigned to him as a convict worker, but by 1793 she may already have been assigned work from which she could not be released. In any case, though he was free, John had not yet received a land grant and would not have been entitled to employ convict labour. There was now plenty of work for the women convicts. The arrival of the Second Fleet, and the *Justinian* storeship, in mid-1790, had brought provisions that included cloth to be made into garments, and needles and thread for making them up. Officers of the New South Wales Corps, raised to replace the marines now returning to England, had been arriving, some with wives, since June 1790: the wives would want convict women to help around the house, and Mary Parker had been a domestic servant. The dreadful total of sick and dying convicts from the Second Fleet, accommodated in 30 tents hastily set up around the hospital, called for more persons to attend them: perhaps John was called back to his hospital work after the redoubt was completed, earning a little money from his labours now he was free, and Mary might have helped with the nursing of the ailing women.[307]

So life continued during the unrecorded years for John and Mary Small, who can be seen only against the background of the times in which they lived. This, after all, is the history of the inarticulate. After March 1792, John was a free man once more, but still, in the state of the colony, dependent on rations from government stores. He could work for others for what he could earn, paid in money or in kind, and perhaps was able to make a small private store of flour or grain to supplement the official ration. After Mary, too, became free in April the following year, John would have to make a decision about their future. He could continue to live in Sydney town, working perhaps as a gardener, carpenter, stock-keeper, for some of the officers and free settlers—marines who had taken up grants in 1792 and needed labourers to work their properties. He could try for a passage home for himself and his little family, either by paying if he had the money, or working on a ship. He might have been able to offer his early skills as bitt-maker, which must have given him experience in a blacksmith's shop: but that was long ago, and may no longer have appealed to him. He could have become an entrepreneur, importing and selling goods to local residents, but John did not have that kind of ambition. Possibly he could have found work at the hospital, but likely enough it was not work congenial to him, to be among the pitifully ill, and to have to see and dress the lacerated backs of constantly flogged men.

There is no record that he himself was ever flogged, either in his sea-going days or in the colony, nor do his ship's logs record any punishment for drunkenness: only for that one aberration in July 1788, when temptation proved too strong and opportunity too easy, was such a verifiable charge ever recorded against him. Phillip had left in December 1792 by the *Atlantic* transport, which also carried home those marines who had not gone earlier on HMS *Gorgon*. For the next two years the colony was left under the authority of Lieutenant Governor Francis Grose, also commandant of the New South Wales Corps. It was from Grose that John received his grant of 30 acres on 20 February 1794, "at the Eastern Farms" (later Kissing Point, and today Ryde). John and Mary had decided to remain in their new country, where John would be a farmer, on property of his own.[308]

17. FARMER, CITIZEN, PATERFAMILIAS

The thirty acres now proudly owned by John and Mary Small in the Eastern Farms area could hardly have had a more delightful situation: high on a hilltop, with breathtaking views across the Parramatta River into Horseshoe Bay, beyond the reach of the floods like those that would so disastrously devastate the farms of the Hawkesbury area opened in January 1794. Twelve settlers had been allocated land in the area before Phillip left in December 1792: at that time, some 53 acres were either under cultivation or cleared of timber, and there were huts and small sheds already erected in the tiny clearings.[309]

John's grant was officially entered as at 20 February 1794 in the regime of Francis Grose. It is likely that he was in actual possession of the land a few months earlier. He is not in the list submitted by Augustus Alt, surveyor general, dated 16 October 1792, but the twelve Eastern Farms settlers shown there are all credited with dates varying from one to two months earlier than the official date of their grants.[310]

John also seems to have been short-changed in the size of the grant. Instructions laid down by George III to Phillip in April 1787 clearly stated that "To every Male [emancipated convict] shall be granted 30 Acres of Land, *and in case he shall be married 20 Acres more, and for every Child who may be with them at the Settlement, at the time of making the said Grant a further Quantity of Ten acres,* free of all Fees, Taxes, Quit Rents, or other acknowledgements whatsoever, for the space of Ten years, provided that the Person to whom the said Land shall have been granted, shall reside within the same, and proceed to the Cultivation and Improvement thereof . . . ."[311]

With a wife and two children, John was entitled to have received 70 acres. Why he did not receive his entitlement is not known, but he seems to have been a quiet man, not pugnacious or particularly ambitious, content with his own small patch of independence, and it is hardly likely that officials, if they had noticed the error, would have taken any initiative in correcting it without prodding. Certainly, a further 20 acres was added to Peter Ellam's 30-acre grant at Prospect Hill in December

123

1792, a month after his first grant, "it not being then known that he was married." Ellam was probably more inclined to stand on his rights than John, or was perhaps more aware.[312]

The Instructions had called for "an assortment of Tools and Utensils and . . . a proportion of Seed Grain, Cattle Sheep, Hogs, &ca" if they could be spared from government stock. Phillip had given to each settler one ewe for breeding, and where possible, a goat, so John may have profited from this arrangement.

When the great day came to take up their grant, John and Mary (she almost certainly pregnant with the son to be born in October) would go upriver in one of the boats that now plied from the east side wharf between Sydney Cove and Rose Hill, carefully stowing their meagre household effects—bedding, clothing, cooking utensils, platters, pots and some garden tools—to avoid losing them overboard, Mary holding tightly to four-year Rebecca and two-year-old Mary, warning them to sit still and not wriggle. At the landing place about seven miles up from Sydney, they were probably greeted jovially by some of the twelve families already settled around the hilltop (but John's section was the crowning one), especially old friends from *Dunkirk* and *Charlotte* days. All except three of the twelve were First Fleeters. Four of them had been on *Dunkirk* with John—William Jones, John Bazeley, John Lawrell and John Jones. The two latter were both *Mercury* men: John Jones and Bazeley had gone out on *Charlotte*. One of the twelve, or all together in a community effort, would already have constructed a rough sled for their own use, on which the Small family's goods would be dragged up the steep slope by willing hands, the two little girls perhaps hitching a ride.[313]

John Callaghan's wife Elizabeth Leonard and William Tyrrell's wife Ann Ward, if not close friends, had shared *Newgate* and *Lady Penrhyn* tribulations with Mary. The two other wives, Betty Mason from Gloucester now married to Richard Hawkes, and Ann Sparrow from the *Lady Juliana*, who had married Joseph Hatton, would be glad to welcome another woman in the community, whatever jealousies and quarrels might develop later. Perhaps, at the beginning, they would have greeted the newcomers with a hot meal from carefully husbanded provisions, which would no doubt be returned in kind in due course.[314]

Poor John Callaghan, convicted at Exeter in July 1782, knew well enough that his time was up in July 1789, and tried to get himself freed from government work under the misapprehension that the stores held two years' provisions for everyone. A long and confused inquiry in the Court of Criminal Judicature held that he had insulted Major Ross by believing him to be the source of information passed to him by Elizabeth Lock. This misapprehension earned him "600 Lashes on his bare Back with a Cat of Nine Tails—& to work in Irons for . . . Six Months. . . ."

Those first years were harsh ones. Callaghan [Cullyhorn] was not to know of Phillip's desperate ration problems, but the flesh of today's reader crawls at the punishment meted out for an honest mistake.[315]

The other Eastern Farms settlers at the time were Thomas Chadwick, from the West Indies, who could trade yarns with John about Caribbean experiences (and ruefully recall their narrow escape in the matter of the stolen hospital wine), and three men who had survived the loss of the *Guardian,* wrecked on an iceberg in December 1790. These were Richard Cheers, William Careless and James Weavers, three of 14 convicts pardoned by Phillip for courage at the time of the disaster, which had seen the loss of most of the valuable cargo—stock bought at the Cape, food, clothing, plants and implements of which the colony was in dire need, as well as two of seven men sent as overseers and five of the 25 convicts on board. A grant offered also to a fourth *Guardian* convict, John Chapman Morris, was forfeited when he failed to cultivate it.[316]

Grants bearing the same date as John's went to James Bradley, and Thomas Jones. Whether Bradley and Jones had already arrived, or would follow shortly, or indeed, came upriver at the same time in a mini-Armada, we cannot know, but the Eastern Farms community was to consist of 15 occupied lots until the end of the year, when Edward Marsh and Ann Thorne received grants dated 19 November, and James Stewart, immediately west of John, in December (Stewart knew Mary's London: he had stolen 70 yards of striped bed ticking from Robert and John Gillow, Oxford Street merchants, when their porter stopped for refreshment at the Crown and Mitre in Bloomsbury). John's nearest neighbour was William Jones, immediately to the east. Bradley's land met John's at the northwest corner, above that of Richard Cheers. James Bradley, whose daughter Rachel would marry John Small's youngest son Samuel in October 1833, had been 21 and "late of the Liberty of the Rolls" (Chancery Lane area) when he stole "a white handkerchief with a purple border" value 1s. from a gentleman in Kensington. After sentence to seven years' transportation at his Old Bailey trial in June 1785, he went to New South Wales on the *Scarborough* transport. Two men named James Bradley were ordered for the First Fleet, thoroughly confusing the authorities and the contractor William Richards. The man who eventually arrived was on the *Justitia* hulk, and ordered to *Alexander,* but the other man, on the *Censor* hulk, was sent in error. This is apparent from the hulk records and comparison of the name order on various lists and warrants. *Alexander's* James Bradley, also 21 and tried London 26 May 1784 for a similar theft, died on board on 12 February 1787.[317]

In 1795 (July), James Squire, a *Charlotte* associate of John's, acquired 30 acres west of Stewart's: the beginning, for him, of enormous expansion into land-owning and experimental brewing. He brought with him a *de facto* wife, Elizabeth Mason (he had left a legal wife and three small children in Kingston, after arrest for the theft from a neighbour's cart of "four Cocks five Hens and divers other Goods and Chattals").

Elizabeth Mason, arrived per *Mary Ann* in 1791, brought with her a small girl, Priscilla, generally accepted as Squire's daughter: but she was baptized "Priscilla Mason daughter of Elizabeth Mason and Philip Morris on 29 May 1792", and could have been Elizabeth's child by a *Mary Ann* seaman with a delayed baptismal date, Priscilla would give John Small a grandson-in-law by her first husband Arthur Devlin, and eight genuine Small grandchildren by her second, John's third son Thomas, in days to come.[318]

There were thus no unoccupied gaps in a tightly knit community, which would have given a greater sense of security from the depredations of marauding natives and escaped convicts, an increasing problem for some time to come. John's life as a free man with his own small estate had begun in a period that saw less growth and stability and more uncertainty and unrest in the settlement than could possibly have been foreseen at Phillip's departure.

On the crest of the hill, John found his precious acres, thick with trees and scrub, perhaps too thick to see the view he would eventually discover across the river: likely enough criss-crossed with the paths tramped by the feet of those earlier settlers, visiting each other, taking short cuts for wood and water, looking for wandering animals. Perhaps his first act, after seeing Mary and the children settled in a tent—or even simply leaving them to rest, breathless from the climb, with the haphazard collection of their household goods around them, before starting the work of preparing shelter—would have been to pace around his boundaries with all the pride of ownership, marking this spot in mind's-eye for the site of the house, that for sheds and fenced yards. Here he would make his garden, plant his fruit trees: there he would keep the animals, there would spread his fields of wheat and maize.

But there was much hard, back-breaking work to be done before that dream turned into reality. As an emigrant to Canada some forty years later would write of her first encounter with her undeveloped land, he may have felt "hemmed in on every side by a thick wall of trees, through the interminable shades of which the eye vainly endeavours to penetrate in search of other objects and other scenes; but so dense is the growth of timber, that all beyond the immediate clearing is wrapped in profound obscurity."[319] For miles around the area great trees for timber-felling still stood awaiting the axe more than thirty years after John and Mary had tamed their own bit of wilderness.

It may be doubted whether the building of John's house or hut was aided by the labour of a convict according to the promise of "government expense" to cover its erection, in the current state of the colony, though perhaps he was reimbursed by extra provisions. He most certainly would have received the tools and seeds needed, or he could not possibly have cultivated his land. Most likely a simple bark shelter, or a tent, sufficed to protect the family and possessions for the first few weeks until a more substantial dwelling could be provided, and this probably with the help of neighbours. John had taken possession in summer: protection from rain and wind would be his main problem. Convict labour, instead of being used as intended for public benefit, and as in fact organized by Phillip, to clear land for government produce and government buildings, had been turned to misuse by self-seeking individuals, to the cost of the settlement. Under the military regime that followed Phillip's departure, the colony had fallen into the hands of officers of the New South Wales Corps, first for two years under Francis Grose and then for another nine months under the senior officer, Captain William Paterson, but more and more under the control of John Macarthur, the arrogant and forceful corps officer who would end up master-minding a mutiny, and whose grip on the economy was too strong to be broken by subsequent governors.[320]

"The whole concerns of the Colony, if I have been rightly inform'd," Governor John Hunter (who returned as governor in September 1795) would write in June 1797, "were taken into the hands of the Military." Thousands of acres were granted to the officers, dozens of convicts from a labour pool that could demand no wages were allotted to work those acres, and limitless fortunes could be made by selling to needy settlers the goods (especially spirits) bought at low cost from arriving ships and sold to the settlers at an exorbitant profit. "The introduction of this destructive trade . . . has done immense Mischief, & by the Ruin of Many of the oldest settlers, has retarded the progress of industry amongst that Class of People, who were before sober & labord hard . . . [a trade] highly disgraceful to Men who hold . . . a Commission signd by His Majesty." Moreover, by keeping most of the livestock for themselves, with the advantage of milk, meat and the dung so necessary to fertilize the land, "the civil & military officers are the only Graziers & Butchers and are enabled by it & actually do keep up the price of meat."[321]

Nevertheless, these were probably happy years for John and Mary. Their first son, baptized 21 October 1794, was named John, for John himself and his father in Birmingham. Ground gradually cleared and planted began to provide fresh vegetables and grain. Rations were erratic, augmented or restricted from time to time as scarcity ruled, or as supplemented by fresh supplies in the arriving ships. In May 1794, John's ration (Mary's at two-thirds allowance, the children's proportionately less) was eight pounds of flour, seven pounds of beef or four of pork and three pints of Indian corn, to last a week. The mills were small, few, and slow-working, and there were tedious journeys to have the grain ground, and tedious waits in the long line of men waiting for the same thing. But by October 1795, John had become self-sufficient (though not enough to support Mary and the children too), and was taken off government stores.[322] The hard work involved in reaching this point of independence has to be imagined: up at sunrise to fell timber, spade and hoe the acres cleared, plant the seed, reap the harvest, build enclosures for the small stock he may have had at the time (a goat, a ewe, a pig?)—and add to the comforts of the small house he and his growing family inhabited. Basic necessities we take for granted had to be added slowly, the enjoyment in their use probably in excess of their actual usefulness: a home-made table, a rough chair, a proper bedstead, a bench, a peg to hang clothes or utensils. What must Mary's pleasure have been when she was able to hang her first window curtain?

There was time for neighbourly intercourse, probably in the evenings: and gossip about the latest successes and tragedies among friends who lived in other settlements. In their own area there was the sad affair that put Joseph Hatton in hospital when his wife Ann stabbed him dangerously in a quarrel in June 1795. When he recovered, "he earnestly requested that no punishment might be inflicted on her, but that she might be put away from him." John (and Thomas Chadwick), perhaps practised in first aid, would have been helpful in conveying the injured man to the hospital: Mary, with the other women, may well have had to comfort a guilty but horrified Ann Hatton. And by January 1805, John Callaghan's wife was gone, cohabiting with another Kissing Point settler, John Curran, earning herself two years of labour for the Crown by making off with "every movable" in his absence.[323]

In 1797, *General Remarks on the District of Kissing Point* intimated to Governor Hunter that "This District is capable of producing a very large quantity of Grain provided the Farmers in it were only able to carry on their Cultivation," and asked for the adoption of such measures that might remedy the grievances. "Many of the old Settlers in this District are also poor." There were constant interruptions to the work: the regular General Musters that sent them to Sydney to be counted: three 8-hour days a week of obligatory road-building, though with time off allowed during planting and reaping seasons. The high wages charged by labourers caused Hunter to draw up a code of charges for various jobs, but quarterly meetings in each area were urged to make sure that no settler undercut the wages (set by the code) to obtain a worker.[324]

Hunter was all too well aware of the profiteering that had improverished so many of the early settlers, most of whom had small acreage and few assets to help them stave off distress. His letters to the Home Secretary in this period show very clearly the ideas he was pondering to help improve their lot. Windmills to add to the small and overused mills already established, where a man had to wait hours for his

turn to have grain ground. Registration and numbering of boats. The
hope that a supply of suitable hooks, lines and fishing gear might
eventually enable government boats to fish in the neighbouring bays. In
June 1797 he outlined the scheme he hoped to adopt for establishing a
Public Store, where settlers would buy clothing, materials, hardware,
tools, sugar, soap, tobacco and other items at reasonable cost, allowing
an additional charge to cover only freight, insurance and the salary of "a
respectable storekeeper". These, he thought, "woud put an Effectual
stop to the impositions practised upon [the settlers] but too often." In
1795 Rev Thomas Fyshe Palmer, exiled from England with three others
(known as the Scottish Martyrs) because of outspoken criticism of
government, had written to a friend, "The officers have monopolized all
the trade of the colony. They suffer no one but themselves to board any
ship that may arrive. They alone buy the cargo, and sell it at 1, 2, 3, 400
and even 1000 per cent profit."[325]

At the general muster in July (John and Mary belonged to the Sydney
district and had to appear on consecutive days at Government House at 8
a.m., which would have meant a very early start indeed), Hunter told the
gathered settlers that he was aware of their grievances and proposed
sending "two gentlemen on whom he had much dependance" to visit
each district and collect the information they wanted made known.
Accordingly, the two investigators, Surgeon Thomas Arndell and the
Reverend Samuel Marsden (who had arrived in March 1794 to assist the
Reverend Richard Johnson) made the round of visits, meeting the
Kissing Point residents in February 1798.[326]

A long preamble summarised what all the settlers felt; unsigned, but
perhaps the work of James Weavers, who with it submitted an account of
his own indebtedness in 1796-7 to the commissary, James Williamson, as
an example of the high charges that had been made.[327]

"Agriculture is the Support of this Colony, and . . . its welfare and
existence depends on the progress and encouragement it receives. The
difficulties and impositions the Farmer in general meets with in this
Colony are owing to the Trading part meeting with too great
Countenance and protection, so that the Farmer in reality is no better
than an abject Slave of the mercenary Trader whose only merit lies in
extortion and Chicanery.

"The Farmer is branded as an infamous, idle, drunk and abandoned
Character—The Trader on the other hand, who has the opportunity
of getting Money and is in fact only a nuisance and pest to the Colony
not doing any one thing for the Support or welfare of it but is the
original cause of every disorder, meets with respect, enjoys all the
comforts of life, and in a very few years makes his Fortune out of
nothing at the expense of the distress'd, and industrious Farmer, and
on Government on whom they so grossly impose . . . The Farmer . . .

is reduced to poverty and want, being obliged by the Forestallers from necessity to pay 400 per Cent for every article of Consumption, or let his Land go uncultivated. . . . The Trading people by their influence, has all the opportunity of getting Goods when shipping come in . . . the Farmer is the Spring from which the Trader must live, and unless they will be more fair and honest, or Government take some steps to prevent their extortion, the Grievances and hardships of the Farmer will remain, and Agriculture rapidly decline. . . . The Writer of this has and still does receive encouragement from Government, and notwithstanding finds it impossible to live comfortably tho' possess'd of a large and fertile Farm, yet without the Assistance afforded him by Government cou'd not maintain his Family. . . ."

The main complaints were lodged against the commissary, James Williamson, whose dealings were discriminatory at the expense of the small settlers and rewarding to his own personal fortunes. Eight settlers submitted individual complaints, including such old residents as James Squire, James Bradley, and John Small. Charles Peat (a *Mercury* mutineer first settled at Kissing Point in 1795), John Callaghan [Kellyhorn], James Weavers and Richard Shrimpton (whose grant was dated November 1799, but who was clearly in possession in 1798) had all found Williamson devious in crediting them with grain and/or pigs brought in: Shrimpton said he was not allowed to keep the seed with which to sow his next crop. Squire and Bradley had both been arrested for Williamson's failure to supply "any Bill specifying the Debt".[328]

John Small minced no words. "Before his Wheat was half in Mr Williamson sent Chapman Morriss to insist on him to thresh the same as he was Indebted to him—this put Small to a great loss and inconvenience in being compell'd to thrash his Wheat, and his Corn sustained a great loss it being overrun with weeds in consequence of the Men being employed in threshing and he will not have half a Crop—he has a large Family (a Wife and four Children)—he has paid him £53 without receiving a Bill—in short this is the Complaint of the whole District who have any Dealing with Mr W—— and the whole or principal part of the Settlers are connected with him, and declare that when they enquire of Mr Williamson the price of Articles that he will never satisfy them."

The submission was signed on 1 March 1798 by 27 Kissing Point settlers.[329]

Hunter did his best to remedy the distresses, issuing orders and regulations designed to help the poorer settlers and hinder the profiteers, but without notable success. The grip of the speculators and self-enrichers was too strong, and would ultimately lead to his recall in 1799 with undeserved "disapprobation" from the Duke of Portland, a judgement by a government in Britain that failed to understand the immense local difficulties. "How perpetually was invention at work on the one hand to impose, and on the other to provide a remedy against the evil!" wrote Collins in June 1798. "No one, from the picture of his arduous situation which these and the preceding pages have held up, will envy the office of the governor, or of those officers who supported his authority, or think that they cheaply earned the salaries that they were allowed."[330]

By 1800, John and Mary had two more sons, William, born 14 December 1796, and Thomas, 7 July 1799, following the name sequence for John's two elder brothers in Birmingham. The muster of 1802 showed that of John's 30 acres, 20 had been cleared, ten were sown in wheat and maize, he had two sheep, ten hogs and three of the family were no longer provisioned from the government. When the *Sydney Gazette* began publication in 1803, reports appeared almost every week of boats arriving at Sydney Wharf from Kissing Point with garden produce and poultry. If the orchard and garden shown as established by John in the muster of three years later was in production in 1803, some of the melons (4s. to 6s. a dozen), pumpkins (5s. to 7s. a dozen) and bushels of maize at storehouse prices—even a few chickens—may have come from John's farm.[331]

Now we must consider certain incidents and episodes that are on record in the names of John Small and Mary Parker. On 23 June 1798 a John Small was charged with riotous and disorderly behaviour, but discharged on a surety of good conduct: and on 4 May the following year, with two others, he was charged with having used a boat hired by another man: they were ordered to compensate the hirer for the time the boat was used. Two months later, John Small was brought before the magistrates on a charge of drunkeness and riotous behaviour, and for this he was sentenced to 100 lashes and 18 months' government work in the gaol gang.[332]

Three weeks after this John Small had been convicted and was enduring his punishment, a charge of theft of a watch from a sleeping drunk was brought against two women, one of them named Mary Parker, who was discharged on a promise to appear when sent for.[333]

One might wonder why John and Mary Small, busily making a home at Kissing Point and raising a family, would so senselessly and dangerously involve themselves in conduct that could prejudice all they had achieved. But we must now look at dates, and at other records. There was in the community by this time another John Small and another Mary Parker. This second John Small, tried 23 May 1787 at the Old Bailey, arrived in Sydney by *Neptune* in 1790: Mary Parker, also convicted at the Old Bailey on 27 October 1790 for breaking and entering (with a male companion) and theft of a quantity of clothing and other goods, had come out on *Mary Ann*, arriving at Port Jackson in July 1791. Both had been sentenced to seven years' transportation.[334]

Looking at dates alone, there is no reason to believe (and much to disbelieve) that John Small and Mary Parker of Kissing Point were the persons in trouble in 1798 and 1799. On 26 July 1799, when the later Mary Parker was on charge for theft, Mary Parker of Kissing Point was nursing her fifth child and third son Thomas, born only three weeks earlier, on 7 July: and at the end of February 1798, John Small was one of the Kissing Point farmers who stated his own grievances among those of his neighbours against high prices for commodities that were imposed on hardworking farmers. It seems unlikely that only five months after making his responsible and legitimate complaint to the investigators, Thomas Arndell and the Reverend Samuel Marsden, he would jeopardize his position in the community by riotous behaviour. If we can lay this incident to the charge of the second John Small, it is even more possible to charge him also with the second and third charges less than a year later, especially the last one. It is hard to see a man like John Small, working hard at Kissing Point to make good, conducting himself in such a way as to earn 100 lashes and enforced absence from his farm, his new-born son and four older children, while he worked for 18 months in a gaol gang. Moreover, of course, such a record would hardly add to his reputation when considered for acceptance as a District Constable in 1808.[335]

However, research shows that in 1806, Mary Parker (*Mary Ann*) is recorded in the community as housekeeper to William [Illegible], while Mary Parker (*Lady Penrhyn*) appears in the same muster list as Mary Small "married to John Small".[336]

In the *Sydney Gazette* of 11 December 1803 a John Small is listed among 20 persons about to leave the colony in the newly launched schooner *Marcia,* which on 4 December had advertised for men for "an Expedition to the Southward for the purposes of Sealing, Oiling, &c." The ship was owned by Simeon Lord, who had arrived as a seven-year convict from Manchester in 1791 and soon began to operate as entrepreneur and shipowner. The *Marcia* returned to Sydney on 21 February 1804. In the 5 May 1805 issue of the *Gazette,* John Small was about to leave the Cove again "to proceed to the southward". In October that year he had permission "to depart the Colony for the southward," this time in the *George,* owned by John Palmer, Esq., and employed sealing in Bass Strait.[337]

Early in February 1806 the *George* was wrecked in Twofold Bay; the captain and five men spent nine days in an open boat before reaching Sydney. By April the vessel was reported a total wreck, though the cargo of skins was saved, and her ironwork retrieved.[338]

It is not possible to say for certain which John Small was the adventurer. It seems possible (though barely) that his sea-going experience could have tempted John Small to leave his Kissing Point farm to add a little to a meagre income by signing on for short-term voyages, the farm left in the care of a convict employee paid at going rates, and with the help of Mary and the little boys. John junior was nine in 1803, 12 in 1806: William was seven in 1803, ten in 1806—both quite old enough in those days of tough childhood to be left in charge of flocks, of gathering wood and water, or doing their share of hoeing and weeding, taking vegetables to the Sydney wharf. In looking at the wreck of the *George,* we can wonder whether John added an extra adventure and another escape to the story of his life. But in all probability it was the second John Small who went "to the southward", footloose as John Small of Kissing Point was not.

At any rate, the 1806 muster shows that John appears to have prospered, at least to the extent that none of the family (now including seven children), nor the one convict and one free man employed by him, were receiving help in victuals from the government. Of his 30 acres, seven were in wheat, ten in maize, one acre was laid out as an orchard and garden, and twelve were pasture. He held four bushels of wheat and 14 of maize in stock. He had neither bulls, cows, nor oxen, but one male and one female sheep, six male and four female hogs. His convict servant was Patrick Hogan, who had arrived on 15 February in the *Tellicherry* from Ireland. By the same ship came five men who were not convicts, but exiles—State Prisoners who had plagued the country for years after the Rebellion of 1798, and finally surrendered on condition that they should not be tried. One of them, Arthur Devlin, we will meet again later.[339]

At this point in his life, then, at the age of 45, John Small could look out at a well developed "estate"—not large, but his own—and find himself and Mary the proud parents of seven sturdy children. Governor Hunter had written in June 1797, "The vast number of women for whom we have very little work, are a heavy weight upon the stores of Government; if we estimate their merits by the charming children with which they have filled the Colony, they will deserve our care." Mary was no burden on the community, and the seven charming children she and John had produced were a source of pride, to them, and would be to their thousands of descendants.[340]

On Friday, 27 April 1804, the last of the seven were born, the twins Samuel and Sarah (once more named for John's Birmingham brother and sister). There is reason to believe that another set of twins, not surviving long enough for baptism and perhaps quietly and sadly buried in a hidden corner of their little estate—a lost corner now covered by homes and gardens or pounded over by 20th century traffic—had been born the year before. At any rate, the *Sydney Gazette* of Sunday 29 April 1804 carried an intriguing entry.

"The Wife of a settler at Kissing Point was on Friday Morning safely delivered of twins, both of whom are thank God in a thriving way. The good woman is as well as can possibly be hoped, and must doubtless be considered an inestimable treasure to her husband, whom she happily complimented with the exact same number scarcely eleven months before."

This would account for the long gap since the birth of the last child, Thomas, in July 1799.

And here, with two small mysteries to contemplate, we will leave them for the moment, survivors of hardship, cruelty, starvation, danger and humiliation, but now respectable and respected members of a stable community in a place of scenic beauty that would have been an ever-present delight. There are other members of the family whose lives and adventures must be followed.

Rebecca Oakes (1789-1883), eldest child of John Small, as a young woman.

Francis Oakes, Rebecca's husband.
Both courtesy of Mrs. B. Hooke.

Thomas Small (1799-1863), 3rd son of John Small and Mary (Parker). Oil portrait.
Grafton Historical Society.

Rebecca Oakes (nee Small) who lived to the age of 93. At her death in 1883 she was the oldest native-born person in the community.
Family photographs by courtesy of the John and Mary Small Descendants Association.

William Small (1796-1891), 2nd son and 4th child of John and Mary Small, with his wife Charlotte (nee Melville) (c1882).

Robert Small (1826-1906) 2nd son of William and Charlotte Small. (Great grandfather of the author).

Eliza Small (nee Hughes) (1828-1921), also a descendant of John Small through her mother Mary. (Great Grandmother of the author).

Rebecca Youdale (1849-1927) (daughter of Eliza and Robert Small) and her husband John. (Grandparents of the author).

Family photographs courtesy of the John and Mary Small Descendants Association and the author.

1. Mathew Hughes

The "charming children" now growing up in the Kissing Point district, helping mothers in the house and fathers in the fields, hoeing, spading, minding flocks, from the earliest possible age, useful for fetching water and wood and running messages to and from neighbours, playing among themselves and with any black children who happened to be around, were in urgent need of schooling.

This was a matter of concern to various community leaders, and in 1799 the Kissing Point district received a schoolmaster, one Mathew Hughes, a convict from Ireland with some education and a great deal of dedication. John Small, through this appointment, was to gain a son-in-law and a grandson-in-law, but that was many years later.[341]

It is something of a shock, searching into the past for one's great-great-grandfather, to find him convicted of *murder*. Further delving, however, brought interesting information and some qualifications. Hughes had arrived in the colony on 27 May 1797 by the transport *Britannia* from Ireland, a small dark Irishman only five feet two and three-quarter inches tall, with ruddy complexion and hazel eyes, then aged about 27, and said to have come from Castlepollard. He had been tried on 19 July 1796 before Mr Justice William Downes at Downpatrick, County Down, and with two companions, Patrick Farrell and Thomas Morris, was declared guilty of murder, and sentenced to hang.[342]

"We hear," reported the London journal *Star* on 28 November 1795, from a story datelined Newry 10 November (this paper printed a lot of Irish news), "that at the fair of Loughbrickland, on Thursday last [the 5th] a dreadful riot took place, between a few of the militia, quartered in that town, and a number of the country people: in the course of which, the former fired on the multitude—either two or three of whom were killed on the spot, and a number wounded; one of the latter, we understand, died this morning, in consequence of the wounds he received. The reports concerning the cause of this melancholy affair, are

135

so various and contradictory, that it would, as yet, be imprudent to place reliance on any of them."

These were the years of unrest that culminated in the Rebellion of 1798 and rumbled on for many following years, if indeed the rumbling has ever stopped: English against Irish, protestant against catholic, landlord against tenant, and tenants divided amongst themselves, Defenders (catholic) against Peep-O'-Day Boys (protestant). The Society of United Irishmen established in 1791 had by 1795 enrolled great numbers, its object to secure catholic emancipation and ultimately the separation of Ireland from Great Britain. In 1795 the Orange lodges were established "to maintain the laws and peace of the country and the Protestant Constitution." In 1793 the government called out the militia of England, Scotland and Ireland, most of the regular army regiments being employed on foreign service: the militia were especially unpopular in Ireland, representing as they did the authority of a protestant government over the Irish population. A mob in Westmeath opposed the ballot for the militia in April 1795 with cries of "No Tythes! No Militia!" In May 1795, Henry Grattan's Bill for the emancipation of catholics in Ireland was rejected by a majority of 71.[343]

To the English press, naturally enough, the Irish people—struggling against high taxes and low prices for their produce, and "an impossibly harsh land system"—were the blameworthy aggressors. The bubbling pot of rebellion, boiling over in country-wide riots, was to be deplored as simple acts of vandalism, and wherever the militia came into face-to-face confrontation with the angry populace, the fault was laid at the door of sedition rather than desperation, of insurrection and not the heartbreaking futility of economic protest. What Thomas Pakenham in *The Year of Liberty* was to call "English imbecility, Irish ferocity" was building up into the 1798 explosion.[344]

Unrest was reported daily in the press. "The Defenders are again at their nefarious practices in various parts of the Country. Near Mullingar they have committed lately several outrages, where many of them have been apprehended and lodged in gaol. Others of the deluded wretches have been guilty of great outrages in the night, from Old Castle to Cavan, where they plundered several houses ... windows entirely demolished. ... Houses in retired situations have the appearance of fortifications: the lower windows are all built up with lime and stone—and embrasures made in the second stories, for the purpose of defence. ... If something be not done immediately, to stop the progress of these infernal plunderers, they may in a short time become too powerful for a small Army to subdue...."[345]

In 1795 Mathew Hughes, with a detachment of the Westmeath militia, was quartered in the lovely small village of Loughbrickland some 60 miles north of Dublin, set in the haunting green of the Irish countryside, the Mountains of Mourne sweeping down to the sea on its eastern side. In the year of Mathew's downfall, the town was described as having "one broad street, at the end of which is the parish church . . . and the town is a great thoroughfare, the turnpike road from *Dublin* to *Belfast* passing through a red bog near it." Even in 1842 it had no more than 123 houses. The name is said to mean "The Lake of the Speckled Trout". It also had a place in history. "The body of *English* forces which were quartered in this part of the N. of Ireland, *anno* 1690, had their first rendezvous at this place under king Wm. IIId. who encamped within a mile of the town." Fairs were held at Loughbrickland in February, March, July, September and November each year.[346]

From Loughbrickland, during the November 1795 fair, when the town was crowded with farmers and their families from neighbouring communities, Thomas Lane, magistrate and agent to Lord Downshire, wrote in agitation to his Lordship on "the calamitous [subject] of *murder*. . . . It seems . . . that a party of the Westmeath Militia . . . on Thursday (that having been the fair day) went with a prostitute into a public house and drank, but the landlord disliking the conduct of the soldiers, desired them to go away, which they affected to do, but when the man remonstrated about pay, they returned and a riot commenced (the house was not licensed and the hour was 12). The soldiers being rather overpowered, the drum was beat. The detachment (at least a considerable part) got arms and in a few minutes they (14 whereof can be identified by the officer . . .) began to fire, notwithstanding his authority and interference. Three fine young men were killed on the spot by the bayonet and ball. . . . I thought the matter of such concern . . . a sufficient stimulus for my hastening to the unhappy scene . . . I found on my getting here the place was thronged—the Westmeath (except 7 in confinement) under arms . . . it is the general opinion that many of the soldiers must be left to the disposal of the civil power. In that case the others (who are indiscreet enough to murmur somewhat like revenge) must be disarmed; and to do that (unless protected by other soldiers) would be leaving them to the mercy of an enraged multitude. Distressing and alarming therefore is the alternative."[347]

Next day (15 November) he was able "to correct . . . [the very hasty and unpleasant letter from hence yesterday] by observing that three only are yet discovered to be dead. The evidence . . . was manifold and tedious, but conclusive against two of the soldiers who are just now going off for D[own] patrick as principals in the murders committed. . . . I am satisfied, if the Westmeaths are not soon and in toto removed, much blood may be shed. . . .

"A corporal is this moment sent off also under examinations and my warrant."

As in so many cases, no transcript of the trial has survived: but the *Belfast News-Letter* of 22-25 July 1796 reported that "Mathew Hughes, Patrick Harrell [sic] and Thomas Morris, privates in the Westmeath regiment of militia, were found guilty of the murders of John Hill, Francis Mossman, and Samuel Gillmer, at Loughbrickland, on the 12th of November last—ordered to be hanged on the 16th inst.—since respited to the 20th of August." A fourth man was acquitted in the same case.[348]

The corporal, Mathew Hughes, sent to Downpatrick later than the two whom the "conclusive evidence" had sent instantly for trial, was according to the law guilty as an accessory, probably as not having been in sufficient control of his men. He therefore shared their sentence of death for murder. It is interesting to note, in this context, that only a year earlier, at a similar riot at Ballymahon Fair between the regiment and civilians, a charge of wilful murder brought against the lieutenant in charge, when a bayonet thrust had killed one man, was quietly dropped.[349]

Reprieved (no surviving record) to transportation for life, Hughes was probably sent to the New Prison in Dublin, where "persons under the rule of transportation, many of whom were transmitted from gaols in the country," would be put on board a vessel at the North Wall, "to be brought down to Cork, and from thence . . . sent to Botany Bay." One of 144 men and 44 women, Mathew Hughes was put on board the *Britannia* (second transport of the name) at the end of November, and sailed from Cork 10 December 1796.[350]

This was to be the disgraceful horror voyage under the brutal captain Thomas Dennott, whose surgeon Augustus Jacob Beyer took no interest in the continual and vicious flogging of the victims, and refused them the medication they so often needed. The convicts were kept below in wet and stinking berths, short of water, confined in irons and chained to the ship's side during their minimal two-hour break on deck. "Their undermost berths were continually wet, and . . . no steps were taken to dry them," Beyer said in his own defence at the subsequent inquiry at Sydney in July 1797. "Several of [the] . . . complaints proceeded from want of cleanliness in apparel, continual wetness in their berths, foul air, bad water (as the ventilators and water-sweetners sent on board by Government were not made use of), in consequence of which a number of their beds and bedding and some of their cloaths were destroyed, and obliged to lay without beds."[351]

One woman and ten men died on the voyage, most of them after sadistic flogging. Perhaps the only thing that saved the lives of the rest was the three-week period spent on an island at Rio (Beyer's suggestion, according to his evidence) while the ship was aired, cleaned and caulked (not greatly improving her leaky condition) and the captain disposed of government goods to his own profit. Although the inquiry clearly established the guilt of captain and surgeon, "to the everlasting shame of the British authorities, neither Dennott nor Beyer were punished, except that they were not again employed in the convict service." It seems like just one more piece of evidence for the complete indifference the government felt about the convicts and their disposal, as long as they had been removed from Britain.[352]

Young Mathew Hughes had a fair education from his Castlepollard boyhood, and wrote a good hand. He was quite early attracted to religion: "he went to attend preaching among Mr Wesley's people in Ireland." If he heard Wesley himself, he was very young and Wesley very old. Not long after his arrival in the colony, he was attracted to the ministry of those London Missionary Society members who had left Tahiti and arrived in Sydney in May 1798. His education and good behaviour—and perhaps because the murder charge had been, in his case, a legal technicality—gained him the permission of Governor John Hunter to accept the position of schoolmaster at Kissing Point in August 1799.[353]

The leader of the missionary group, the Reverend William Henry, had been trying, not too successfully, to establish preaching appearances in various parts of the colony. But at Kissing Point, "they have begun of late to attend something better . . . & have requested me to continue longer to preach amongst them, & am now building a house for the purpose of a School & Chapel. They are allowed a Schoolmaster by their Excellency the Governor, & I am happy to say that him whom they are now about to have for one is, I believe, a real convert. He is an Irishman named Matt^w Hews, & before his transportation from Ireland was a Corporal in the Militia, but was convicted in consequence of some soldiers who were under his charge (who are now here with him) killing some persons in a skirmish . . . When we came to the Colony he was exceedingly glad, & soon endeavoured to get acquaint with us, & seemed to be then under some serious impressions. I believe now enjoys the comfort, and in his walk & conversation is truely exemplary & circumspect, so that I hope if he continueth here, prove a blessing to the children who may be placed under his care."[354]

So Mathew Hughes got his schoolroom and a place to dwell, "a house 3.0 feet by 14 wide, with a side-room for the master to sleep in, about 9 feet by 7." A subscription had been opened, "which met with encouragement" though at 22 April 1800 the missionary and preacher Rowland Hassall found it had cost him "£40.12s.2d., which is £26.7s.1d. more than I have received at this date." However, Mr Henry was grateful that "His Excilency Governor Hunter gave us a man of our own appointment to instruct the children, which are in number 18 or 20 . . . and we have every reason to believe that he his truly taught of God. In My general visit to the school, weather to catechise the children or superintend other affears, I find them in good order, and they make pretty good progress in their book, so that some of them can now read in the Testament."[355]

In June 1802 Hughes was given a conditional pardon by Governor King. In the following year he was victim of a robbery, when his future brother-in-law, Francis Oakes, offered (in the *Sydney Gazette*, 15 May 1803) a £5 reward for information about "a WATCH . . . Nine Shillings in Money, One Piece of Nankeen, Two pair of New Shoes, and Five pair of Stockings, the property of M. HUGHES, Schoolmaster; also a Curtain which was used in partitioning part of the Room for the use of the Minister." A heavy loss for a young man trying to build a life for himself.

Here, probably first as a pupil at the school, and later, when in 1806 she was living in the household of Rowland Hassall near her older sister Rebecca Oakes (herself less than a year married), Mary Small got to know Mat Hughes, and at the age of seventeen she married him in St John's Church, Parramatta, on 6 October 1808, though it seems to have been a civil ceremony performed by James Mileham on the orders of Lieutenant Governor Joseph Foveaux—much, one may be sure, against Mathew's strong religious sentiments. They were remarried on 12 March 1810 by the Reverend Henry Fulton, who considered the first marriage to be illegal: they must have rejoiced in a proper religious ceremony.[356]

When Governor Macquarie, arriving to assume office on New Year's day 1810, cancelled all earlier appointments, grants and other privileges made by the usurping government that had taken over from William Bligh, Hughes lost his ration privileges temporarily (but they had been granted by Governor Hunter in 1799: his appointment was a longstanding one. Did Macquarie believe him to have been a supporter of the rebel regime because his appointment had continued without opposition from this group?) He was worried about the neglect of the education of the "above fifty children in the district", and wrote to say that as a result of his loss of rations he was "compell'd to relinquish the school in part . . . [and] labour in the field in order to supply the necessary wants of me and my wife."[357] One assumes he would have been working for John Small, his father-in-law. Mat Hughes was always to be deeply concerned about his pupils' welfare. A new arrangement was made almost at once, by which he agreed to provide six children with free education and take any others that might choose to come "at the rate of eight pence per week for spelling and reading and one shilling per week for writing and accounts", plus one ration daily from government stores.

Susannah, the first child of 14 in the family of Mathew and Mary Hughes, was born 18 March 1810; the last one, Henry, born in 1839, died in 1930 at the age of 91, unmarried. In 1818 Mathew was given an absolute pardon, and lived at Richmond, where he was master of the public school until his death in December 1845 at the age of 75.[358]

In 1822 he was paid £30 (£37.10s. in the less valuable "currency"), and fees for the past three years had averaged £12. He also held the office of chaplain's clerk at Windsor, and rations from H.M. Stores for himself, wife and four children were allowed. He had an allowance of £10 currency for firewood and received £5 p.a. currency for surplice fees, and a ration for an assistant. The average number of pupils was 60.

In 1825 he had received £30 plus £9 in fees, and was allowed a residence in the school house. He was also allowed to cultivate four acres and received commutation money and rations. His fees as chaplain's clerk were £1.10s. and the pupils averaged 30. In the next year he held no other job, was still allowed a house and received no fees for children in actual attendance. In 1827 his salary was £50 with house, and an allowance of 3d. for each child attending.

By 1828 an extra £10 was received by his wife, as teacher of needlework, scholars numbered 31, and this continued until his death, the pupils ranging from 42 to 90, with ½d. allowed for pupils whose parents could not pay.

From 1831 one of his daughters sometimes took over as needlework teacher. (Ann is mentioned by name in 1835). Mathew appears as master of the public school at the Parish of Ham Common (Richmond NSW). Teaching was based on the Madras system, in which older pupils were used to teach younger ones. He apparently did not receive the pension he asked for, and remained teaching until his death in December 1845.

This is not his biography, and we must leave him here, only pausing to note the tenderness and care in the will made in 1840 for the younger of his 14 children. "I most earnestly request both of their mother and my Executors that my little children whose minds are young and tender shall have that instruction given them . . . so that they may be early impressed with the importance of religious truth. . . ." His goods were sworn at £300, and his executors were his wife Mary, James Devlin and William Bowman.[359]

THE IRISH CONNECTION

2. ARTHUR DEVLIN

An Irish political prisoner whose eldest son would one day marry Susannah Hughes as his second wife was, five years before that son's birth, featured in a letter to Governor Philip Gidley King from the Lord Lieutenant of Ireland. On 17 August 1805, a warrant had been signed to send 130 male and 36 female convicts on the *Tellicherry* transport from Cork to New South Wales.

"Among the number are five Men," the Lord Lieutenant's secretary explained, "Michael Dwyer, John Mernagh, Hugh Byrne, Martin Burke and Arthur Develin, who were engaged in treasonable practices here and who have requested to be allowed to banish themselves for Life to New South Wales to avoid being brought to trial, And as it has been deemed expedient to make such a compromise with them they are sent there. Not having been convicted they claimed the advantage of this distinction, the effect of which is not however to prevent their being subjected to all the Laws and Dicipline of the Settlement and that any further indulgence is to be earned by their behaviour of which there has been no reason to complain during the Time of their confinement here."

Governor King was unhappy that they were not to be held under the usual restrictions of convicts. But "I have very clearly explained to them," he replied on 22 February 1806, "the footing they are on: and on their Promises of being circumspect in their Conduct and not giving Cause for any Complaint, I have allowed them to become Settlers with the Encouragement generally given to free Settlers sent from England."[360]

Devlin was part of a strong family connection that, with other dissidents, had kept the terrible Irish Rebellion of 1798 flickering through Wicklow and Wexford until more or less driven to surrender at the end of 1803. Irish papers had reported firings, shootings, uproars, narrow escapes, and mounting exasperation as "the Dwyer gang" slipped in and out of the Wicklow mountains for several years, often nearly cornered, but always escaping, though not always without loss. A proclamation was published at the end of 1803 offering £500 reward for information leading to the capture of Dwyer and his associates: and Dwyer, many of his adherents either killed or captured, realizing his own time at large was almost exhausted, surrendered on 14 December 1803 at Humewood, the residence of William Hoare Hume, who had succeeded his father in the Wicklow election early in 1799. Hugh Byrne gave himself up on the 16th, with the information that the rest intended to do the same as soon as they could safely reach Humewood without being captured en route. Burke had been taken on the 10th: Devlin was reported surrendered on the 29th.[361]

There is some uncertainty about which of three men of the same name he was. Of three brothers, Bryan, Harry and Patrick, all seem to have had sons named Arthur, according to evidence from Bryan and his wife and various neighbours: two, particularly, known as Big Arthur and Little Arthur, but not distinguished from each other in the evidence ("witness never having seen any other Arthur Develin, cannot say whether the one abovementd (and who was a middle sized man) was called Big or Little Arthur") were closely involved with Dwyer—who, incidentally, was the son of Bryan's wife Winny's sister Mary and thus first cousin of Bryan's daughter Ann and by extension to all (or both) Arthurs.[362]

It seems fairly certain, however, by the evidence of his cousin Ann (Bryan's daughter Nanny) and by the evidence of others examined at the time, that the Arthur Devlin who came to Australia was Patrick's son, "Big Arthur", that he had left the Dwyer gang a few years earlier to enlist briefly in the army "for safety", had been in France, and on return, "fell in with some of Mr Emmet's party ... to carry out the freedom of Ireland." It was claimed that he had acted as messenger, picking up ammunition (deposited possibly by Nanny) to carry to Emmet's headquarters. Robert Emmet, honoured by a Dublin statue today, distinguished student, a leader of the United Irishmen, had tried for French help for invasion, and began to pile up weapons in Dublin in the genuine belief that Ireland should be freed. He was betrayed by confusion and stupidity: the projected rising "had become a mere street brawl": he was captured and hanged in September 1803. As much as anything, this could have taken the heart out of Dwyer's Wicklow rebels.[363]

Devlin has been described by a contemporary as "a handsome, fine young fellow, about 5ft. 10in. and 13½ stone weight, not given to drink or any other vice. He was remarkably quiet, and as true hearted and as worthy a fellow as ever lived:" though in view of his age at death in New South Wales (recorded in hospital returns as 36 in 1820 but on his tombstone as 39) he must surely have been absurdly young to have been involved in rebellious activities for so many years. Myles Ronan, writing in 1944 from Luke Cullen's contemporary manuscript account of the incidents, quotes his age at "about 24 or 25 years of age at the commencement of the insurrection."[364]

Another contemporary, Thomas Cloney, held in the Tower in the Castle at Dublin, reported seeing "one of the most noted and active partisans of the famous Dwyer ... brought to the Tower, and ordered to walk about the Castle-yard for several days, with some well-trained agents in infamy there, in order that I might see him.... This man whose name was Arthur Develin, and who was well known to be one of Mr. Emmett's confidential agents, was there made to appear to me in the character of an informer against the state prisoners. After keeping Develin, who proved himself to be a firm and decided character, among a gang of unprincipled vagabonds for several days to no purpose, they then sent him to Kilmainham prison." Probably mature for his age in those hard days, Arthur Devlin could have been a mere boy when he became a useful member of Dwyer's gang and Emmet's messenger.[365]

At Kilmainham, none of the political prisoners seem to have been badly treated, except for being refused permission, as they said they had been promised, to go to the United States, and for being held there for some 19 months before being sent anywhere. Dwyer was allowed to have his wife and children in Kilmainham with him, and took her and two of his children to New South Wales. Byrne also took his wife and three of the six children Governor King reported coming with them. One of these appears to have been Mernagh's. Francis Plowden, writing a history of Ireland published in 1811, says the Government gave them each £100 "either to indemnify them for their confinement or for their having consented to transport themselves to Botany Bay."[366]

The 100-acre grant given to each of the five in the district of Cabramatta is dated May 1809, but that they took immediate possession after arrival is clear from the report in the muster of 1806. Byrne had leased an additional 100 acres, of which 73 were pasture, 14 in wheat, 12 in maize and one in potatoes. He owned five male and five female sheep, 12 male and 12 female hogs, had four bushels of wheat and ten of maize in hand, employed one convict victualled from stores (he, his wife and three children were also), and two convicts not victualled.[367]

Dwyer and his wife were receiving government victuals, though one child seems to have been off the public stores. Each of these exiles had one convict publicly victualled (Dwyer had two, plus one not victualled, 40 acres in maize, and 12 hogs, seven male and five female). John Mernagh and one child were publicly victualled, and though Devlin and his convict helper were victualled from the stores, his wife was not: he had managed to acquire a wife since arrival, and was producing sufficient food to maintain her from his own produce. For Arthur Devlin, before the end of 1806, had married Priscilla Squire, then perhaps only 14 years old.[368]

What took Devlin into the Kissing Point orbit will probably never be known for certain, the area where Priscilla lived with James Squire and his family; Squire already held large sections of the land. In January 1806 he was announcing action to be taken against people found removing timber from "the undermentioned farms my property", which now included Lawrell's, Chadwick's, Tyrell's, Callaghan's and Hatton's, they possibly holding them then by lease from Squire. John Small was soon to be among the only remaining original owners.[369]

The *Tellicherry* convicts were sent up the river to Parramatta to work, but Devlin and his fellows were not convicts, and were not to be assigned to any public work in the colony. At this time the 1806 muster shows a convict from *Tellicherry* working for John Small, by the name of Patrick Hogan. Did Devlin strike up some acquaintance with this man on the voyage and receive hospitality from John as a temporary resting place? Here he would have met the young Priscilla, Squire's adopted daughter. An unreliable document supposed to be recollections of another *Tellicherry* man, James Sheedy, states that Devlin was *assigned* to John, but Devlin was not assigned to anyone—and Sheedy himself had become a bushranger by November, saved from hanging only by a last-minute pardon. His grandiose tales of close friendship with and favours from Major George Johnston (who only two years earlier had suppressed an Irish convict rebellion) ring decidedly false, and his information about Mary Parker's presence as midwife to Esther Abrahams' Newgate-born child is definitely untrue (Mary was on *Lady Penrhyn* at Portsmouth at the time). Wherever and however they met, Arthur Devlin and Priscilla Squire lived in happy marriage until his death in November 1820 from "phrenitis", leaving "a disconsolate widow and six children."[370]

She did not have to remain disconsolate for long. On 17 December 1821, aged 29, she married John Small's third son Thomas, aged 22, and added eight Small children to her six surviving Devlins. On 15 September 1834, her eldest Devlin son James, then 26, married Mathew and Mary Hughes's eldest daughter Susannah, then 24, thus linking the Devlins twice with the Smalls.[371]

The house "Willandra" standing almost in the centre of John Small's original grant, was begun in June 1841 and then known as Ryde House. It is said to be "perhaps the finest of the numerous two-storey Colonial Georgian houses with encircling single storey verandah built in N.S.W." The spectacular views from its upper windows are the familiar sights John and Mary Small knew so well while they were owners and dwellers on this magnificent 30 acres of land, through which the main shopping street of Ryde, Devlin Street, today runs almost down the centre of the lot to the Ryde Bridge.[372]

Willandra (Ryde House). Home of James Devlin — built c.1845. Drawn by Mrs. Pat Smyth.
Courtesy Ryde Historical Society.

19. TOWARDS PROSPERITY

In August 1789 a night watch had been established, suggested (so Collins says) by John Harris, a convict who had been a *Mercury* mutineer and who was tried in London for his escape, after returning by the Exeter coach, presumably to reach his wife and three small children. The watch consisted of twelve of the most trustworthy convicts Governor Phillip could find, who were to patrol the settlement "to secure all persons . . . who should be found straggling from the huts at improper hours." Such persons included seamen, and (at first) soldiers until the marine commandant Major Ross took exception to his men being charged by convicts.[373]

Constables, later chosen from free settlers or ex-convicts, were continued in all districts and charged with innumerable duties. In November 1796, Governor Hunter proposed a more formal and better organized system. "We shall have Watchmen chosen from amongst the inhabitants to guard during the Night their respective Divisions, and a Constable will also be chosen who shall have proper instructions. This regulation I propose shall take place in every district of the Colony." A document was drawn up headed "Encouragement to People acting as Constables at Sydney, Parramatta, Toongabbe & the Hawkesbury" [Kissing Point was in the Sydney district], making the following points.

"1st. Each to have an additional suit of cloathing annually in order that their having at all times a more respectable appearance.

2d. To have a pint of Spirits served to each every Saturday.

3d. To have the same Ration served to them which is issued to the Military & free people.

N.B. This does not relate to quantity, for that is the same to all descriptions of People, but in the particular articles, it being impossible to regulate that so as to avoid making some distinction; in such case the preference is given to the Military & free People.

4th. Those who may have been sent to this Country for 7 years, & who shall officiate as a Constable to the satisfaction of the magistrates of the district in which he acts for the space of three years, from his appointment as such, shall be intitled to Emancipation, and be at liberty to leave the settlement whenever he chooses.

5th. Those who may have been sent to this country for 14 years, & who shall officiate as above for the space of 7 years, shall be intitled to the same reward & advantages.

6th. Those who may have been transported for Life & who shall officiate as above for the space of ten years, shall be intitled to the above advantages, & to conditional Emancipation, i.e. Freedom in this Country & liberty to become settlers."[374]

From around this date John may have undertaken gradually increasing constabulary duties in his area, perhaps as one of what were known as "inferior" constables who would help the district constable, but he first began to serve as district constable himself in the Kissing Point area from 1809. In 1798 it was reported that December was the time when constables and watchmen for the following year were selected, so he was probably appointed in December 1808 to begin serving in January 1809. At any rate, he was a "Constable of 17 years service" when his first pension of £9.2s.6d. was paid on 1 December 1825, and he received this sum annually until his death, with an extra 6d. for each leap year. Two different convicts who had absconded from public service as servants to "Mr Small district constable, Kissing Point", were advertised in the *Sydney Gazettes* of 25 June and 11 July 1809.[375]

Constables led an arduous life, constantly called on for duties other than maintaining law and order: cautioned against allowing worthless persons to lurk about the farms, and required to present the commanding officer with monthly accounts of men, women and children residing in the area: every new employee taken on in the district to be instantly notified to the Chief Constable in Sydney: returns to be collected of wheat and maize reaped, especially at each harvest, and the number and kind of livestock in the district: convicts locally employed must be kept at regular church attendance on Sundays: constables were urged to be "extreamly vigilant" in locating and reporting illicit stills. They were required to list for the local magistrate the settlers employed on road building, and the number of days so worked, and they would be expected to offer help as far as possible in other areas when huge disasters occurred, as in the terrible Hawkesbury floods of April 1806, when John Chapman Morris, who had chosen to forfeit his Kissing Point grant in 1794 and then lived in the Hawkesbury area, was tragically drowned.[376]

How did a man like John Small manage, without reading or writing? Perhaps by now he had worked out his own system, aided by the schoolmaster Mathew Hughes, whose schoolhouse had adjoined his farm: or perhaps he had an excellent memory.

The little house on the hill at Kissing Point was gradually becoming more homelike and comfortable, with furniture and even a few frills added. From the Parramatta store opened by Rowland Hassall, one of the Tahiti missionaries, John Small bought a teapot for 2s. in 1803, some tobacco, rice, tea and sugar, half a yard of window blind, 2½ yards of black "Figerd Ribbam". In 1804, sugar, soup, tobacco, tea and bottles of oil were among various purchases, sometimes paid for in maize, and sometimes it is noted that Mrs Small was the purchaser. Mary probably made many a journey by boat to Parramatta, especially after her 15-year-old namesake daughter Mary went to live with Mrs Hassall, probably as household help, in 1806, and her first daughter Rebecca was married to Francis Oakes on 27 January the same year at St John's Parramatta.[377]

Oakes was another of the missionaries who had come from Tahiti in 1798.[378] He had been appointed chief constable of Parramatta in the September previous to his wedding. In view of the date of this wedding, one must wonder again whether the John Small who went "to the southward" in the ill-fated private colonial vessel George was in fact John Small of Kissing Point, or the second convict of this name who had arrived by Neptune in 1790. Possibly (though improbably) a daughter's wedding could have been less important than the need to improve his economic situation. It has been suggested, too, that the William Small who came out free on Canada at the end of 1801 was John's elder brother, but there is no family or official confirmation of this.

John's first son-in-law, Francis Oakes, had been baptized as "Francis Oaks" at Coleshill, Warwickshire, in April 1770,[379] and was more than twice the age of his young wife. His name occurs repeatedly in colonial documents as "farmer, baker, shop-keeper and contractor . . . inspector of slaughtering houses . . . clerk of the public market . . . auctioneer"—altogether a busy entrepreneur: and from 1814 he was superintendent of the Female Factory at Parramatta. Of the 14 children Rebecca bore him, two sons became members of parliament: George, who was to die in a tram accident at Parramatta in 1881, had replied to a taunt in 1850 about his convict ancestry, only days before his grandfather's death, that "whatever respectability he might possess, he owed it entirely to his early education."[380]

Philip Gidley King, successively second officer of Sirius, lieutenant governor of Norfolk Island and succeeding Hunter as governor of New South Wales on 28 September 1800, was little more successful than Hunter in releasing the grip of the insolent military officers, unsupported by government in Britain just as Hunter had been. In the various turbulent events involving John Macarthur, Francis Oakes had a part to play in opposition to this powerful officer after Captain William Bligh had become governor in August 1806, being directly involved in the arrest of Macarthur on 15 December 1807, an arrest contemptuously refused by Macarthur, but achieved by Oakes (with an armed guard this time) next day.[381]

Bligh had been welcomed by addresses from the free settlers, who made it very plain that they wanted to be rid of the monopolists, naming Macarthur directly as the chief cause of their difficulties. Bligh's vigorous measures to restore order, to eliminate the rum trade, and to impede the activities of those ex-convicts and NSW Corps personnel most active in profiteering and subverting justice, naturally banded more closely together those whose bank accounts would be most severely savaged as a result. The whole period up to the time when it erupted into disgraceful mutiny with the seizure of Bligh on 26 January 1808 was littered with lawsuits, crammed with criminal charges, cluttered with courtmartials and rampant with recriminations, together with more than a little touch of terror. What could poverty-stricken settlers do against a drunken, armed soldiery? (what, in the event, could even a *governor* do?)

Twenty-five signatures, including that of Francis Oakes, were appended to the petition to Lord Castlereagh, the colonial secretary, dated 4 November 1808 asking for reinstatement of Bligh, "who, by his most salutory orders put a stop to the bartering of spirits and the stroling dealers who were generally employ'd by our trading officers, suppressing extortion and the Colonial cash notes, the drawers of which were making a trade of them by chargeing from 25 to 40 p'r c't. whenever any of the holders of such bills presented them for consolidation. . . . N.B. Several hundred more signatures could have been obtained, but the system of terror which reigns in the colony prevented us from venturing further."[382]

Francis Oakes was to pay a heavy price for a few years for being at the sharp end of the spearhead Macarthur was directing against the colony. "He was deprived of his office [of chief constable] on account of his fidelity to His Majesty's Governor . . . by which himself and family were exposed to great inconveniences and expence, and afterwards deprived of his Government servants, and other advantages arising from the situation, and that he was continually persecuted until the arrival of Governor Macquarie, when he was ordered Home as an evidence for the Crown." This was to attend the court martial in England of George Johnston, when "he [Oakes] was put to considerable expence fitting himself out for the voyage, besides the expence incurred by his family during his absence. . . ." His petition was dated 12 August 1811 and directed to the Lord Liverpool, while Oakes was in England: he was reinstated in his office on his return home, to which other appointments were added in following years.[383]

It might have been dangerous for John Small to have Oakes as a son-in-law, except that Macarthur's spite would hardly have extended to those inferiors he considered less than the insects that abounded in New South Wales. Kissing Point seems to have been a fairly isolated small community, on the road to nowhere important, its inhabitants in general living quietly undisturbed lives. The peaceful beauty of Ryde (as it is known today), even in 1888 was ascribed to being too little known "through lack of communication with the metropolis:" still a place where one could enjoy "the quiet of country life and the shade of the big trees in the summer."[384]

As it was, John Small went his way through the Bligh crisis without any recorded problems. On 20 April 1809 he had received a grant of a further 30 acres from Lieutenant Governor William Paterson, but when Lachlan Macquarie was sent as governor to clean up the mess made during the interregnum after Bligh's arrest, all grants issued by the illegal government were called in, and John's was surrendered on 10 January 1810. When the lands were re-granted on 18 October 1811, John Small's 30 acres were given as at Parramatta, "under Date the 1st January 1810".[385]

"The humble petition of John Small, a Constable and a Settler at Kissing Point" addressed to "His Excellency Laughlan Macquarie Esq." at the time of surrender informed the governor that his petitioner "has been in this Colony upwards of Twenty years, has a large family, a wife and Seven children, which he has supported by extreme industry, that in consequence of his land being nearly exhausted by constant tillage", Lieutenant Governor Paterson had been "pleased to grant him, thirty acres more; & it was further His Honor's intention to have given petitioner another addition, had His Honor remain'd in the Command." John referred Macquarie to Paterson "and most of the officers" for a character, hoped he might receive consideration from the governor, "a protector to his large family", and promised to continue in the ways of virtue he had hitherto followed.[386]

So, through the second decade of the 19th century, John and Mary Small continued a quiet family life in the expanding community, John carrying out his civic duties, making a 10s. contribution to the chapel and school in 1813, appointed pound-keeper in November. The two boys, John and William, were apprentices in 1814, William to the trade of bootmaker. When he was 92 years old (the oldest living native-born resident of Sydney in 1888 as his sister Rebecca Oakes had been in her turn when she died in 1883, aged 93), William recalled the days of their childhood.[387]

"I remember this place when we were a handful of white men camping in an unknown country crowded with hostile or doubting blacks. Even during the day we scarcely dared to go outside the house unarmed, and constant alarms added to the toils of us first settlers. My father had to raise his own grain and meat . . . we had to grind our wheat ourselves in hand steel mills. There wasn't much choice of food in my time or his either and we have all thriven the better for our simple fare. . . . When I

"Williamsdale" which still stands in Bridge Street, North Ryde. Showing William Small (centre) 2nd son of John Small and Mary (Parker). Photograph believed to have been taken on 26 January, 1888. Henry Small (on left of William) 7th child of William and Charlotte. (On Henry's left) Janette his wife. Charlotte Gertrude Small (later Walker) 2nd child of Henry (to right of William). Eva Davies (nee Small) 6th child of Henry (on right of Charlotte). Robert Small 3rd child of Henry (far right).

Courtesy John and Mary Small Descendants Association.

Elizabeth Wicks (nee Betsy Small, eldest child of William), 90th birthday gathering at the old Ryde Town Hall, 1911.

Courtesy Mrs R. Pollard, Goulburn.

was a boy I learned all sorts of things from the blackfellows. They soon got friendly, and I was sorry to see them gradually dying out. I had many playmates amongst them, and I haven't forgotten the principal words of the tribes round here yet."

Mary, the second daughter of John and Mary Small, had given them their third grandchild, Susannah Hughes, in April 1810. Only in February that year had her husband's ration privileges been restored, with the aid of the Reverend William Cowper, minister of St Philip's Church in Sydney since August 1809. Cowper had acted quickly in response to Mathew Hughes's letter of 24 January. On 5 February his ration was restored: he agreed to teach six children without charge, and for each child above that number the fee would be "eight pence per week for spelling and reading and one shilling per week for writing and accounts." This would supply the rest of his family's needs.

After their move to Richmond, the family seems to have been comfortably situated, his regular small salary augmented by Mary's as needlework teacher, a small stipend for the time he was parish clerk at Windsor, and the produce of his few acres. In the 1828 census he is shown as holding 16 acres, all cleared and cultivated, with three horses and 51 horned cattle, with ten of his 14 children then born; only one of them had died in infancy. He held lot No 3 in Section 16 on a chart drawn up in 1820, approximately 1½ miles east of what is today Pugh's Lagoon.

In 1820 three more Small weddings were celebrated, all at St Philip's Church. On 18 June, William married Charlotte Melville, and in a double wedding on 31 October, John married Elizabeth Patfield and his young sister Sarah married Elizabeth's brother George.[388]

"My wife," William would say in January 1888, ". . . was also born in the colony, dying two years ago at the age of 82 years." Charlotte's mother Elizabeth had gamely chosen to accompany her husband Robert on HMS *Glatton* when as Pannel [accused] at the Tolbooth of Perth, Scotland, he had confessed to "the Crime of Robbery and Theft" (the indictment, alas, has been lost): he received sentence of life transportation on 10 April 1801. Melville's free pardon from Paterson in June 1809 was surrendered under Macquarie's orders in February 1810, but reissued in February 1812. He became a landholder and constable at Broken Bay, raised a family, and was a dedicated member of the Presbyterian church in Sydney. He died in May 1853 aged 83: his wife, "a native of Glasgow", had predeceased him on 31 August 1841.[389]

The young Smalls and the young Patfields had grown up and played together in the fields and woods at Kissing Point since George Patfield senior, who had arrived in the colony by *Neptune* in June 1790, had acquired a grant of land in 1798 to the north and west of John Small's. He had been sentenced (as George Paddle) at Taunton, Somerset, on 17 March 1788, to serve seven years' transportation for the theft, with

Thomas Hill, of two she-asses and two he-asses from two different owners, total value £4. His wife, Mary O'Brien, whom he married at St John's, Parramatta, on 14 August 1793, had arrived by the *Bellona* the year before, sentenced to seven years at Exeter on 22 August 1791 for stealing a cotton gown and petticoat, with other goods, value 22s.[390]

George Patfield's farm was prosperous: by 1802 he had cleared 40 of his 60 acres, and sown them in wheat and maize: he owned six sheep and ten hogs, and his family of five was off government stores. It was a tremendous shock to the neighbourhood, therefore, when in October 1809 he was found to have "put an end to his own existence by strangling himself with a handkerchief one end of which he tied fast about his neck, and the other to a branch of a tree not of sufficient height to prevent his knees from almost touching the ground."[391]

Only hours earlier he had shared some pots of "Squires's Beer" with friends, but neighbours who had seen him later on "Small's Hill" did not seem to think he had been really intoxicated. John, testifying, said "he judged he had been drinking a little, But states he appeared to be in good Health and in perfect senses." There was some hint that he might have been brooding over "a temporary embarrassment of a pecuniary nature," but though the verdict was suicide, the evidence could just as easily point to an accident, the end of his neckerchief tangling on a protruding branch as he stumbled while inspecting his sheep feeding on the hill, and the knot tightening as he struggled to free himself.

St. Anne's Church, Ryde — commenced 1826. Drawn by Mrs. Pat Smyth.

The grandchildren (eventually to number 74) had begun arriving in 1806, first with three Oakes girls (Elizabeth on 23 December 1806, Ann on 6 September 1808 and Mary on 24 August 1810), followed by Susannah Hughes on 18 April 1810. The first grandson, George Oakes, was born on 8 August 1813: of the 74 grandchildren, boys would outnumber girls by six. Of William's ten children, eight were sons, all of whom lived to healthy old age, the shortest-lived (Henry) dying at 63, and old John would live to see the birth of all but the last two. Their grandmother had the joy of knowing 23 of these young second-generation Australians, though she had had to mourn the death of little Robert Hughes at the age of two in 1818, and baby Samuel Oakes, who survived for only three weeks. But in April 1824, real tragedy entered the life of John senior: Mary, his wife and helpmeet for 36 years, was found drowned in "a large hole of seven feet depth of water, close to which is a foot path," and which supplied the neighbourhood with water.[392]

John junior had been visiting his brother William about six o'clock that evening, when William's Charlotte asked her husband to bring a pail of water from the hole. The two brothers set off, chatting amiably, no doubt, about personal and local affairs, when "near the well [John] saw two shoes and a woman's Cap, floating on the surface". William at once reached for one of the shoes, and recognized it as his mother's. Leaving John at the well, he rushed to his parents' house, and found that Mary had been gone for some time.

Meanwhile, John had got a pole and manoeuvred the body to the surface, when to his horror, he *"took her out, and found it to be his. Mother"*. His wife, seeing from their own house that something was amiss, came "running down the hill, crying, John, John, what is the matter?"

William, who had discovered from his younger brother Samuel (still living with his parents) that their mother had been gone for some time, now could only fear the worst. Samuel had not seen her since two o'clock, when he had lain down to sleep, "having been upon business the night before". Now rushing breathlessly back to the well, William found the group joined by Isaac Shepherd and his sister, who had been passing by on their way to chapel. They advised taking Mary back to her house and trying resuscitation, which was done without effect. Mary was beyond help.

The inquest was held next day by the coroner, John Eyre, before twelve "good and lawful men" of the district, among whom were such old friends as Richard Hawkes, Joseph Hatton and James Bradley, whose daughter Rachel was to marry Samuel Small in 1833. The jury questioned William, to be sure there had been no foul play, about his mother's relations with his father.

"Had you seen your Mother in the course of the day?

"Yes, about 1 o'clock, but was some distance off; she was standing at the door.

"What state has your mother been in lately, has she shown any symptoms of derangement?

"I have thought that she has at times appeared childish, but have supposed it to be the infirmity of old age.

"Do you know if your father and mother have had any quarrel lately?

"They have had no quarrel lately, they were as sociable yesterday as ever."

Isaac Shepherd said he had noticed Mary "walking down the wheat stubble . . . near the house", and that she appeared "as usual". Samuel, before retiring to his rest, "saw nothing particular the matter with her," and was as emphatic as William had been about the relationship of his parents.

"Have you any reason to believe there had been any quarrel between her and her husband?" "No," replied Samuel, "not any."

The verdict was a foregone conclusion. "Accidentally, Casually, and by Misfortune, she, the said *Mary Small fell into the water,* of foresaid large hole and then and there *was suffocated and drowned,* of which suffocation and drowning, she the said Mary Small then and there instantly died, and . . . by Misfortune came to her death, and not otherwise."

The affection that had persisted between John and Mary was underlined and emphasized by many examples. The constant appearance of family names—John, Rebecca, Mary, William, Samuel, Thomas, Sarah—in the next generations, showed a family closeness, as well as the choice of the sons to live nearby and often visit their old home. The phrase "as sociable as ever" has a nice ring. It is a heart-warming phrase, speaking of affinity, affability, common interests, amiable family conversations, and of a partnership from which both had drawn strength and tenderness. The daughters-in-law would have comforted John in bereavement as lovingly as his own daughters. It was perhaps as well for him at this time that he had the close company of his youngest son Samuel.

Thomas had been renting his father's farm since around 1825, and felt well enough established to stand up to Thomas Bowden, an influential landowner in the area, when Thomas tried to have closed a road across the Small farm which John had kept open for the convenience of his neighbours. Bowden, who had recently gone into enforced retirement after years of competent school teaching, and taken to drink, was protesting that the road had been open for enough years to make it a public one. Thomas (in a good distinctive hand) explained that John had accepted payment from Bowden for the use of the road for his carriage "until he knocked the Chimney from the House which he would not repair again . . . I should think it very hard," wrote Thomas, "for Individual to Injure me by thus passing through this Farm and damaging my Crops, or other things I may have on the Ground." By 1828 Thomas was largely running his father's property, listed with his father as residing at "Small's Farm" in the 1828 census signed by John junior, who had been district constable since 1826: but he was also a publican, operating a successful and popular tavern beside the river. Alexander Harris, a free emigrant, who spent 16 years in what he called "the Australian Backwoods", wrote of his visit there.[393]

"I landed at Tom Small's, a native of the colony, who had very large timber concerns in the bush and a good public-house on the river bank. The evening was so far advanced and so dark that I could see no farther than the landing place where I got ashore; but the sounds that came from some little distance quite clearly indicated in what direction I must look for the public-house. . . . Reaching the little snug homestead I found a company of about twenty men of all sorts, sizes, aspects, and degrees of sobriety in the tap-room. . . . The mistress found me a very good bed (of course, it being a licensed house) for payment. . . ."

The mistress was of course Tom's wife Priscilla, married to him a year after the death of her first husband Arthur Devlin: they had grown up together, Priscilla (some seven years older than Tom) the adoptive daughter of James Squire, whose now extensive property was down the hill from John Small's.[394]

By 1828 Thomas was taking much of the responsibility for his father's property: old John, retired as district constable, was receiving his pension from December in the year after Mary's death. Samuel had left the parental home, already perhaps preparing the orchards in Lane Cove for the bride (Rachel Bradley) he would bring to them in October 1833. John junior (now district constable himself) had his own 17 acres adjoining the family estate: and William had given up his bootmaking ("which I carried on at Richmond"), joined the police force for ten years, and eventually found himself at "Williamsdale" (still standing, though altered), the home he built near the family farm when his health needed outdoor work.[395]

"Just then I had a splendid offer from Captain Rossi, the police magistrate, whose family still lives at Goulburn. He asked me to overseer his run up there, and even offered me one-third of the increase of the stock as an inducement to serve under him. My wife thought Goulburn altogether 'too outlandish,' however, so I told him that, though in Australia, 'we must draw the line somewhere,' as we objected to being buried alive. It was a generous offer, but we have never regretted settling in Ryde. Country life agreed with me, and though I had to sow, reap, thresh and grind the wheat myself, I was none the worse for it, and my sons—all steady, good lads—were soon old enough to give me a hand with it. I was not sorry to give up the force, where, nevertheless, I had warm friends and got on well."

Among the festivities for the centenary celebration of Australia's first hundred years, a Citizens' Banquet was held on 30 January 1888 in the Town Hall, to which "some aged Australian natives and others, representative of the history of the colony," were invited. Among these—the oldest—was William, John Small's fourth child and second son, then aged 92, "born at Kissing Point, near Ryde, in 1796". Each was individually introduced to the company of about 150 guests by the Hon. George Thornton (MLA and himself son of a convict mother) "with very evident pride." William "recapitulated several incidents in his and his family's career . . . but it was so feebly uttered as to render it quite inaudible. Nevertheless the orator was vociferously cheered. His listeners sang, 'For he is a jolly good fellow,' and it was demanded of the band that they should play 'A fine old English Gentleman.' Missing the signal they gave 'Rule Britannia' instead." His father would have felt himself more than redeemed.[396]

Alexander Harris was made to feel very much aware (to his admitted mortification) of the clannishness of those settlers with convict ancestry when he tried to find work as a sawyer in the Kissing Point and Lane Cove areas. "They all behaved very civilly and hospitably to me: but there was unmistakeably a general disinclination to work with a free emigrant. . . . The galling sense of my superiority in this particular was not to be neutralized even by the strong law of fellowship inherent in the trade." A lady resident writing a few years earlier saw the same distinction throughout New South Wales society, a distinction not to be overcome for several generations: but she tended to perpetuate it herself by her reference (from her own eminence of wealth and free status) to "the lower classes", and the "eager rivalry . . . in a colony, where all, with very rare exceptions, have sprung from needy emigrants or transported criminals." The taint of "criminal" was hard to overcome, even though the criminality was often due more to poverty and more often than not on a level far lower than that committed openly and legally by the better-off and the lucky. There was (as now) a belief in the existence of a "criminal class", when there was, as always, no such "class", but only *criminals,* to be found in all "classes". No wonder, though, that a certain reticence was observed in the next generations about their parents' past. Those who came later were left to wonder.[397]

Alexander Harris, however, has given a strong picture of the kind of work going on at this stage of settlement. "The whole bush in this part of the country was then thronged, as indeed it was also almost all round Sydney, with men who get their living by various kinds of bush work; some felling and squaring whole trees with the squaring axe for girders, &c., &c., to use in the colony or export, some splitting out of wood the slatelike shingles with which the houses are here covered in; some splitting posts, rails, paling, for fences; some sawing the various sorts of building stuff, and some cutting and splitting firewood for domestic purposes at Sydney, or for the use of the various steam-engines that were already in operation on water and on land. Each of these pairs of bushmen (for owing to the nature of the work it is best to work in pairs) knocks up a little temporary hut on setting in to work; shifting only as the job is finished or as it becomes necessary to move on for fresh timber. . . . I could not but take notice of the immense numbers of tree stumps. . . . Several times I was induced to wander off the road . . . to where I saw the form of a hut, in the hope of getting a light for my pipe: but found only some deserted pit or falling hut, with docks and other such plants growing all around . . . the spot where the fire had been, and in the pit where the earth is covered with sawdust, are the only exceptions."

He also noticed "the general style of dress . . . lace-up boots, duck trousers, check shirt, coloured silk neckerchief [like the one that had strangled poor George Patfield all those years earlier?] and straw hat. One or two had got so far as whity brown socks and pumps, with a stylish blue jacket and waistcoat and black hat for Sundays."

The silent woods-covered area of Sydney Cove as John and Mary had first seen it had altered beyond recognition, long before Mary's death. As early as 1810 the street names had been altered: "High Street, Spring Row or Serjeant Major's Row" had become George Street: Windmill Row was Prince Street, Chapel Row was Castlereagh Street. Six sons of George III, the dukes of York, Clarence, Kent, Cumberland, Sussex and Cambridge gave their names to Barrack Street, Middle Soldiers' Row, Back Soldiers' Row and three streets without name. The governors were commemorated: Back Row East became Phillip Street, Bell Street turned into Hunter Street, Bell Row became Bligh Street, Macquarie gave his name to a "No Name" street. South Street turned into O'Connell Street,

Bridge Street retained its former name: other no-name streets became Bent, Market and Park Streets, and Spring Row.[398]

The harbour was thronged with shipping from dozens of nations, busily unloading the goods that stuffed the warehouses: muslins, stockings, lace, bed furniture, japanned wares, glass and iron ware. John and Mary would have recognized (had they been on deck to see it in 1788) the entrance to Port Jackson as it appeared to the newcomer some 50-odd years later, with only the lighthouse and signal station added. . . . "grand in the extreme. The high, dark cliffs . . . suddenly terminate in an abrupt precipice, called the South Head. . . . The North Head is a similar cliff, a bare bluff promontory of dark horizontal rocks; and between these grand stupendous pillars, as through a colossal gate, we entered Port Jackson."[399]

But in 1839, as there were not in 1788, between many of the bays and inlets "on some fine lawny promontory or rocky mount, white villas, and handsome cottages appeared, encircled with gardens and shrubberies . . . and perched amid as picturesque, but less cultivated scenery, were the cottages of pilots, fishermen, &c.". The tiny islet known as Pinchgut to the unlucky convicts once marooned there as punishment (this innocent observer called it "an unmeaning name") now bore a small fort. Sydney was seen as "a large busy town . . . with many good buildings, though few have any pretension to architectural beauty. . . . One long street traverses its whole length . . . full of good shops exhibiting every variety of merchandise; and in the afternoon, when the ladies of the place drive out, whole strings of carriages may be seen rolling about or waiting near the more 'fashionable emporiums', that being the term in which Australian shopkeepers especially delight."

Sydney had changed, but the insects remained the same (Ralph Clark would have recognized them). "Flies are another nuisance; they swarm in every room in tens of thousands, and blacken the . . . table as soon as the viands appear." Mosquitoes, too, "nearly as numerous, and infinitely more detestable." And ants—"myriads of ants . . . running hither and thither, up and down the smooth-barked gum-trees, in long lines reaching from the ground far beyond my sight into the tall branches." And birds—"Parrots . . . were flying from tree to tree . . . all as gay and happy as splendid colours and glad freedom could make them . . . like living gems and gold, so vividly bright they shone in the sun."

Bushrangers abounded, holding up travellers on the road to Parramatta and the other towns, Liverpool, Richmond, Windsor. One wonders if John, remembering his own past, was sympathetic or outraged by such boldness. Probably outraged: he had been driven to robbery in different circumstances, not from a desire to prey on society.[400]

The family association with St Anne's Church, in whose grounds so many of the Smalls would be buried, had begun with a transaction by

Thomas. "I find," wrote an officer of the Church and School Corporation in April 1834, "that the scite of the Church & Burial ground forms part of the 30 Acres given by [the deed of grant] to Will<u>m</u> Jones but subsequently purchased by Thos. Small and that Small effected an Exchange of the above Land with the Corporation for the Northern part of John Jones's land which had been purchased by the Corporation." Mary would not be buried here: she lay in an unmarked grave after her drowning.[401]

Old John Small would have been proud to read that though Ryde (which he had known as Kissing Point) was too little known a hundred years later, in 1888, "through lack of convenient communication with the metropolis", it was nevertheless—and perhaps *because* of its isolation—"a paradise of green grass and shady trees, of verdant vineyard and blushing orchard . . . Nowhere else so close to town can be seen such evidence of glad fruitfulness. . . . The homely English flowers that grace the gardens, the orchards loaded with fruit and blossom, and the smooth red roads, give the district an old-world look, impressed as deeply upon no other part of the colony except the south coast."[402]

He who had lived to see all but two of his 74 grandchildren born would have been proud, too, to learn that in 1888 "every third person you meet between Gladesville and Ryde is named Small, the family being real 'sons of the soil' and dearly loving the birthplace of their forefathers." John had much reason to feel satisfied at the end of his life, saddened only by the loss of his wife. All his seven children lived long and useful lives, none of them dying before the age of 64. Two of them were each the oldest living native-born residents at the time of their death, Rebecca in 1883 at the age of 93 and William in his turn in 1891, at the age of almost 95.

By 1840, Britain had ceased transporting convicts to New South Wales, largely because of colonial protest, though not to other parts of Australia until 1867. In 1850 debate had begun again in England about resuming transportation to New South Wales, causing furious anti-transportation meetings and reports in Sydney newspapers. On 18 September the *Sydney Morning Herald* (the former *Sydney Herald,* owned since 1841 by John Fairfax, whose son James Reading Fairfax married John Small's great-granddaughter Lucy Armstrong in 1857) published more than 19 columns on an anti-transportation meeting at Barrack Square: on 4 October 1850 the debate had run to more than 31 columns.

Next day, while the furore was at its height, John Small was buried, aged almost 89: he had died on the 2nd. Of all the convicts who landed at Sydney Cove on 26 January 1788, he was the last known survivor.[403]

REFERENCE NOTES

1. *Morning Post*, 28 Jan: Cockburn p. 52.
2. Devon Assizes (Assi 23/8).
3. HO 42/5 f 103: Howard (1792) pp. 382-3, (1789) p. 185.
4. HO 13/3 p. 24: for writings of Paul, Zouch, Montagu, Dr Smith, Hanway, Jebb, see bibliography.
5. Cal. of prisoners 1784-85, Devon RO. Information was taken by a magistrate from a suspect before committal to a gaol.
6. Devon Assizes: *Bristol Journal* 6 Nov 1784 and other papers for Bliss.
7. Howard (1792) p. 467: HO 42/7 f 315.
8. *Exeter Flying Post* 17 Mar 1785: *Bristol Journal* op. cit.
9. HO. 47/3, report on Devon Assizes 26 Mar 1785: Mark Domingo, sentenced to 14 years, died on the hulk 24 Aug 1786 aged 35.
10. See n. 282 infra.
11. See n. 403 infra.
12. No 21 on *Charlotte* transport (CO 201/2 f 245): Carmichael in 1926 and Rumsey in 1937 recorded some of this erroneous information as probable fact.
13. Parish records Stoke Damerel (Devon RO): *Fame* muster Adm 36 7362: *Bristol Journal* 16 Feb 1788.
14. Devon RO, 74B/MT 200-98 no 33: QSB 1784-5 3 B/2/7 no 22, 3/4A/101 Recognisance no 22.
15. *Sherborne Mercury* 21 Mar 1785 p. 4.
16. Devon RO, Q/RLv5, L/V 1779-84 return for 1784: St Budeaux parish registers 1780 and 1783: Gillespie pp. 272, 278: Lloyd p. 263.
17. *Europe* muster no 28 SVO: *Nemesis* muster (Adm 36/10164) marine no 76.
18. Captain's log *Europe*.
19. John Herbert no 660 on muster. Phillip would go out as the New South Wales colony's first governor (see ADB for comprehensive biography). Others who would later be associated with the colony appear on this muster—Lt. P. G. King, Henry Brewer (clerk), Andrew Miller and Edward Spain (captain's servants). See Edward Spain, Reminiscences, 1774-1802. ML C266,. Miller would become commissary at Sydney Cove, Brewer provost marshal. Naval logbooks (so named from 15th century custom of measuring distance travelled by a log line attached to a wooden board, or log, run out as the ship moved ahead) recorded daily information about weather, distance travelled, navigation, land sighted, punishments administered, deaths, men "Run", ships sighted or "chaced", arrival, departure, etc.
20. *Caton* muster, marine no 104.
21. *Augusta* muster, marine no 60.
22. Adm 1/5308 pt 3, court martial for the loss of *Augusta*: Marshall vol 1 p. 157.
23. Talbot p. 26.
24. Captain's log *Eagle*.
25. Adm 36/7898 (*Somerset* muster) Davenport marine no 15: Massachusetts vol. XX p. 101: Adm 1/489 f 147: photographs sent to author showing timbers of *Somerset* on beach.

26. Adm 36/8770 (*Renown* muster) Ourry no 334, 12 Feb 1779: *Dublin* muster, Davenport marine no 9: *Dublin* master's log.
27. *Dublin* master's log 25-28 Dec 1779.
28. Adm 36/8875 (*Diligente* muster), Adm 36/9479 (*Monarch* muster), Adm 36/9172 (*Cormorant* muster), Adm 36/9720 (*Nymph* muster, in muster for *La Nymphe*).
29. Adm 36/10401 (*Nymph* muster, Davenport marine no 39): Adm 1/312 f 332: *Caton* muster, paybook: Tortola is one of the Virgin Islands in the Caribbean.
30. Blumberg p. 179.
31. Adm 106/2611: *Whitehall E P*, 13 Feb 1783.
32. HO 42/5 f 282: OBSP 10 Jan 1787 p. 315: *Lady Penrhyn* log 12 July 1787.
33. Ship musters Adm 36/10079 (*Superb*): Adm 36/8996 (*Invincible*): Adm 36/10356 (*Leocadia*): Adm 36/8922 (*Alcide*): Adm 36/9945 (*Alcmene*): Adm 36/9816 (*Sulphur*): Adm 36/8745 (*Warspite*): Adm 36/8617 (*Monsieur*): Adm 36/8775 (*Diligente*): Adm 36/8725 (*Courageux*): Adm 36/9417 (*Belleisle*): Adm 36/10117 (*Sultan*): Adm 36/9137 (*London*): Adm 36/8327 (*Diligente*).
34. Adm 36/8328: see *DNB* for Major John Small: will, PROB 11/1275(279) PRO London.
35. Nelson, Adm 36/9847: Christian, of *Bounty* fame, Adm 36/10358: White, Adm 36/9816 and Adm 106/2611, 28 Jan, 1 Feb 1783: Anstis, Adm 51/4376, (no muster for *Surprize*), Adm 36/9856, 9936, 10138: Considen, Adm 36/9749, 9936, 10079: Southwell, Adm 36/8732: Bradley, Adm 36/10521: Faddy, Adm 36/9749: Tench, Adm 36/10482, 10452: Balmain, Adm 36/10702.
36. Various ship musters.
37. *Medway* muster, marine no 254.
38. Adm 102/663 (1774-83, persons lodged in private quarters 1781).
39. Haslar Hospital, minutes of council 1779-83, book 7, 17 Jan 1783. Haslar is the naval hospital at Gosport, Portsmouth.
40. Adm 14/48 f 3333.
41. Adm 158/283.
42. *Medway* muster, logs. *Medway* was a 4th rate 60 gun ship (Colledge). Warships of sailing navies were grouped according to the number of guns carried, line of battle ships being in the first three rates. This applied to ships built between 1757 and 1792, after which more guns were carried in each rate.
43. *Medway* logs, various dates: de Grasse, see n 88 infra: ships armed *en flûte* have had some guns removed to provide extra accommodation for troops or stores (*Companion* p. 318): *PH* 22 col. 917.
44. *Medway* logs, various dates: *PH* 22 col. 918. Charles James Fox was a leading Whig statesman (see *DNB*): *AR* 1782 p. 102.
45. Adm 36/8953 (*Kite* muster): Ancell pp. 94, 96-97: Gibraltar p. 29. The Barbary coast lay in the Berber country, Morocco, across the Straits of Gibraltar.
46. Mann p. 260.
47. Ancell p. 112: Gibraltar p. 29: *AR* 1782 p. 103: BL Add Mss 38,681 f 81.
48. BL Add Mss 38,681 f 82v: Ancell p. 104.
49. BL Add Mss 38,681 f 83v: Gibraltar p. 31.
50. Master's log, *Medway*.
51. ibid: *Encyc. Brit.* (St Helena).
52. Sir Richard Grenville (1541?-1591), naval commander of *Revenge* under Lord Thomas Howard, sent to Azores to watch for Spanish treasure fleet in 1591. See DNB and Tennyson's poem, *The Revenge*.
53. Musters, logs and paybook, *Medway*.
54. Musters and logs of *Lively*, *Perseus*, *Medway*.
55. Letter to author from aunt Miss E. P. Youdale, 14 June 1951: Carmichael p. 5. Miss Youdale lived in the same house as her grandmother, Eliza Hughes Small, for some 16 years.
56. This and following baptismal records from the registers of St Martin's parish church and St Philip's cathedral, Birmingham, and from parish rate books (rates collected to sustain public works, support of poor, belonging to the parish). These are in Birmingham Public Library, reference section. Dates of birth were not often recorded, but baptism within three weeks of birth was encouraged.

57. Rate books, op. cit: cf. contemporary maps with those of today.
58. Rate books, Kingston upon Thames RO (KG 3/2/12): Squire lived on Heathen Street, now Eden Street.
59. Hutton, various pp.
60. ibid: Dent vol 1 p. 99: Crowe p. 45.
61. Young vol 3: *Encyc. Brit*: Boulton, see *DNB*: Bruce, in *The Engineer* 8 Mar 1957 for Dr Small.
62. Young op cit: St Fond p. 346.
63. See illustration of Birmingham within this volume: Langford, various pp. and *Birmingham Gazette* 1750-1785 (the verse quoted by Langford, 6 Nov 1769).
64. Langford and *Birmingham Gazette*, various dates.
65. Little p. 13: Langford 13 Feb 1769.
66. Adm 158/283 f 95v-96.
67. *DT* 23 Jan 1888.
68. *OED*.
69. Grover p. 19: 29 Geo II c 6: Reports (3) 1833 vol VII pp. 3156, 3188.
70. Adm 1/5246 p. 61. Prince George was appointed Lord High Admiral in May 1702.
71. WO 26/21 f 85, 28 Feb 1746/7: Observations p. 45: 29 Geo II c 4.
72. Gillespie p. 256.
73. RM Mus. Acq nos P/9/6, P/9/14.
74. Woodforde pp. 522-23.
75. Adm 96/153 ff 14-18: *Derby Mercury* 6-13 Jan 1758.
76. 21 Geo III c 9: Act for the regulation of HM's marine forces while on shore (similar to Acts in preceding and following years). The regulation of marine forces at sea was governed by the Navy Act (22 Geo II c 33) which put marines under the command of the captain, subject to the same laws as seamen. The Navy Act was not repealed until 1860.
77. ibid.
78. Personal service documents 1755-1800, RM Acq 591/76 (C)—Arch 11/12/20 (4), enlistment of John Palmer 1798: the "inlisting money" was two guineas (Blumberg p. 7 and *Gazetteer*, London, 7 Dec 1778).
79. RM Archs (11/12/20, Item 121/71(B)).
80. Gen. Collins, various dates, RM Archives.
81. *Observations* pp. 13-14, 18-19. Kersey was a coarse woollen cloth.
82. Blumberg p. 110: Adm 14/49, 22 Apr 1783.
83. 20 Geo III c 13, p. 282.
84. *Observations* pp. 53-57, 72.
85. *Lively* muster: RM Mus. Acq P/9/6 op. cit.
86. *Lively* logs, muster. John Small, marine no 6.
87. Colledge p. 321: Sir Samuel Hood (1762-1814) had a brilliant naval career (see DNB). He appears on *Lively* muster Adm 36/10137 no 92.
88. *Lively* logs various dates: the comte de Grasse was the French admiral who captured Chesapeake Bay and caused havoc among British shipping in the West Indies. He was captured with his flagship *Ville de Paris* in mid-April 1783 near Dominica, by Admiral Rodney (see *DNB*): Adm 7/575.
89. *Lively* logs, muster: oakum was rope untwisted and teased out to stuff into ships' seams.
90. From HMS *Sphynx* (Adm 36/10014).
91. Masefield pp. 64 ff.
92. *Lively* logs, various dates. (*Hussar, Zebra, Pearl, Ostrich*).
93. Admiral Thomas Graves (1725?-1802), commander in chief of North American station, was succeeded in July 1781 by Rear Admiral Robert Digby (1732-1815), who had been appointed governor to Prince William Henry (third son of George III and later King William IV). Graves had been second in command under Admiral George Darby at the relief of Gibraltar early in 1781 in which Irish John Small took part in *Medway*. Graves had been unable to make conclusive engagement with the French when de Grasse took control of Chesapeake Bay at the end of August 1781.
94. Ziegler p. 38 (RA 44630, 27 Sep 1781): Talbot p. 106: Barney p. 72 ff, Onderdonk p. 235: Adm 7/575 p. 221.

95. *Lively* logs: Adm 7/575 op. cit.
96. Adm 7/575: Pasley p. 257 (Sir George Brydges Rodney (1719-1792) received a peerage in June 1783: *DNB*).
97. *Lively* logs: Pasley p. 133.
98. *Lively* logs, muster: Cuthbert had been a prisoner of war for two years in San Domingo, released on exchange in May 1779 (Adm 14/40 p. 514).
99. *Lively* logs and muster: Stanhope, see n 24 supra, n 132 infra.
100. Pasley p. 276: Sir Guy Carleton, later Lord Dorchester, had been governor of Quebec, commander of the army in Canada, defeating an American siege in 1776. Appointed in 1782 as commander-in-chief in America, "by a consistent policy of clemency he did much to conciliate the Americans", and after the peace he evacuated New York in November 1783. As Lord Dorchester he returned to Quebec as governor until 1796 (*DNB*).
101. *Lively* logs. Halifax, Nova Scotia was an important British port: a battalion of marines was stationed there (Adm 96/153).
102. Talbot, Barney, Onderdonk, op. cit: Adm 14/56 no 2109, Cuthbert.
103. *Lively* paybook. Balmain was born near Rhynd, about ten miles from Newborough [Newburgh].
104. Adm 1/313 f 513v. Admiral Hugh Pigot (1721?-1792) appointed a lord of the admiralty, promoted rear admiral of the blue and commander-in-chief in West Indies, superceded Rodney.
105. Colledge p. 294: *Jupiter* logs (see map).
106. Adm 1/313 f 540: elephants' teeth—perhaps walrus tusks?
107. *Lively, Jupiter* logs.
108. ibid: Adm 1/5323 (court martial on the loss of *Lively*).
109. Adm 1/313 ff 514, 540-41: *Jupiter* logs, Pasley p. 259.
110. Adm 1/5323. Much of this and following information is found in this record of the court martial into the loss of *Lively*. The sequence of events is a little confusing. Also see *Lively's* muster and logs.
111. It is uncertain who the supercargo [passenger] was. He is not identified as such in *Lively's* muster of prisoners.
112. Floyd, carpenter, said Whitmore was "Mate or Sailing Master of the Ship Prize." (p. 29 of court martial transcript): Bell, the surgeon, said "He had been Mate of a Vessel, and was going a Passenger when he was taken." (p. 34 of court martial transcript—see reference 110 supra).
113. Oakes was an American. Yeoman [PR]—"an officer under the boatswain or gunner of a ship of war usually charged with the stowage, account, and distribution of their respective stores" (Falconer). PR—powder room. "Ab" stands for *Able* seaman (*Companion* p. 1).
114. "What became of the girl?" the Court asked (p. 14 of court martial). "She went to St Augustine with the captain," said Lt. Walton—presumably when the officers were released by cartel. There had been some talk about the captain's wanting to go to St Augustine to settle about the prize. The girl was not the supercargo on *St Helena*: she had been on *Lively* with Stanhope.
115. Quoted in *Whitehall Evening Post* 22 February 1783.
116. *Belisarius* logs and muster.
117. Adm 1/1704, Durell: Adm 36/7571, *Cygnet* muster log Adm 52/1200 (1767).
118. Adm 36/9057: *Vulture* was at St Augustine in Nov 1782 (*Belisarius* log) and may have taken Stanhope and officers to New York (see n. 114 supra).
119. Onderdonk, Talbot, Barney, op. cit: see note 164 infra re Cowdry. Muffin no 260 *Lively* paybook: his mother Ann received his pay in Jan 1786.
120. Philip Allwood, Adm 1/489 f 314.
121. These were captains of merchant ships. Navy captains would have been exchanged by cartel (a ship sailing under a flag of truce).
122. Quoted in *Whitehall E P* 28-30 Jan 1783.
123. *Diamond* logs, muster: *Diamond*, 5th rate, 710 tons (Colledge p. 163): Adm L/D/104 (NMM): Adm 1/5522, court martial on loss of *Tickler*. Warp: to move the ship from place to place by hauling on a rope attached to a small anchor.

124. Adm 7/575 p. 170: Sir Augustus d'Este was son of the Duke of Sussex (6th son of George III) and Lady Augusta Murray. His journal, unpublished, has been donated to the PRO and is located at PRO 30/93. He had fought at the battle of New Orleans in 1815.
125. *Diamond* muster (Clark was no 74 in marine list).
126. Adm 1/5322 *Tickler*, op. cit.:
127. Adm 36/9957, Adm 51/4110. The *Fortunee* was later used as a prison hulk in Portsmouth (Langstone Harbour): see n. 165 infra.
128. *Diamond* log.
129. *Actas* op cit., ff 248v-249v, 260.
130. *Diamond* muster and log.
131. Adm 1/5323, *Lively* court martial op cit, and *Lively* muster.
132. PC 2/129 p. 4: Adm 107/7 f 95: *Adams's Weekly Courant* 19 Oct 1779 p. 2 col. 1. Stanhope was first cousin to Philip Stanhope (son of Arthur Charles Stanhope) who became 5th Earl of Chesterfield, all collateral descendants of the 4th earl whose letters to his natural son, published in 1774, remain popular for wit and wisdom. Michael Stanhope had had a long and honourable naval career from his first appearance as Ab on *Cygnet* in 1765, serving on *Fowey, Alarm, Tartar, Gaspee, Eagle, Renown, Serapis, Fox, Belliqueux* and *Prothee.* He was serving on *Serapis* when she fought with the famous American naval commander John Paul Jones on *Bonhomme Richard.* The battle was fought in the North Sea in full view of thousands of English spectators who gathered on shore on 23 September 1779 near Scarborough. Stanhope was wounded, and spent some time as prisoner of war in the Netherlands. Date of death not traced as yet, but apparently after 1806, when his wife's will described her as "wife of Michael Stanhope Esqr".
133. Adm 36/8637 *Edgar* muster, marine no 257: Adm 36/9039 *Standard* muster, marine no 283, Adm 51/859 captain's log.
134. *Perseus, Diamond* musters. Perseus, 6th rate, 432 tons (Colledge p. 416).
135. Adm 1/2307 no 28.
136. *Perseus* master's log: Fryer came on board on 9 October 1783.
137. *Perseus* paybook, no 31. He may have died in sick quarters: the annotation in the muster book is unclear.
138. "In ordinary"—an old naval term for ships laid up in this manner (Companion p. 617).
139. Blumberg pp. 184, 188, 190.
140. *Diamond, Lively* paybooks.
141. *Caton,* Adm 34/538 *Nymph* paybooks: Adm 36/10164, Adm 34/541, *Nemesis* muster, paybook: *Europe* muster, paybook.
142. *Morning Post* 7 Jan 1785.
143. *Exeter Flying Post* 24 Mar 1785.
144. HO 13/3 pp. 50-52.
145. Ann Goodiff (OBSP 4 Dec 1782 p. 16) was sent to the *Swift* transport for America (PCOM 2/170, week 28 Jly 1783) for 7 years transportation for theft of a bundle of laundry. Maryland records show her as received in Baltimore 31 December 1783 (Maryland Hall of Records, Record of Convicts, Baltimore City Court, 1772-1783, ff 383-89, signed by W. Gibson clerk). This list, however, repeats the names of *all* the convicts sent, many of whom had escaped when the *Swift* convicts took over the ship near Rye and had been long since captured and some hanged. It is therefore not possible to know whether Ann Goodiff survived the voyage and reached America.
146. Quoted in Cockburn p. 3: Devon Assizes: Ayton vol 2 p. 108.
147. T 1/841, with letter 12 Nov 1785. For *Mercury,* sss n. 163 infra.
148. Stubbs, various pp.
149. Hotham, Buller, see n. 1 supra. Beaumont Hotham (1737-1815) was knighted in May 1813. He was "a man of strong commonsense, of a kindly temperament and polished manners." Francis Buller (1746-1800), made a puisne judge of the King's Bench at the age of 32, was said to have been the youngest man ever created an English judge. He was considered hasty and prejudiced, often subject of severe criticism. Short, but "of handsome features, with a piercing eye and a commanding forehead." He was made a baronet in January 1790. (*DNB*): Cottu p. 43.

150. Cottu op. cit.
151. Halevy vol. 3 p. 152.
152. Hotham Papers, 9 Sep 1783.
153. Sermons (Clayton): Curwen p. 67, Prov. 14, 34: Smith, Rev. S.: *General Evening Post*, 4-6 Jan 1785.
154. Cottu pp. 103-4.
155. Madan pp. 148, 153. See *DNB*.
156. Modbury: Ayton vol. 2 p. 108.
157. Treatise.
158. Madan pp. 23, 28, 26, 29. The grand jury was a jury of inquiry, composed of gentlemen of the county who examined the individual charges to decide if they were a "True Bill" and should go to trial. The petty (trial jury) heard the evidence and decided on guilt or acquittal.
159. *Exeter Flying Post* 7 Apr 1785: Jenkins, p. 222: *Public Advertiser* 7 Apr 1785.
160. *Exeter Flying Post* 16 Mar 1785: Madan pp. 40, 79, 110, 40.
161. HO 47/3, 26 Mar 1785: HO 13/3 pp. 50-52, 62.
162. Assi 24/26, Devon, n.d.: *Exeter Flying Post* 2 Feb 1786.
163. HO 13/4 p. 84: Adm 106/2611, 12 Feb 1783: Colledge p. 177: HO 7/1, 27 Apr 1785 (p. 8 of Beauchamps Committee on Convicts): Adm 106/2619, 28 Oct 1785. The *Mercury* was the second vessel to try to resume transportation of convicts to America after the war ended (the earlier one was the *Swift*) and some convicts from both vessels mutinied and escaped. Those convicts from *Swift* who did not escape were accepted at Baltimore, *Mercury's* weren't. These ended up in British Honduras. Two First Fleeters (William Blatherhorn and Joseph Hall) and possibly three (John Jones) were in both mutinies.
164. HO 13/2 p. 120, 11 Jun 1784: HO 42/3 ff 72-3: T 54/44 p. 642: HO 42/4 f 26: IOR/F/1/2 p. 44: HO 42/8, letters 11 (f 20), 17 Mar 1786. Cowdry wanted to retain the contract.
165. *Exeter Flying Post* 2 Feb 1786: Treasurer's Account Book 1785-9 (A/1/12, Devon RO): *Dunkirk* HO 42/8, 1786: Adm 106/2619, letter 3 Nov 1785: Colledge p. 219 (the ship that took Prince William Henry into Havana).
166. HO 42/7, 20 Sep 1785: HO 13/3 pp. 281, 265: HO 36/5, 19 Jan 1786: HO 29/2 p. 53: Banks Corresp., Kew, B.C. 1 f 203: HO 42/8, 22 Jan 1786: *Morning Chronicle* 6 Jan 1786.
167. *Dunkirk* (HO 42/8): *Morning Chronicle* 11 Jan 1786, *Morning Herald* 12 Jan 1786.
168. *Dunkirk* (HO 42/8): T 1/644 (*Dunkirk* Dec 1786-Mar 1787): HO 13/4 pp. 45, 86, *Exeter Flying Post* 17 May 1786: HO 42/10 ff 205, 350, 352-3: OBSP 10 Sep 1783 p. 940: T 1/645 (*Censor* Jan-Apr 1787).
169. T 1/647 (*Dunkirk* Apr-Jne 1787), T 1/676 (*Dunkirk* Jly-Sep 1789): T 1/693 f 10. Liddy had stolen some ostrich plumes from a hearse (OBSP 14 Jan 1784 p. 177).
170. *Dunkirk* (HO 42/8): HO 42/5 f 110: Adm 1/807, 28 Nov 1784. The soldiers were indicated only as "Regulars". See text, notes 189 and 192, Mary Bond re women on hulks. *Mercury* women were held on *Dunkirk* from 1784, and this hulk would receive women from county gaols destined for Botany Bay from October 1786.
171. Adm 106/2615, 2 Jly 1784: HO 28/4 f 339: HO 42/8, 22 Jan 1786, James Hill.
172. HO 42/5 f 368: HO 13/2 p. 292: Smith, W., p. 83.
173. HO 36/5 p. 15: HO 13/4 p. 116: T 1/643, *Fortunee* and *Lion*, and HO 42/15 f 257.
174. Smith, W., op cit. p. 83 ff.
175. T 1/605, Holt to Lord Sydney 14 Jun 1784.
176. T 1/620 f 264: Assi 23/8, Devon Lent Assizes 1783: *Helena* muster 1 Mar-30 Apr 1784 (Adm 36/10412): T 1/645 (*Censor* Jan-Apr 1787): Honduras p. 140 ff.
177. OBSP 10 Sep 1783 p. 941: *Morning Herald* 3 Jun 1784: Clark p. 78; HO 42/5 in Carrington's 5 Sep 1784 f 118: HO 42/4, Carrington's 14 Jun 1784: OBSP 3 Jun 1778 p. 255; 11 and 18 Sep 1782 pp. 558 and 646. Chancellor Carrington was the Exeter magistrate most closely concerned with the aftermath of the *Mercury* mutiny.
178. Adm 1/4151, letter 5 Nov 1784: HO 42/5, f 47.
179. Assi 23/8, Devon Summer Assizes 1782: HO 13/1 p. 2: T 1/617 ff 151-55: HO 13/3 p. 77: T 1/637 *Censor* Apr-Jly 1786: T 1/645 *Censor* Jan-Apr 1787. *Compter* is an old name for a debtor's prison. At this time there were two prisons in London using this

166

name—Wood Street Compter and Poultry Compter. The dungeons of Wood Street Compter are used today to store wine and spirits.

180. SP 37/13 f 11: T 1/614 ff 31-41, 34-38, 48-59: HO 42/5 f 461.
181. *Whitehall Evening Post,* 18 Jan 1783: Edward Willes, an assize judge called to bar 1726, died 14 Jan 1787 (Foss).
182. *Morning Chronicle* 2 Nov 1782 and PCOM 2/170, week 28 Oct 1782: T 1/539 Pt. 2, Woolwich hulks 6 Jly-8 Sep 1778, no 188. Tried at Westminster; OB/SR 10 Sep 1783. Ind. no 78 (GLRO): OBSP 8 Oct 1782 p. 851.
183. T 70/33 p. 53: OBSP 10 Sep 1783 p. 851: E 370/41 bundle 13. Goree, an island off the coast of French Equatorial Africa (now Senegal). Cape Coast Castle on West African Gold Coast (now Ghana).
184. HO 13/1 p. 143: OBSP 7 Jly 1784 p. 874: OBSP 26 May 1784 p. 775. Harris was a wax chandler with wife and two children (HO 42/2 f 62) who reached London after escaping from the *Mercury* transport. Peat had also reached London from the *Mercury,* and both men were tried there. Potten, HO 77/1 p. 167, HO 47/5, letter re Ann Randall/Cox and Mary Potten/Rine [listed elsewhere as ux Kime], both taken in Bristol Jun 1784. No prosecution; sent to London and maintained at Corporation's expense. Potten absconded and was sent to NSW (HO 11/1 p. 16). Nowland, T 1/678 (*Fortunee* Nov 1789-Feb 1790 no 300).
185. HO 42/8 1 May 1786: *GM* 1785, ii, 1003: HO 42/7 ff 28-31: HO 42/1 ff 409, 428-31: *Public Advertiser* 9 Dec 1786, "Letter to a Respectable Nobleman".
186. HO 42/7 f 40 ff.
187. HO 28/5 ff 116, 118: Adm 51/627 (*Nautilus* log) 17 May 1786: T 1/639 ff 142-62.
188. *Exeter Flying Post* 11 Jan 1787: HO 42/9 f 20.
189. T 1/641 (*Dunkirk* Sep-Dec 1786): HO 13/6 p. 33: HO 13/4 pp 260 ff passim: HO 42/10 ff 410, 405.
190. *Friendship, Charlotte* logs.
191. *Charlotte* log: *Friendship* log: T 1/644 (*Dunkirk* Dec 1786-Mar 1787): HO 13/5 p. 70.
192. HO 13/4 p. 254: T 1/692 f 231: T 1/693 f 8: *Dunkirk* returns showing Mary Bond, T 1/647, 661, 651, 655, 657, 663, 667, 672: also CO 201/4 f 177 showing 315 men and *one woman* on *Neptune* from *Dunkirk.*
193. *Alexander, Borrowdale, Charlotte, Fishburn* logs: *Friendship, Golden Grove, Lady Penrhyn, Prince of Wales, Scarborough* logs: *Sirius* logs: *Supply* master's log.
194. HO 13/5 f 5: *Gazetteer* 8 Jan 1787: PCOM 2/173 and HO 77/1 p. 451 ff (marginal notes): *Lady Penrhyn* log: HO 13/4 pp. 309-338 passim: HO 13/5 p. 29: Bradley p. 6.
195. CO 201/2 pt. 1 f 123: John Turnpenny Altree, a volunteer surgeon, was reported inefficient, but may have been ill. He is mentioned frequently in Bowes ("found him dangerously ill taking medicines of Mr. White's prescribing"—Bowes p. 11). He went to Norfolk Island with the first contingent under Lt. King (*Supply* muster 14 Feb 1788).
196. PCOM 2/173 week 1 Jan 1786, marginal note.
197. Cf Horwood with contemporary map of area.
198. Bedford archives: Dobie p. 201.
199. *Public Advertiser* 25 Nov 1784: parish registers of St George's church, Bloomsbury (GLRO).
200. Willan p. 254.
201. Cole/Postgate p. 83.
202. Bedford archives; Land Tax Assessment Books, St. George's, Bloomsbury, GLRO 1781-87 vols: Dobie p. 201.
203. Murray p. 5.
204. St George's parish registers, op cit.
205. HO 42/8, women transports 1 Jan [1787]: OBSP 14 Sep 1785 p. 1114: OB/SR 14 MJ/OBS Book 18, Ind. 91 (GLRO).
206. PCOM 2/172.
207. Ilive, passim.
208. ibid: MJ/SPC W 364C, 365C, 366C (GLRO).
209. Details about this trial are taken from GLRO/MJ/OBSP 1786 Apr 22, MJ/OBSR 26 Apr 1786 Ind. 2, and OBSP 26 Apr 1786 p. 505. Mary Parker was brought to Newgate

20 Apr 1786 (PCOM 2/172). Until 1836 (6 & 7 Wm IV c 114) counsel for prisoners were supposed to advise on legal points only: prisoners had to conduct their own defence.

210. FF logs: CO 201/2 f 251.
211. HO 13/4 p. 220: T 70/33 p. 53: CO 201/1 f 58: CO 201/2 f 88 n.d.: GM 1791, i, 79.
212. HO 13/4 p. 220: Adm 1/4289, George Rose 21 Oct 1786: FF logs.
213. *Justitia* had 185 transportation convicts at that date, *Censor* 253, *Ceres* 281 (T 1/641): HO 13/2 p. 342. There seems no apparent reason governing the choice of the 202 men ordered by warrant for delivery to the transport *Alexander* (HO 13/5) except that in these and other warrants the name order seems to have been taken almost directly from the most recent hulk returns, name for name in the case of the *Dunkirk*, which was intended to be cleared and sold, though this was in fact postponed.
214. HO 13/5 ff 31, 65: *Alexander, Scarborough* logs: T 1/644, 645: Adm 1/929, 18 Mar 1787: Collins p. lvii: CO 201/3 f 56.
215. HO 13/5 f 39 ff passim: the three men were Peter Ellam, Thomas Oldfield and George Youngson. Only three men went from Newgate (Francis Fowkes, Hardwicke Richardson and John Lockley).
216. Adm 1/989, 21 Mar 1787. Captain Marshall was port officer. Many (perhaps most) of these men served their full terms on the hulks and were never transported.
217. Wilkie p. 565.
218. White pp. 50, 48, 49.
219. CO 201/2, Ross's lists ff 233-251, Richards' lists ff 256-90: Williams no 3 on *Stanislaus* Jne-Sep 1792 (T 1/703): FF logs: PCOM 2/175 week 12 Mar 1787 (marginal note).
220. CO 201/2 f 105v: quoted in Dugan p. 72: *Royal George*—there are several interesting small books on this event with good descriptions of Portsmouth and Spithead.
221. *Sirius* log: see n 93 supra.
222. The surgeon was John Turnpenny Altree (see n. 195 supra): Bowes, various pp.
223. *Lady Penrhyn* log: OBSP 13 Dec 1786 p. 68.
224. OBSP 26 May 1784 p. 756: OBSP 10 Jan 1787 p. 315: HO 42/10 f 405 (see n 189): Collins p. 45: NIVB AO reel 2747 (convicts' children no 4): Adm 35/285B (no 5, *Buffalo*); Adm 51/1564, 3 Aug 1798 ("at 8 P.M. missed Edward Parkinson Boy who could not be found and imagined he was washed out of the Head Drown'd as nobody could give any account of him since 6 O'Clock").
225. *Lady Penrhyn* log: there is confusion about Ann Morton—Bowes calls her Ann Morton (p. 43): the log records Ann Moulton, but there was no convict of this name. She was perhaps Mary Morton: Sheedy, CY ML Mss 1337.
226. Arthur Phillip (1738-1814) had had solid but not outstanding naval experience, some of it with the Portuguese navy. He was humane, conscientious, capable and careful, and FF convicts owed a safe and healthy voyage largely to these qualities in their leader. His plans for NSW were to some extent frustrated by antagonism between him and Major Ross, marine commandant and lieutenant governor, from handicaps imposed on him by government's lack of proper supplies and provisions, by lack of necessary officials such as overseers, and of skilled persons to perform necessary work, and by the self-interest of opportunists who developed the liquor trade and for private purposes diverted convict labour from government projects.

When the Fleet sailed the "opera" *Botany Bay* had drawn to its inevitable close. "The Botany Bay petite piece was interesting, and the characters well supported," the *World's* critic had written after it opened on 9 April. "the *cargo* bound for that part of the world, was surely the best that the *Borough, Rotherhithe*, or the purlieus of the *Dog and Duck* [all unsavoury areas] could have afforded." Botany Bay's risqué songs were bellowed with other topical bawdy songs by the crowds in St. Paul's churchyard, consigning Pitt and his new taxes to the horrors of Botany Bay: Bowes p. 16.
227. White p. 52, 232: FF logs.
228. FF logs: Collins p. lviii.
229. ibid, lvi: Bowes p. 39 (6 Oct 1787).

230. Bradley p. 19: Bowes p. 18: Collins p. lix. Teneriffe, in the Canary Islands, Spanish-owned.
231. *Charlotte* log: *Lively* master's log 28 Jun 1782.
232. Collins p. lxvi: Pasley p. 247.
233. White p. 67: Southwell letters BL Add Mss 16,381 f 17v.
234. Bowes, various pp. (16, 25, 27 etc.).
235. Phillip, see *ADB* and n 226 supra: Clark p. 37.
236. Bowes p. 33: CO 201/2 f 184.
237. Bowes, various pp.
238. White p. 89.
239. Bowes, various pp.
240. Collins p. ixxviii: Bradley pp. 41-2: *Alexander* log 19 Jan 1787.
241. Collins p. lxxvii: Bowes p. 40: Bradley p. 41.
242. Clark pp. 36, 54: Bowes pp. 47, 67.
243. Bowes p. 48: Clark p. 33.
244. CO 201/2 ff 156, 182, 183. Cassava is tapioca: "Russia", a coarse linen or hempen textile (*OED*).
245. FF logs.
246. *Lady Penrhyn* log: BL Add Mss 16,381 f 23: Worgan pp. 12-13, 42-44.
247. Clark pp. 8-10, 65.
248. *Dunkirk* (HO 42/8) nos 137 and 75: White p. 102.
249. *Prince of Wales* log: White p. 102: Bowes pp. 44-45, Adm 1/4152 f 67, White p. 103.
250. Bowes p. 47: Clark p. 74: Tench p. 32: White p. 113.
251. Bowes p. 45.
252. ibid pp. 45-47.
253. Clark p. 49: OBSP 10 Sep 1783 p. 940: Easty p. 73: CO 201/3 f 191-92: CO 201/40 ff 20-21, 1788: SG 28 Apr, 4 May 1806.
254. Bowes pp. 52-55.
255. ibid pp. 44, 63.
256. Hunter p. 28, Collins p. 2. King p. 36 writes that this short voyage was made by *Supply*, with a company of marines and 40 convicts.
257. White p. 211, Collins p. 4.
258. Bowes pp. 63-64, Clark p. 93, Bowes p. 64.
259. Tench p. 38, White p. 112, Collins p. 3, Bowes p. 62, Clark p. 93, Worgan p. 7.
260. BL Add Mss 16,381 ff 27v-28r: *Fishburn* log 26 Jan 1788.
261. Poem by Erasmus Darwin (1731-1802) published in Phillip p. xxiii.
262. King p. 36.
263. Collins pp. 4-5, Worgan p. 8.
264. Clark p. 95.
265. Adm 106/2622, 8 Nov 1786 (Transport Service): CO 201/3 f 24: Clark p. 90: FF logs.
266. Collins p. 5: *Lady Penrhyn* log: Bowes p. 65: *Dunkirk* (HO 42/8) no 66.
267. Bowes p. 67: Tench p. 39.
268. *Charlotte* log: Tench p. 38: White p. 113: *Sirius* log.
269. Bowes p. 66. *Lady Penrhyn's* log records the discharge of five women to *Supply* on 14 Feb 1788 when the latter sailed for Norfolk Island.
270. See n. 208 supra.
271. Collins pp. 6-7: Clark p. 96: Bowes pp. 67-8.
272. CO 201/2 f 37: Bowes p. 69.
273. CO 201/3 f 9: Collins p. 19: CO 201/3 ff 95, 8, 29. The information was not sent to Phillip until February 1791 in letter from Nepean (no 10) 19 February 1791 (HO 31/1, annotation on copies of Orders in Council).
274. CO 201/3 ff 95v, 56, 62: Adm 51/832A (*Sirius* log): CO 201/3 ff 62, 95v-96v.
275. CO 201/3 f 60: White, p. 155. CO 201/3 f 45v.
276. Collins pp. 5-6: Worgan p. 12.
277. CO 201/3 f 55v: Collins pp. 31, 33: CO 201/3 f 54.
278. Collins pp. 544 (n. 1), 33.
279. CO 201/3 f 12.
280. Clark p. 97, Collins p. 13.
281. Clark p. 94: Collins p. 538 (n. 3).

282. Details of this incident and trial are found in records of Court of Criminal Jurisdiction, 1788-1794, AO 5/1147A, pp. 45-55 (AO reel 2391).
283. Collins p. 28.
284. CO 201/2 f 340: *Dunkirk* (HO 42/8) nos 139, 102, 135: AO COD 382 photocopy of St Philips parish register p. 217: OBSP 7 Jly 1784 p. 738. John Small's assignment to the laboratory tent lends substance to the legend that he was a "ship's *apothecary*".
285. Marriages in the Parish of St Philip. no 63 Vol 4 Registry of B.D.M. Sydney. The Rev. Richard Johnson (1753-1827) was appointed by royal warrant in October 1786 as chaplain to the colony and travelled on the *Golden Grove* storeship with wife and servant. He preached the first sermon in Sydney under the trees: it was not until 1793 that he had a church, built at his own expense. A daughter and son were born in NSW. Apart from the convict priests James Harold, James Dixon and Peter O'Neil the first official Roman Catholic chaplains (though two priests offered to go without pay, CO 201/2 f 213) were Fr J. J. Therry and Fr Philip Conolly in 1820.
286. T 70/33 p. 53 (see n. 183): CO 201/5 f 36: CO 201/2 f 115v: Tench p. 71.
287. White p. 114.
288. There is no way to be quite sure of the actual number of convicts in the First Fleet: all records have discrepancies, omissions and duplications: Collins 108.
289. Meredith p. 50.
290. AO COD 17, Bench of Magistrates, Co. Cumberland pp. 83, 236-7.
291. CO 201/3 ff 71, 95v.
292. This was sometimes dangerous work. Samuel Davis and William Okey, two friends from Gloucestershire (see Cobley for both) were killed by natives while cutting rushes (Collins p. 24).
293. Collins p. 28.
294. AO COD 17 p. 95.
295. AO COD 17 p. 44. Frances Williams was capitally convicted in Mold, Flint County, Wales, for theft, sentence commuted to 7 years' transportation. Elizabeth Powley/Pulley was similarly sentenced and pardoned at Thetford, Norfolk. Anthony Rope was an Essex convict, guilty of stealing a large quantity of goods, sentenced to 7 years' transportation (see Cobley).
296. The escape of Mary Braund and William Bryant was sensational (see White p. 239 and ADB, Mary Bryant). The couple escaped on 28 March 1791 with their two young children and seven male convicts in a stolen government boat. William and his baby son died in Batavia after arrest at Koepang, Timor: on the way to the Cape of Good Hope, in custody, two of the convicts died and one fell overboard. The rest were embarked on HMS *Gorgon* for England: the older child died on the passage. The survivors were tried and ordered to Newgate to complete their sentences. Mary was released through James Boswell's interest, pardoned 2 May 1793 and returned to her family in Fowey, Cornwall.
297. Eliza Hughes, 10th child of Mathew Hughes and Mary, John's Small's second child, was born 1 Nov 1828, when her eldest sister Susannah (later to marry James Devlin) was 18. She married her cousin Robert (son of John Small's fourth child and second son William) in 1848—her grandfather still alive—and died in May 1921, aged almost 93. For James Devlin, see chapter 18 pt 2.
298. *Fishburn* log 29 Feb 1788.
299. Collins pp. 24, 34: White pp. 132, 134: *Dunkirk* (HO 42/8) nos 11, 29.
300. Collins p. 57, Clark pp. 96, 102, Collins pp. 23, 28, 33, 54.
301. Collins pp. 40, 46, 37.
302. CO 201/5 ff 281-83.
303. Bowes p. 70: AO COD 17 (see Note 290) pp. 210-17.
     283r PRO reel 3 AO COD 17 (see Note 290) pp. 210-17.
304. *Dunkirk* (HO 42/8) nos 10, 126: Corbett [Cormick], T 1/641, (*Ceres* Oct 1786-Jan 1787 no 205): White pp. 133, 142-43: Tench p. 145: Collins pp. 49, 70: AO COD 17 pp. 155-174: *Dunkirk* (HO 42/8) no 79. Sidaway had been a baker in the community, and died in 1809, "much respected" (*SG* 15 October 1809 p. 2).
305. CO 201/1 f 7: OBSP end 15 Jan sessions p. 328: *Lady Penrhyn* log 24 Apr, 8 Feb, 23 Oct, 31 May 1787.

306. Sailors among the convicts included John Boyle, William Thompson, John Hall, Thomas Crowder, James Dodding, Jacob Messiah/Massias, Hardwicke Richardson and many others (CO 201/9 f 265 ff). Francis Fowke was a former midshipman (OBSP 13 Dec 1786 p. 111). Bradley pp. 194-199. After the wreck of *Sirius* on 19 March 1790, Bradley, who had been first lieutenant, was left at Norfolk Island for 11 months, to his great disgust, returning to Sydney by *Supply* in February 1791, thence to England on the chartered Dutch ship *Waaksamheyd* (see *ADB*, Bradley).

307. Collins pp. 97, 99, 108. Plan to raise a special corps (NSW Corps) to replace marines, T 1/671 (no 998), WO to T, 20 May 1789. Major Francis Grose raised four companies by Sep: two more were raised in Feb-Mar 1791. The men went out to NSW in small detachments as guards on convict ships: Grose himself arrived in Feb 1792 (see *H NSW* vol 2 pp. 90-111) John Macarthur had arrived in June 1790 as lieutenant in the NSW Corps and almost at once began a career of speculation and self-enrichment that, with his arrogance and tenacity, soon brought him "crucial control of the colony's rudimentary resources" (*ADB* vol. 2 p. 154). This brought him into violent conflict with Governor Bligh after the latter's arrival in August 1806. Macarthur's reputation as the father of the Australian sheep industry is deserved, but his enterprise was undertaken for self-interest and not for the ultimate good of the colony. His life was a series of triumphs, quarrels and reverses: he died insane in April 1834.

308. Easty (a private marine) gives an account of the voyage home on *Atlantic*. CO 201/11 f 37v (Land Grants p. 21).

309. Collins pp. 285, 209.

310. CO 201/7 ff 111v-112.

311. CO 202/5 f 37 (author's italics).

312. CO 201/8 f 58.

313. Collins p. 40: Sydney Lands Office plan S.W. Sheet PH. Hunter's Hill Co Cumberland: *Dunkirk* (HO 42/8) nos 124, 111, 74, 90.

314. Callaghan married 19 Feb, Tyrell 6 Apr 1788, Hawkes 14 Feb 1790 (St Philip's Register MLD362 ff 14, 16, 20): Hatton married at Parramatta 18 Mar 1792 (*Sydney Cove* vol. 3 p. 227).

315. Devon Summer Assizes 1782 (Assi 23/8) for burglary: Court of Criminal Jurisdiction, 1788-1794, AO 5/1147A, pp. 117-133 (AO reel 2391).

316. See no. 284: Collins pp. 93-95, 103, 189: Land Grants p. 9. Other land grants for which references to primary sources have been given are listed in this book also.

317. CO 201/11 f 37: Land Grants pp. 21, 36, 43: OBSP 21 Apr 1784 p. 575. There were other men named Thomas Jones in the colony at this time, but in a group of grants given largely to First Fleeters, it is possible that this Thomas Jones was one of the two FF men of this name. Both were sent to Norfolk Island; Thomas Jones (1) in 1788 by the *Golden Grove*, and Thomas Jones (2) by *Sirius* in Mar 1790. Thomas Jones (1) left the island by *Kitty* (NIVB, male convicts no 5) and shows as a Kissing Point settler in 1806: GLRO/OB/SR 29 June 1785 no 59, 7 years to parts beyond the seas: OBSP 29 June 1785 pp. 908, 940: PC 2/131 pp. 494, 513: T 1/645 (*Justitia* Jan-Apr 1787 no 228): OBSP 26 May 1784 pp. 782, 863: Adm 51/4375 (*Alexander* log).

318. HO 42/7 f 110: parish registers, Kingston upon Thames RO.

319. Traill p. 196.

320. Macarthur, see n. 307 supra and *ADB*.

321. CO 201/14 ff 3, 364 r and v.

322. CO 201/12 f 107.

323. Collins p. 352: *SG* 13 Jan 1805.

324. CO 201/14 f 149v.

325. CO 201/13 f 218v: CO 201/14 f 10: *Star*, 28 July 1796.

326. Collins II p. 66.

327. CO 201/123 ff 615-619v. Williamson was temporary commissary in the absence of Palmer (see n. 337 infra and *ADB*).

328. Charles Peat reached London and was tried there after escaping from the *Mercury* (sometimes called the *Grand Duke of Tuscany*), OBSP 7 Jly 1784 p. 874) see n. 184 supra. After an earlier trial for highway robbery in 1781, he had been pardoned to

join the navy (HO 13/1 p. 143), where he served on *Prince Edward* for two months and then ran from *Belleisle* (Adm 36/8810, Adm 36/9417). He spent nine months in Newgate before dispatch to the *Censor* hulk, where he remained until 27 Feb 1787 to embark on *Scarborough* at Portsmouth (T 1/644, *Censor* Jan-Apr 1787). He married Hannah Mullens at Sydney 22 Feb 1788 (MLD362 f. 15).

329. CO 201/123 f 619v.
330. Collins II p. 84.
331. CO 201/25 f 163v: HO 10/37 f 76.
332. AO COD 76 Bench of Magistrates, Sydney p. 22: AO COD 77 pp. 75, 91.
333. AO COD 77 p. 105.
334. AO COD Convict Indents 1788-1799 pp. 75, 85.
335. See n. 329 supra.
336. NSW 1806 Muster, HO 10/37 ff 129, 143.
337. John Palmer had been purser on *Sirius* (muster, no 165). After the wreck of *Sirius*, Palmer was appointed commissary 2 Jun 1791 when Andrew Miller resigned because of ill-health (see *ADB*). He seems to have been well liked.
338. SG 16 Feb, 6 Apr 1806.
339. HO 10/37 ff 1, 76. The five men were Michael Dwyer, John Mernagh, Martin Burke, Hugh Byrne and Arthur Devlin (see chapter 18 pt 2 infra).
340. CO 201/14 f 15.
341. Mathew Hughes spelt his first name with one "t" (holograph letter MLA h 48/2).
342. AO 4/4427 COD 18 Return of Absolute and Conditional Pardons 1810-1819, p. 898 AP no 325: *Belfast Newsletter* 22-23 Jly 1796. No relevant Castlepollard and militia records have survived.
343. *Secret Committee* pp. 1-8, 76: *Encyc. Brit.* vol 16 p. 844: HO 100/17 ff 163-70, 1785: *DNB*, Grattan, vol XXII p. 421: *Sun* 20 Apr 1795, May 4, 9, 1795.
344. Pakenham pp. 31, 180.
345. *Sun* 29 Jan 1795.
346. Lewis, Seward (Loughbrickland).
347. Downshire Papers, Belfast PRO (D607/C/164A and 165). The Newry dateline of 10 November quoted in the *Star* was evidently a misprint.
348. *Hibernian* p. 95, 12 Nov, gives the murdered men's names as John Fell, Francis Mossman and — Gillmor.
349. WO/68/329 f 1.
350. *Star* 18 Aug 1796 (Dublin, 12 Aug).
351. The subsequent inquiry is found in CO 201/14 ff 31-53, also printed in HRA I, ii, pp. 36-67.
352. *HRA* I, ii, p. 64: Bateson p. 165.
353. Wesley, *Journal* vol 4, various pp.: LMS, pp. 114-116.
354. MLBT Box 49 op. cit. The missionary group, including Francis Oakes, had come to Sydney in 1798 after disagreements with Tahiti natives.
355. *HRNSW* vol. IV p. 75, Hassall to London Missionary Society 22 Apr 1800.
356. HO 10/37 NSW Muster, 1806 p. 144: St John's parish register, Parramatta: CP surrendered to be cancelled for an AP dated 31 Jan 1818 (AO COD 18). The first marriage was recorded as "on order of Lt. Gov. Foveaux" (NSW Corps officer who, promoted to Lt-colonel in 1802, was Lt-governor at Sydney until Col. Paterson, his senior officer, returned from Van Diemen's Land in January 1809: see *ADB* Foveaux, Paterson). Fulton arrived as an Irish political prisoner by the *Minerva* in January 1800, was given a CP in November, after departure of the Rev. Richard Johnson. He served on Norfolk Island and returned to Sydney in 1806. His loyalty to Bligh earned him suspension from Jan 1808 to Jan 1810 (see *ADB*).
357. *HRNSW* vol VII pp. 277 and 284.
358. This and following details are found in Blue Books CO 206/63-87 under the heading Education. His own letter (MLA h. 48/2 op. cit.) in 1841 gives his teaching service as eleven years at Kissing Point, three years at Windsor and 27 years at Richmond. The pension seems not to have been granted, and he was teaching until his death in 1845.
359. Will, Supreme Court, Registry of Probate, NSW Series I, 5574, made 23 Sep 1840, left goods valued at £300 to his wife (and children) while she lived and to his

youngest son, Henry Francis, the property, on her death. Henry Francis lived there as a farmer until shortly before his death in a home for the aged in 1930. This writer knew him as a very old man with distinctive "Small" features.

360. CO 201/39 ff 3-4.
361. *Saunders's News-Letter*, 14 Dec, 25 Nov 1803, *Dublin Journal* various dates 1799-1803: examinations taken after surrender, ISPO 620/13/168/3.
362. ISPO 620/11/38/8, 620/11/138/22.
363. Cullen Mss 9761 p. 21, Nat. Lib. of Ireland: Dickson p. 339.
364. Ronan p. 51: CO 201/24 f 401.
365. Cloney pp. 164-65.
366. CO 201/39 f 1: Plowden vol 1 p. 240.
367. *Land Grants* pp. 201-202 May 1809: NSW 1806 Muster HO 10/37 f 10.
368. HO 10/37 op. cit.: Arthur Devlin married Priscilla Squire 2 Apr 1806—St John's Parramatta.
369. *SG* 5 January 1806 p. 1.
370. Hogan, HO 10/37 f 76: Sheedy, CY ML 1337, *SG* 30 Nov 1806: Bigge Report CO 201/124 f 401 and tombstone (now at Bunnerong). *Gravestone Inscriptions Sydney Burial Ground* vol 1, p. 4.
371. Small family genealogy.
372. See contemporary maps of area and *Welcome to Willandra*, Ryde, N.S.W. (1980).
373. CO 201/5 f 8: Collins p. 63.
374. CO 201/13 f 24-26: CO 201/13 f 218-219v.
375. CO 201/15 f 60: sworn in 16 Aug 1808 (AO COD 231 Bench of Magistrates Co. Cumberland 1808-1810). "Inferior" constables would be those in the area serving under the district constables. The record of John Small's service and pension payments from 1 December 1825 until the year of his death in 1850 are found in Blue Books CO 206/69-92.
376. Governor Hunter's Instructions to Watchmen and Constables, 16 Nov 1796, ML CY Reel 365) and CO 201/13 ff 24-26.
377. ML A861 Hassall's Day Sales Book 1803-4: HO 10/37 NSW Muster, 1806 f 144.
378. See *ADB* Vol. 2 (Oakes) and text, n 379, 380 infra.
379. Coleshill parish register, Warwick, England.
380. Oakes *ADB* op cit: *SMH* 16 Sep 1850.
381. Evatt pp. 161-64.
382. *HRNSW* vol. VI pp. 802-804.
383. *HRNSW* vol VII pp. 575-576.
384. *DT*, Sydney, 23 Jan 1888.
385. *HRA* I, VII, p. 309: AO 4/1822 Colonial Secretary, Memorials re land, 1810 p. 295 and Land Grants p. 197: *HRA* I, vii, p. 439. A grant of 100 acres at Richmond Hill is listed for a John Small in *Land-Holders* p. 47: this and one of 30 acres at Bankstown may have been made to the other John Small (no date is given, but the lot numbers were 44 and 50 respectively).
386. AO 4/1822 p. 295 op. cit.
387. *SG* 11 Jly, 13 Nov. 1813: *SMH* 31 Jan 1883: *DT* 31 Jan 1888, from which following details also come.
388. *HRNSW* vol VII pp. 277-78: HO 10/23 Census of NSW (PRO Copy): CO 201/123 ff 425, 427.
389. *DT* 23 Jan 1888: Scottish RO, JC/11/46: AO 4/4427 Returns of Pardons 1810-1819 p. 692: *SG* 11 Feb 1815: *SMH* 17, 18 May 1853, 31 Aug 1841.
390. Devon Lent Assizes 1788 (Assi 23/8): HO 11/1 p. 191, Devon Summer Assizes 1791, (Assi 23/8).
391. CO 201/25 f 163: AO 4/1819 Coroner's Inquests, 1809-1822 pp. 503-13.
392. Small family genealogy: AO 2/8289 Reports of Inquests, 1796-Apr 1824 pp. 77-84 (Reel 2232-33) from which account of Mary's death is taken.
393. AO 4/1814 Colonial Secretary, Letters from John Oxley 1810-1826 ff 157-59, 2 Jan 1826: AO reel 2551 Original Householders Returns, Census of NSW 1828: Harris pp. 157-58.
394. Priscilla Devlin married Thomas Small 17 Dec 1821—St Philips, Sydney.
395. CO 206/92 Returns of the Colony (Blue Books) f 266. *DT* 23 Jan 1888.

396. *DT* 31 Jan 1888. Francis Nicholas Rossi, superintendent of police in NSW, retired in 1834 and lived on his Goulburn property until his death in 1851 (*ADB*).
397. Harris pp. 160-62: Meredith p. 52.
398. *SG* 6 Oct 1810.
399. For this and following paragraphs, Meredith pp. 34, 35, 38, 44, 47, 69.
400. Meredith op. cit.
401. ML A165,'8 Apr 1834. Though Mary's grave has not been discovered, an unknown skeleton has been found in the area and may be hers.
402. *DT* 23 Jan 1888.
403. Burials in the Parish of Hunter's Hill, 302 Vol. 36A. John died on 2 October and was buried on 5 Oct 1850 (NSW Registry BDM, Sydney). He was buried in St Anne's churchyard, Ryde, his tombstone later moved to the Field of Mars Cemetery.

GENEALOGICAL TABLE

JOHN SMALL (son of John and Rebecca Small)   MARY PARKER
Bapt. 11 Dec. 1761   Born c.1758
St Martins, Birmingham, War, ENG.   Died 4 April 1824
Died 2 Oct. 1850, Ryde, N.S.W., AUS.   Ryde, N.S.W., AUS.
Married 12 Oct. 1788, Sydney, N.S.W.

CHILDREN	MARRIED	SPOUSE	GRANDCHILDREN
1. REBECCA SMALL		FRANCIS OAKES	
b. 22 Sep. 1789 Sydney	27 Jan. 1806	b. 15 Apr. 1770	7 sons
d. 30 Jan. 1883 Parramatta.	Parramatta.	d. 15 Feb. 1844	7 daus.
2. MARY SMALL		MATHEW HUGHES	
b. 13 Dec. 1791 Sydney	17 Oct. 1808	b. c.1770	6 sons
d. 21 Nov. 1879 Richmond.	Parramatta.	d. 25 Dec. 1845	8 daus.
3. JOHN SMALL		ELIZABETH PATFIELD	
b. 21 Oct. 1794 Kissing Pt.	31 Oct. 1820	b. 6 Oct. 1802	4 sons
d. 15 Apr. 1883 Brushgrove.	Sydney.	d. 29 May 1870	7 daus.
4. WILLIAM SMALL		CHARLOTTE MELVILLE	
b. 14 Dec. 1796 Kissing Pt.	8 Aug. 1820	b. 21 Aug. 1803	8 sons
d. 9 Nov. 1891 Ryde.	Sydney.	d. 23 Sep. 1885	2 daus.
5. THOMAS SMALL		PRISCILLA DEVLIN (nee SQUIRE)	
b. 7 Jly. 1799 Kissing Pt.	17 Dec. 1821	b. 29 May 1792	4 sons
d. 12 Nov. 1863 Ryde.	Sydney.	d. 28 Jun. 1862	4 daus.
6. SARAH SMALL		GEORGE PATFIELD	
b. 27 Apr. 1804 Kissing Pt.	31 Oct. 1820	b. 10 Oct. 1797	5 sons
d.	Sydney.	d. 3 Jly. 1863	3 daus.
7. SAMUEL SMALL		RACHEL REBECCA BRADLEY	
b. 27 Apr. 1804 Kissing Pt.	14 Oct. 1833	b. 27 Mar. 1811	6 sons
d. 18 Apr. 1889 Ryde.	Ryde.	d. 19 Feb. 1891	3 daus.

Research: B. M. Bridle, F. R. Fleming, M. Gillen, B. I. M. Hooke, W. J. Pollock.

BIBLIOGRAPHY.

Bibliography, with key abbreviations: All journals read in manuscript or first editions, but quotations for convenience refer to pages in any later reprint.

Actas: Actas Capitulares del Ayuntamiento de la Habana trasuntadas de 1º de enerio de 1782 a 22 de diciembre de 1783: Havana City Museum.

ADB: *Australian Dictionary of Biography, 1788-1850.*

Adm: Admiralty papers, PRO London.

Adm (NMM):   Ådmiralty papers, National Maritime Museum, Greenwich.

Alexander (transport): log, Adm 51/4375 (PRO London).

Ancell: *Journal of the blockade and siege of Gibraltar from ... 1669 to ...* 1783, Samuel Ancell, 3rd edn 1786.

AO: Archives Office of NSW, Sydney.

AP: Absolute pardon.

AR: *Annual Register,* various years.

Assi: Assize records, PRO, London.

Augusta (HMS):   muster Adm 36/7709, log (captain's) Adm 51/4120, paybook Adm 34/76B

Ayton: *A Voyage around Britain ... in 1813,* Richard Ayton, London 1814.

Barry: *Gallant John Barry,* W. B. Clark, NY 1938.

Bateson: *The Convict Ships,* Charles Bateson 1969.

Bayley: Thomas Butterworth Bayley, acting magistrate Lancashire, letters in HO 42/6, PRO, London.

BB: Botany Bay.

Bedford: Archives of the Duke of Bedford, London.

Belisarius (HMS):   muster Adm 36/9592, logs 51/97, 52/2161.

Bigge, Commissioner John Thomas (1780-1843):
                    Report 1822 CO 201/114-117 PRO reels 104-105.
                    Appendix: (Documents; Evidences; Returns; Memorials; Correspondence; Despatches 1819-1823) CO 201/118-142.

Birmingham Gazette: various years, esp. 1783, 1784, 1785.

BL: British Library, London.

Blagden: *Banks Corresp.* Kew, B.C.I f 203, 10 Sep 1785.

Blue Books: CO 206/63-145, PRO, London.

Blumberg: RM Records 1755-92, compiled by Gen. Sir H. E. Blumberg (typescript) RM Museum, Portsmouth.

Book of Trades, London 1820.

Borrowdale storeship: log Adm 51/4375, PRO London.

Bowes: *The Journal of Arthur Bowes Smyth* (ML Mss 995): BL Add Mss 47,966: published, ed. Fidlon and Ryan, Sydney 1979. He came on *Lady Penrhyn.*

Bradley: *A Voyage to New South Wales,* William Bradley (facsimile copy from original manuscript), Ure Smith Sydney 1969.

Carmichael: Ryde 1790-1926, ed. R. Carmichael, 1926.

Caton (HMS):	muster, Adm 36/9582, logs Adm 51/170, 52/1649, paybook, adm 34/214.
Charlotte (transport):	log Adm 51/4375.
Clark:	*Journal and Letters of Lt. Ralph Clark 1787-1792* (ML/C219, C220) published 1981, ed. Fidlon and Ryan. He came on *Friendship*.
Cloney:	*Personal narrative of the transactions of the County of Wexford during 1798*, Thomas Cloney, Dublin 1832.
CO:	Colonial Office papers, PRO London.
Cobley:	*Crimes of the First Fleet Convicts*, John Cobley, Sydney 1970.
Cockburn:	*History of English Assizes 1558-1714*, London 1972.
Cole/Postgate:	*The Common People*, G. D. H. Cole and Raymone Postgate, London, 1966.
Colledge:	*Ships of the Royal Navy* (Vol. 1), J. J. Colledge, Newton Abbot, 1969.
Collins:	*Account of the English Colony in New South Wales*, David Collins, 1798: reprinted as Vol 1, ed. Brian H. Fletcher, Sydney 1975.
Collins 2:	Vol. 2, 1802, reprinted as Vol. 2, 1975, ed. Brian H. Fletcher.
Collins, Gen.:	*General Collins' Order Book* (RM Museum, Portsmouth).
Companion:	*Oxford Companion to Ships and the Sea*, ed. P. Kemp, 1979 edn.
Cottu:	*On the Administration of Justice in England*, Charles Cottu, 1822.
CP:	Conditional pardon.
Crowe:	*St. Martin's-in-the-Bull Ring*, Rev. Philip Crowe, 1975.
Cullen:	*Life of Ann Devlin*, Luke Cullen, Mss 9761, National Library of Ireland.
Curwen:	*Journal and Letters of the late Samuel Curwen . . . an American refugee . . . from 1775 to 1784*, London 1842.
Dent:	*Old and New Birmingham*, R. H. Dent 1879.
Devon Assizes:	Assi 23/8, PRO, London.
Devon RO:	Devon Record Office.
Diamond (HMS):	muster Adm 36/9216, logs Adm 51/245, 52/2249, paybook Adm 34/259.
Dickson:	*Life of Michael Dwyer*, Charles Dickson, Dublin 1944.
Directories:	*Kent's* London 1785, 1786, 1788, 1937: *Merchants' and tradesmen* London 1787: *Lowndes* London 1784: *Sands'* Sydney various years: *Boyle's* Court Guide, London;: *Wakefield's* General Directory, London: *Bailey's* British Directory 1784: *Birmingham Directory* 1781.
DNB:	*Dictionary of National Biography.*
Dobie:	*History of the United Parishes of St Giles in the Fields and St George's, Bloomsbury*, Rowland Dobie, London 1829.
Downshire:	Downshire Papers, PRO Belfast.
DT:	*Daily Telegraph*, Sydney, January 1888.
Dublin (HMS):	muster Adm 36/8850, Log, Adm 52/1703, paybook Adm 34/238.
Dugan:	*The Great Mutiny*, J. Dugan 1967 (Signet edn).
Dunkirk:	(HO 42/8): Returns Apr-Jne 1786.
E:	Exchequer papers, PRO London.
Eagle (HMS):	muster Adm 36/8334, log 51/293, paybook Adm 34/272.
Easty:	*Memorandum . . . of a Voyage from England to Botany Bay 1787-93:* John Easty, Sydney 1965. John Easty was on the *Scarborough* and his journal includes his stay in N.S.W. and his return home on the *Atlantic*.
E.F.P.:	*Exeter Flying Post:* various dates.
Encyc. Brit:	*Encyclopaedia Britannica*, 1958 see n p. 12 text.
Europe (HMS):	muster Adm 36/9517, logs Adm 51/324, 52/2288, paybook Adm 34/289.

Evatt:	*The Rum Rebellion*, H. V. Evatt, Sydney (1978 edn.).
Falconer:	*Falconer's Marine Dictionary: An Universal Dictionary of the Marine*, William Falconer, London 1780.
First Fleet:	see alphabetical listing for *Alexander, Borrowdale, Charlotte, Fishburn, Friendship, Golden Grove, Lady Penrhyn, Prince of Wales, Scarborough, Sirius (HMS), Supply (HMS).*
Fishburn (storeship):	log Adm 51/4375, PRO London.
FO:	Foreign Office papers, PRO London.
Foss:	*Biographical Dictionary of the Judges of England*, London, 4 vols 1848-64.
FP:	Free pardon.
Friendship transport:	log Adm 51/4376, PRO London.
George, D.:	*London life in the 18th century*, D. George, Harper Torchbooks 1965.
Gibraltar:	*A description of Gibraltar*, London 1782 (Anon.).
Gillespie:	*Historical review of the RM Corps to 1803*, Alexander Gillespie, Birmingham 1803.
GLRO:	Greater London Record Office.
GM:	*Gentleman's Magazine*, various years.
Golden Grove storeship:	log Adm 51/4376.
Grover:	*Short History of the Marines*, Col. G. W. M. Grover, 1959.
Halévy:	*History of the English people in 1815*, Eric Halévy, Pelican edn. 3 vols.
Harris:	*Settlers and Convicts*, or Recollections of sixteen years' labour in the Australian Backwoods, London 1847.
Hibernian:	*Walker's Hibernian Magazine*, July 1796.
Hist. NSW:	*History of New South Wales*, ed. G. B. Barton, Vol. 1 (1783-89).
HNSW:	*History of New South Wales*, Alexander Britton, ed. F. M. Bladen, 1894 vol 2.
HO:	Home Office papers, PRO, London.
Hobart Gazette:	vol 1 (1816) . . . . .
Honduras:	*Archives of British Honduras*, vol 1, ed. Sir John Alder Burdon, London 1931.
Horwood:	Plan of London Westminster Southwark & Parts Adjoining 1792-1799 (Guildhall Library London).
Hotham:	Hotham Papers, Brynmor Jones Library, University of Hull.
Howard:	*An Account of Prisons, House of Correction, and Hospitals, in London and Westminster*, London 1789.
	State of Prisons in England and Wales, 1789, 1792 edns.
HRA:	*Historical Records of Australia*, ed. F. Watson.
HRNSW:	*Historical Records of New South Wales*, ed. F. M. Baden 1901, various volumes.
Hunter:	*An Historical Journal of events at Sydney and at sea.* John Hunter, London 1793: reprinted 1968 Sydney, ed. J. Bach.
Hutton:	*History of Birmingham*, Wm Hutton, various editions from 1781.
Ilive:	*Reasons . . . for the reformation of the House of Correction in Clerkenwell*, Jacob Ilive London 1757.
Ind.:	Indictment.
IOR:	India Office Records, London.
Ireland:	*Parliamentary Gazette of Ireland* 1844-45 (1846).
ISPO:	Irish State Paper Office, Dublin.
Jebb:	*Thoughts on . . . Prisons*, London 1786.
Jenkins:	*History of Exeter*, A. Jenkins, Exeter 1806.
Jupiter (HMS):	logs Adm 51/482, 52/4365.
King:	*Journal of Philip Gidley King, Lieutenant, R.N. 1787-1790*, ed. Fidlon and Ryan, Sydney 1980.

Lady Penrhyn transport:	log Adm 51/4376, PRO London.
Land Grants 1788-1809:	ed. R. J. Ryan, Sydney 1974.
Land-Holders:	*An Accurate List of . . . Land-Holders in . . . New South Wales,* London 1814, corrected to 1813.
Langford:	*A century of Birmingham life . . . from 1741 to 1841,* J. A. Langford, 2 vols, 1868.
Lewis:	*Topographical Dictionary of Ireland,* S. Lewis, London 1837, 1842.
Little:	*Birmingham Buildings,* Bryan Little, 1971.
Lively (HMS):	muster Adm 36.10138, logs Adm 51/526, 52/1835, paybook, Adm 34/473.
Lloyd:	*The British Seaman,* Christopher Lloyd, London 1968 (Paladin edn 1970).
Lloyd's List:	various years.
Lloyd's Register:	various years.
LMS:	London Missionary Society Mss, William Henry to the Society 29 August 1799, ML Bonwick Transcripts Box 49.
Logs:	See under ships' names: Captains' logs, Adm class 36, masters' logs Adm class 52, PRO London.
Madan:	*Thoughts on Executive Justice,* Martin Madan: by A Sincere Well-Wisher to the Public. London 1785.
Mann:	*History of Gibraltar and its Sieges,* J. H. Mann, London 1870.
Marshall:	*Passages from the diary of Christopher Marshall,* 1774-77, ed. Wm. Duane 1839-49.
Masefield:	*Sea Life in Nelson's Time,* John Masefield, London 1905.
Massachusetts:	*Acts . . . of the Province of Massachusetts Bay . . . Vol. XX,* 1777-8, Boston 1918.
Medway (HMS):	muster Adm 36/8855-8, logs Adm 51/595, 52/2400, paybook Adm 34/510.
Meredith:	*Notes and sketches of New South Wales,* Louisa Anne (Mrs Charles) Meredith, London 1844: reprinted Sydney 1973.
ML:	Mitchell Library, Sydney NSW.
Modbury:	Diaries of John Andrews, Devon RO.
Murray:	*Remarks on the situation of the poor in the metropolis . . .* Y. A. Murray, London 1801.
NIVB:	Norfolk Island Victualling Book, 1792-1796, MLA 1958 (AO Reel 2747).
NMM:	National Maritime Museum, Greenwich.
NSW:	New South Wales.
OBSP:	*Old Bailey Sessions Papers,* Guildhall, London.
Observations:	*Observations, Explanations &c. Relating to the Establishment, most humbly proposed, for His MAJESTY's Marine Forces,* Anon, London [1757].
OED:	*Oxford English Dictionary.*
Offley:	*The Assize Ball,* Mrs Offley, Dorchester 1820.
Onderdonk:	*British prisons and prison ships at New York,* Henry Onderdonk, New York, 1849.
Pakenham:	*The Year of Liberty,* Thomas Pakenham, Panther 1972.
Parish Registers:	St George's, Bloomsbury, London: Kingston upon Thames RO: Stoke Damerel, Devon RO: St Budeaux, Devon RO: St Martin's, St. Philip's, Birmingham Ref. Library: St Philip's, Sydney (ML).
Parl. Gaz:	*Parliamentary Gazette of Ireland,* 1844-5, vol 2.
Pasley:	*Sea Journals, Thomas Pasley,* ed. Sir R. Pasley, London 1931.
PC:	Privy Council records, PRO London.
PCOM:	Prison Commission records, PRO London.

Perseus (HMS):	muster Adm 36/10572, logs Adm 51/585, 52/2429, paybook Adm 34/611.
PH:	*Parliamentary History, BL* London.
Phillip:	*The Voyage of Governor Phillip to Botany Bay,* London 1789, to which are added the Journals of Lts. Shortland, Watts, Ball and Capt. Marshall, London 1789. Reprinted 1970 annotated by J. J. Auchmuchty.
Pitcairn-Jones:	Sea Officers List 1600-1815, PRO London.
PJ:	Port Jackson.
Plowden:	*History of Ireland 1801-10,* Frances Plowden 1811, 3 vols.
Port Admiral:	*The Port Admiral,* vol 1 (Anon.).
Postgate:	See Cole.
PP:	*Parliamentary Papers,* London (BL London).
PR:	*Parliamentary Register,* London (BL London).
Prince of Wales transport:	log Adm 51/4376, PRO London.
PRO:	Public Record Office, London.
PRO (PRO):	PRO class, papers donated to PRO London.
Reports:	Reports and Committees, House of Commons, London.
RM Mus:	Royal Marines Museum, Portsmouth.
RO:	Record Office.
Ronan:	*Resurgent Wicklow,* Myles Ronan 1947.
Royal George (HMS):	*Narrative of the loss of the Royal George at Spithead* August 1782, London 1840. (Anon.).
Rumsey:	*The Pioneers of Sydney Cove,* H. J. Rumsey, Sydney 1937.
SAG:	Society of Australian Genealogists, Sydney.
St. Fond:	Journey through England . . . in 1784. Faugas de St Fond, ed. Sir A. Geikie 1907.
St George's:	Parish registers of St George's Bloomsbury (GLRO).
Scarborough transport:	log Adm 51/4376 (PRO).
Scot. RO:	Scottish Record Office, Edinburgh.
Scott:	*Remarks on a passage to Botany Bay,* James Scott, Sydney 1963. He was on *Prince of Wales.*
Secret Committee:	Report from the Secret Committee of the House of Commons, Dublin, 1798.
Sermons:	Clayton, John (preached at the Lancaster Assize 1736, Rom. 13 pt v. 4: Journal and Letters of late S. Curwen . . . an American refugee . . . from 1775 to 1784, 30 Jly 1776, Prov. 14, 34: Sermon preached in . . . York 26 Mar 1824, Rev. Sydney Smith.
Seward:	*Topographia Hibernica,* Wm. Seward, 1795.
SG:	*Sydney Gazette.*
Sincere Well-Wisher:	see Madan.
Sirius (HMS):	muster Adm 36/10978, logs Adm 51/832A, 52/2516.
Slater:	*Slater's Topography of Ireland* 1826.
Small:	"Dr William Small" (*The Engineer,* 8 Mar 1957), London, A. K. Bruce.
Small family genealogy:	prepared by Mrs B. I. M. Hooke and Committee, John Small & Mary Parker Family Association, from records in the Registry B.D.M., Sydney.
SMH:	*Sydney Morning Herald.*
Smith:	*Sermon . . . in the cathedral of St Peter, York,* 26 Mar 1824, Acts 23:3, Rev. Sydney Smith.
Smith, W.:	*State of the gaols in London, Westminster and Borough of Southwark . . .*[and] Account of the present state of convicts sentenced to hard labour on board the Justitia in the River Thames, William Smith MD, London 1776.

Smyth:	See Bowes Smyth.
Southwell:	Letters, BL Add Mss 16,381.
SP:	State Papers, PRO London.
SPO Ireland:	State Paper Office, Dublin.
Star:	London, various years.
Statutes:	Acts of Parliament, Great Britain.
Stubbs:	*Crown Circuit Companion*, Stubbs & Talmash, 1799 edn and others (published since 1762).
Student:	*Proposals . . . for preventing . . . executions and exportations of convicts*, Student in Politics, London 1754.
Sun:	London, various years.
Supply (HMS):	Muster Adm 36/10981, log Adm 52/2557.
SVO:	Supernumeraries for victuals only (on ships).
Sydney Cove:	*Sydney Cove 1788, Sydney Cove 1789-1798, Sydney Cove 1791-1792, Sydney Cove 1793-1795*, John Cobley, Sydney 1962-1983.
T:	Treasurery papers, PRO London.
Talbot:	*Life and surprising adventures of Capt. Talbot*, London 1803.
Taylor/Skinner:	*The Roads of Ireland*, Taylor & Skinner.
Tench:	*Narrative of the Expedition to Botany Bay and a Complete Account of the Settlement at PJ*, 1793: reprinted 1979, annotated by L. F. Fitzhardinge, as *Sydney's First Four Years:* Captain Watkin Tench.
Traill:	*The Backwoods of Canada:* Letters from the wife of an emigrant officer, Catherine Parr Traill, 1836 edn.
Treatise:	Treatise on Procedure, Western Circuit, c. 1807, PRO/Assi 24/19(2).
Walker:	*Walker's Hibernian Magazine*, Jly 1796.
White:	*Journal of a Voyage to New South Wales*, John White, London 1790, reprinted 1962 Sydney, ed. Alec H. Chisholm.
Whitehall EP:	*Whitehall Evening Post*, London.
Wilkie:	"Recollections of the early life of a sailor", ed. Lt-Col Wilkie, (*United Service Magazine* 1846 pt. 3).
Willan:	*The Diseases in London*, Robert Willan, London 1801.
WO:	War Office papers, PRO, London.
Woodforde:	*Diary of a Country Parson*, James Woodforde, London 1978, OUP paperback edn.
Worgan:	*Journal of a First Fleet Surgeon* (MLB1463), George Bouchier Worgan, published 1978, LAH, Sydney.
Young:	*Six months Tour through the North of England*, 4 vols 1770, Arthur Young, London.
Ziegler:	*King William IV*,Philip Ziegler, London 1971.

SELECT LIST OF SUPPLEMENTARY SOURCES

Adderley, C. B.: *Transportation not necessary* . . . London 1851.
Adshead, J. *Prisons and Prisoners*, London 1845.
Anon., *The Progress of the War*, London 1740.
Army List, various years.
Australian Encyclopaedia, various vols.
Balfour, J. O., *A Sketch of New South Wales*, London 1845.
Barney, J., *Biographical Memoirs*, ed. Mary Barney, Boston 1837.
Barrington, G., *History of New Holland . . . [and] . . . discourse on Banishment by Rt. Hon. W. Eden*, London 1787 and 1808.
Beaglehole, J. C., *Life of Captain James Cook*, London 1974.
Beames, T., *The Rookeries of London*, 1850.
Bennett, G., *Wanderings in New South Wales*, 2 vols. London 1832-34.
Benson, M. K. & J. E., *St. Anne's, Ryde*, 1976.
Biden, W. D., *History and antiquities, Kingston upon Thames*, London 1852.
Blackstone, W., *Commentaries on the Laws of England*, Oxford 1765 and 1783 (last edn. annotated by Blackstone).
Blainey, G., *The Tyranny of Distance*, Sydney 1968.
Blizard, Dr. W., *Desultory Reflections on Police*, London 1785.
Bracken, C. W., *History of Plymouth*, 1934.
Branch-Johnson, W., *The English prison hulks*, 1957.
Broadbridge, S. R., *The Birmingham Canal*, 1974.
Bunce, J. T., *History of Old St Martin's*, Birmingham 1875.
Byrne, M., *Some Notes of an Irish Exile of 1798*, Dublin 1910.
Carlisle, —, *Topographical dictionary of Ireland*, 1810.
Chesterton, G., *Revelations of Prison Life*, 2 vols, London 1856.
Clinton, Lt-Gen. Sir H., *Narrative* . . . 1783.
Clowes, Sir W. L., *The Royal Navy*, 7 vols, London, 1897-1903.
Cobley, J., *Crimes of the First Fleet Convicts*, 1970.
Cobley, J., *Sydney Cove*, 4 vols, Sydney, 1962-83.
Coghlan, T. A., *Wealth and Progress of New South Wales*, 1891.
Colquhoun, P., *The Police of the Metropolis*, London 1800.
Coldham, P. W., *English convicts in colonial America*, vol. 1, New Orleans 1974.
Commons Journals, relevant years.
Crooks, J. J., *Records relating to the Gold Coast settlements, 1756-1874*, Dublin 1923.
Cunningham, P., *Two years in New South Wales*, 2 vols, London 1827.
Currey, C. H., *Transportation, escape and pardoning of Mary Bryant*, Sydney 1963.
Dalrymple, A., *Serious Admonition . . . on the intended Thief-Colony at Botany Bay*, London 1786.
Dent, R. K., *Old and New Birmingham*, Birmingham 1879.
Dibdin, Charles, *Royal Circus epitomized*, London 1784.
Dixon, H., *The London Prisons*, London 1850.
Dyer, G., *Complaints of the poor*, London 1793.

Eden, Sir F. M., *State of the Poor*, 2 vols, London 1797.

Ellis, M. H., *Lachlan Macquarie*, Sydney, 1952.

Fielding, Henry, *Enquiry into the causes of the late increase of robbers*, London 1751.

Flanagan, R., *History of New South Wales*, 2 vols, London 1838-61.

Gardner, J. A., *Above and Under Hatches*, ed. C. C. Lloyd, London.

Geeves, P., *A Place of Pioneers*, Sydney, 1970.

George, M. D., *London life in the eighteenth century*, London, 1925.

Gilbert, T., *Voyage from NSW to Canton*, London 1789.

Gladstone, H. S., *Thomas Watling, Limner of Dumfries*, Dumfries 1938.

Gordon, C.,*The Old Bailey & Newgate*, London 1902.

Gore, M., *Dwellings of the Poor . . .* London 1851.

Gouger, R., *A letter from Sydney*, ed. R. Gouger, London 1829.

Griffiths, A., *Chronicles of Newgate*, 2 vols, London 1884.

Hall, R. S., *State of NSW in Dec. 1830*, London 1831.

Hanway, J., *Distributive Justice and Mercy*, London 1781.

Hanway, J., *Earnest appeal for . . . the children of the poor*, London 1766.

Harris, P., *Historical Record of the Royal Marines*, London 1845.

Havana: *Description of the Spanish Islands and Settlements on the coast of the West Indies*, T. Jefferys, 1774.

    Standard Guide to Cuba, 1905.

    The Island of Cuba, A. Humboldt, NY 1856.

    History of Cuba, M. M. Ballou, 1854.

    Letters from Havanna during 1820, London 1821.

    Encyclopaedia Americana.

Hay, D., *Albion's Fatal Tree* (with P. Linebaugh, J. G. Rule, E. P. Thompson and C. Winslow), London 1975.

Hibbert, C., *The Roots of Evil*, London 1963.

Hinde, R. S. E., *The British Penal System 1773-1950*, London 1951.

Holt, J., *Memoirs*, ed. T. C. Croker, 2 vols, London 1838.

Hoskins, W. G., *Old Exeter*, London 1952.

Ignatieff, M., *A Just measure of pain*, London 1978.

Jebb, J., *Thoughts on . . . Prisons*, London 1786.

Jewett, L., *History of Plymouth*, London 1873.

Journal of the Royal Australian Historical Society, Sydney, various vols.

Kennedy, G., *Bligh*, London 1978.

Kiernan, T. M., *Irish Exiles in Australia*, Dublin 1954.

Land Tax Assessment Books, parish of St George's, Bloomsbury, GLRO (Middlesex), various years.

Lang, J. D., *Historical and statistical account of NSW*, 2 vols, 1852.

Lettsom, J. C., *. . . The Prison of Newgate*, London 1960.

Lewis, M., *A Social history of the Navy*, London 1960.

Lloyd's List, relevant years.

Lloyd's Register, relevant years.

Lords' Journals, relevant years.

Lovett, R., *History of the London Missionary Society 1795-1895*, 2 vols, London 1899.

Lycett, J.,*Views in Australia*, London 1824.

McAnally, Sir H., *The Irish Militia 1793-1816*, London 1949.

Mackaness, G., *Life of . . . William Bligh*, 2 vols, Sydney 1931.

Malton, T., *Picturesque tour through . . . London and Westminster*, 2 vols 1792.

Mann, D. D., *Present picture of NSW*, London 1811.

Marsden, S., *Letters and Journals 1765-1838*, ed. J. Rawson, Dunedin, 1932.

Marshall, D., *The English poor*, London 1926.

Martin, G., *The Founding of Australia*, ed. G. Martin, Sydney 1970.

Maxwell, C., *Country and Town in Ireland under the Georges*, 1940.

Mayhew, H. and Binny, J., *The Criminal Prisons of London*, London 1862.

Meister, H., *Letters . . . during a residence in England*, London 1799.

Montagu, B., *Opinions . . . upon the punishment of death*, London 1809.

Moritz, C. P., *Travels . . . in England in 1782*, London 1795.
Musgrave, Sir R., *Memoirs of the different rebellions in Ireland*, 1801.
Navy List, various years.
Nield, J., *State of prisons in England, Scotland and Wales*, London 1812.
Noorthouck, J., *New History of London . . . Westminster and Southwark*, London 1773.
O'Brien, E., *Foundation of Australia*, London 1937.
Officer, *An authentic . . . narrative of the late expedition to Botany Bay . . .* London 1789.
Oldham, W., Administration of the system of transportation of British convicts 1763-1793, unpublished thesis, Univ. of London 1933.
Partridge, Col. S. G., *Prisoner's Progress*, London 1935.
Paul, Sir G., . . . *The Defects of Prisons*, London 1784.
Paul, Sir G., *Proceedings of the Grand Juries . . . of Gloucester*, London 1808.
Pemberton, C. R., *Autobiography of Pel Verjuice*, ed. E. Partridge, London 1929.
Phillips, H., *Mid-Georgian London*, London 1964.
Pinks, W. J., *History of Clerkenwell*, ed. E. J. Wood, London 1881.
Preston, W., *An historical account of the colony of N.S.W.*, London 1821.
Pyne, W. H., *Microcosm . . . of arts, agriculture, manufactures etc. of Great Britain*, vol 1, London 1806.
Radzinowicz, Leon, *History of English criminal law*, London 1948.
Regulations . . . for H.M.'s service at sea, London 1790 and 1808.
Rienits, R. and T., *Early Artists of Australia*, Sydney 1963.
Robinson, W., *Nautical Economy . . . by a sailor . . . Jack Nasty-face*, London 1836.
Robson, L. L., *The Convict Settlers of Australia*, Melbourne 1965.
Romilly, Sir S., *Observations on the Criminal Law . . .* London 1810.
Ronan, M. V., *Irish martyrs of the penal laws*, 1935.
Royal Marines, *Instructions . . . re pay*, London 1806.
Rudé, G., *Crime and Punishment*, London 1978.
Ruffhead, Owen, *The Statutes at Large*, London 1769.
Rumbelow, D., *I spy Blue*, London 1971.
Rumsey, H. J., *The Pioneers of Sydney Cove*, Sydney 1937.
Rutter, O., *The First Fleet*, London 1937.
Sessions Books, Corporation of London RO.
Shaw, A. G. L., *Convicts and the Colonies*, London 1966.
Sinclair, Sir J., *History of the Public Revenue of the British Empire*, vol 2, London 1803.
Slater's *Topography of Ireland*, 1806.
Smith, A. E., "The transportation of convicts to the American Colonies in the 17th century" (*American Historical Review* vol. 39, 1934).
Smith, A. E., *Colonists in bondage*, Univ. of N. Carolina, 1947.
Stephen, Sir J. F., *General view of the criminal laws of England*, London 1863.
Storer and Cromwell, *History of Clerkenwell*, 2 vols, London 1828.
Teeling, C. H., *Personal Narrative of the "Irish Rebellion" of 1798*, London 1828.
Tuckey, J. H., *Account of a voyage to establish a colony at Port Phillip*, London 1805.
Upton, C., *The siege of Gibraltar*, London 1781.
Walling, R. J., *Story of Plymouth*, 1950.
Watling, T., *Letters from an exile . . .* 1791.
Wedderburn, A., *Observations on the state of English prisons*, London 1793.
Wentworth, W. C., *Statistical Historical and Political Description of NSW*, London 1820.
Wesley, *Journal*, 4 vols, London 1902.
Worth, R. N., *History of Plymouth*, Plymouth 1890.
Zouch, H., *Observations on the bill . . . to punish . . . certain offenders*, London 1779.
Zouch, H., *Hints respecting the public police*, London 1786.

CORRIGENDA

Publication of this book in October 1985 has brought to light (as always happens) new information that either corrects or augments what had to that point been found. I find this gratifying: it is only by this kind of development that historical distortion can be corrected. I am therefore happy to be able to add a note to this edition.

On the 200th anniversary of the marriage of John Small and Mary Parker it is good to discover that John Small's parents are no longer a mystery, discovered already by the late Bruce Rudd, one of their descendants. John Small married Rebecca Ashford at Harborne, Staffordshire, near Birmingham, on 4 April 1749 (*The Bruce Rudd Story*, Yvonne Browning, 1986).

Also, publication of the portrait "believed to be John Small" has solved the puzzle of the identity of the sitter. His great-granddaughter Enid Dillon was able to clear up the mystery. He was John McGregor, who did, in fact, have a collateral connection with the Smalls; his granddaughter Johanna married John Small's grandson James, son of John Small Junior.

And later research has discovered that the original John Small was not, after all, the very last survivor of the First Fleeters, though numbered among these long-lived persons. That distinction belongs to Elizabeth King (Thackery) 1856. Although John Small does appear to be the last of the male convicts.

It is only a pity that time ran out before the later research could be completed in time for the book.

Mollie Gillen
London 1988

Record of enlistment of both John Smalls in the Marine Corps, John Small (1) of Newry in 1780, John Small (2) Birmingham, in 1781.

		Age	Height	County	Place		Town
1779 Aug.¹ 18	Ebenezer Rawles	17	5.1½	Somerset	Ashgate		Bath
" 1	Robert Bethel	25	5.7½	Kent	Northam		Chester
" 25	John Nichols	45	5.6	York	Miller		Aydle
8ᵗʰ May 3	Edward Clewe						
1779 March 13	John Witham	22	5.6½	Suffolk	Yoxbrook		Ipswich
" Apr 6	Wm Woodhead	28	5.3¼	Nottingham	Nottingham	St Mary's	Nott.
" May 1	Mich O'Brien	23	5.4½	Wexford	Enniscorthy		Carnelough on
" 6	David Carroll	21	5.5½	Tipperary	M Crarbey		Carlow
" 20	Path. Wardlow	20	5.11½	Cork	Dunvea		Carlow
" 7	Richard Davis	18	5.5	Worcester	Moseley		Worcester
June 6	Thomas Margan	15	5.2¾	Gloucester	Vineard		Sudbury
" August 23	John Small (1)	18	5.8	Down	Newry		Dublin
1780 Sep 13	James Sandford	38	5.4½	Worcester	Broadway		Worcester
1781 May 7	Rich.ᵈ Morris (1)	9		Devon	Dock	Stoke Damerell	Plym
" Jan.ʸ 31	Wm Edwards	16	5.3	Surry	Mitcham	Stoke	Bxbridge
" Ap.ˡ 12	Evan Roberts	47	5.7½	Denbigh	Derwen		Chester
" April 16	John Small (2)	19	5.6	Warwick	Birmingham		Birmingham
" 26	Path Curron	21	5.7½	Carlow	Carlow		Carlow
" July 1	Hugh Quail	24	5.3¼	Wexford	Curnew		Dublin
" " 17	Jacob Reeves	23	5.5	Somerset	Bristol	Amble	Somer
" Oct.ʳ 4	James Bott	22	5.6½	Wilts	Lockington		Chester
" Aug.ᵈ 10	John Griffis	47	5.5¾	Stafford	Bloxwich		Birming
" " 11	John Stewart	43	5.6½	Antrim	Belfast		Ballymena
1782 Jan.ʸ 3	John Collins (2)	43	5.5	Somerset	Simsbury		Green
" " 17	John Clink	26	5.8½	ditto	West Chinick		Wells
" Feb.ʸ 11	Thomas Sivage	18	5.8½	Gloucester	Tedbury		Northum
" March 6	Richard Harris (2)	21	5.9½	Hereford	Bromyard		Bromyard
" " 10	Joseph Lewis	17	5.2¾	Gloucester	Tewksbury	Forthampton	Tewksbury
" " 21	George Hill	34	5.6½	Stafford	Tipton Green		Bristol
" May 22	Richard Turner	19	5.7½	Worcester	Sandbury		Worcester
" June 15	Rob.ᵗ or Jn.ᵒ Alexander	20	5.6¾	Northumberland	Shields		Chudleig
" May 21	James Kennedy	20	5.6	Tipperary	Burros O'Kane		Carrick on
" June 12	Daniel Pearce	18	5.5¾	Limerick	Limerick		ditto
" July 1	John Lane	27	5.4½	Kildare	Ballyshannon		Waterford
	Daniel Mahoney	44	5.6¾	Cork	Bandon		Cork
1782 June 22	John Baptist	24	5.7	Flanders	Ostend		Plymouth
" May 20	Rich.ᵈ Hutchenson	23	5.3	Lancashire	Prestage		Manchest

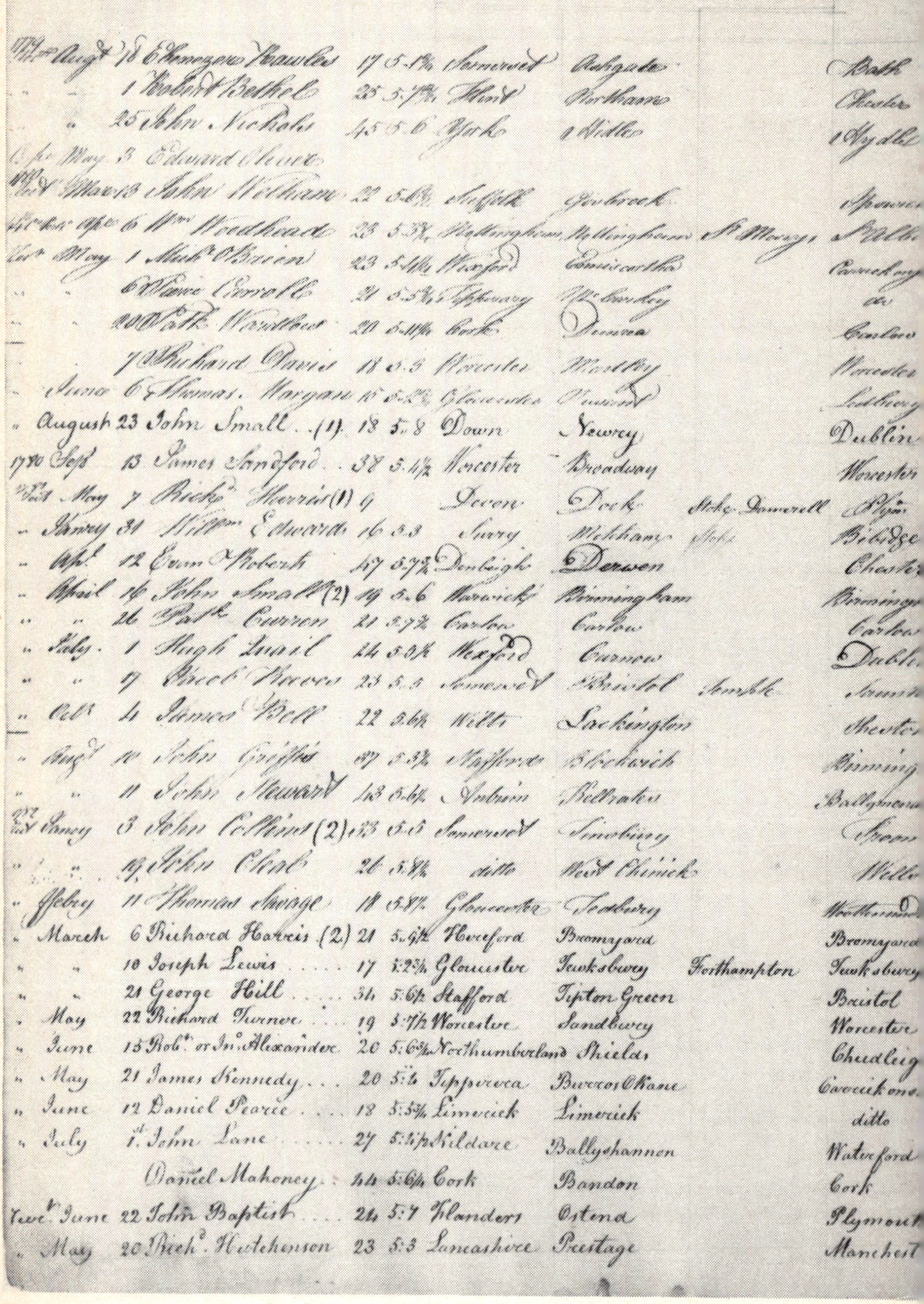

		Brown	fresh	grey	. . . . 3 July 83 Disch
		Do.	fair	brown	pockmarked . . . . 2 Janry 82 Disch
	Ch. Hd. 15 years			fresh	grey
		Lt.	fair	hazle	. . . . 25 Oct 90 Disch
		Brown	fresh	Grey	
		Do.			scar forehead & slight eye brow . . . . .
			fair	hazle	scar right side forehead . . . 1 Sept 83 48 Co.
	5 years 4 years	M.		little	pockmarked
		Red	fresh	hazle	
		Lt.	fair		pockmarked . . . . 2 Oct 83 Disch
Baker		do.	fair	do.	. . . . 1 April 83 2 Co.
	34 Regt 6 years	Black	dark	Brown	scar upon his forehead . . . 22 July 84 Disch
	Red	fair	Grey	Disc'd 31 May 81
		Lt.	fair	hazle	
	Mil. 4 years	Do.	fresh	hazle	scar right Cheek & under his Chin
Maker		Do.	fair	hazle	. . . . 1 Sept 83 64 Co.
		Do.			. . . . 1 Sept 83 13 Co.
		Do.	fresh	hazle	. . . . 4 July 83 Disch
Maker		do.	fair	grey	. . . . 23 April 83 Disc'd
		Lt.	fair	grey	large Marks left cheek & Chin . 1 Sept 83 9 Co.
		Lt.	fair	hazle	
		Do.			
		Do.		Grey	. . . . 31 May 83 Disch
		Do.			hook'd . . . 12 Augt 83 Disch
		Do.			
	Militia 3 years	Do.	do.	hazle	cut forehead . . . 1 Sept 83 51 Co.
Weaver		do.	do.	grey	little Pock marked
smith	31 Regt 11 years	do.	swarthy	hazle	. . . . . . 11 Nov 83 Disch
		Lt.	fresh	do.	Pock Marked . . . . . 7 Feby 83 Disch
		Do.	fair	do.	. . . . 26 Oct 83 Disch
		Fair	fair	Grey	. . . . . . 1 Sept 11 Co.
		Lt.	ditto	ditto	Pock marked . . . . 9 Sept 83 42 Co.
		Lt.	ditto	hazle	. . . . 1 Sept 83 9 Co.
		Do.	fresh	grey	Pock marked . . . . 26 Feb 83 Disch
...ainer	Spanish Service	Brd.	swarthy	Brown	Pock marked
...wer		Do.	fresh	Brown	Scar Chin & forehead . . . . 2 Sept 83 Disch

PENSIONS.

NAME OF THE PARTY.	Amount of the Pension in Sterling.			Authority under which the Pension was granted.
	£	s.	d.	
				Police Cont.ᵈ
John Purcell	20			The Governor
Daniel Geary	18	5	0	Ditto
John Small *	9	2	6	Ditto
John Williams	5	6	5½	Ditto
				Medical
⁎ Matthew Anderson Esq.ʳ †	110	per annum Jan		The Secretary of State
George Brooks Esq.ʳ	132	Ditto		Ditto

Paid from the Military Source out of Sums voted by Parliament for Convict Service in New South Wales

By the Deputy Commissary General

* To 3.ᵈ October 1850   Dead
† To 31. March „   Dead

PENSIONS.

Date from which the Pension has been paid.	Service for which the Pension was granted.	Amount of Emolument when last employed in Public Service.			Present Age of Pensioner.	Cause of Retirement.
		£	s.	d.		
1. January 1832	Late Chief Constable Penrith	100	—		74	Exhaustion of weight day occasioned by Cold whilst on Duty
1. April 1831	As a Constable					Invalided by Wounds received on Duty
1. December 1825	As a Constable					Length of service 17 years
1. May 1843	As a Constable					Having lost his sight whilst on Duty.
1. October 1841	Late Surgeon on the Convict Medical Establishment	469	7	6	62	Impaired health and incapable of further Service.
1. May 1847	Ditto Ditto	323	—		52	Ditto Ditto

"Blue Book" record of John Small's death and final pension payment as Constable of 17 years' service.